The Sport Business Future

Aaron Smith
and
Hans Westerbeek

palgrave
macmillan

First published 2004 by
PALGRAVE MACMILLAN
Houndmills, Basingstoke, Hampshire RG21 6XS and
175 Fifth Avenue, New York, N.Y. 10010
Companies and representatives throughout the world

PALGRAVE MACMILLAN is the global academic imprint of the Palgrave
Macmillan division of St. Martin's Press, LLC and of Palgrave Macmillan Ltd.
Macmillan® is a registered trademark in the United States, United Kingdom
and other countries. Palgrave is a registered trademark in the European
Union and other countries.

ISBN 1–4039–1267–X

This book is printed on paper suitable for recycling and made from fully
managed and sustained forest sources.

A catalogue record for this book is available from the British Library.

Library of Congress Cataloging-in-Publication Data
Smith, Aaron, 1972–
     The sport business future / Aaron Smith & Hans Westerbeek
        p. cm.
     Includes bibliographical references and index.
     ISBN 1–4039–1267–X (cloth)
        1. Sports administration—Forecasting. 2. Sports—Economic aspects. 3. Sports—
     Technological innovations. 4. Sports—Social aspects. I. Westerbeek, Hans. II. Title.

GV713.S58 2004
796′.06′9—dc22   2004044507

10   9   8   7   6   5   4   3   2   1
13 12 11 10 09 08 07 06 05 04

Printed and bound in Great Britain by
Creative Print & Design (Ebbw Vale), Wales

Contents

Contents

LIST OF FIGURES AND TABLES

Figures

Tables

This is no 'Back to the Future' book. It is an academic adventure that moves the reader forward at Formula One 'Grand Prix' speed. The authors, Aaron Smith and Hans Westerbeek, are consulting professionals committed to contributing to the direction of the global sport industry, and not merely responding to it. Their style and approach can scarcely be described as 'cautious'. On the contrary, they bring a bold, courageous, highly imaginative and often contestable approach to their subject.

Given my own experience as an Olympic athlete, sports administrator and business executive, I have always held that sport in all its forms is a reflection of a changing society, motivated by varying degrees of achieving excellence. When I think back some fifty years to my competition days and compare those with the present, I wonder if any of us could have foreseen the changes that embrace the sport business: the universal migration from amateurism to professionalism, the astonishing progress in performance, the advance in technique, the emergence of sports medicine and bio-mechanics, the impact of international media obsession, the relentless surge of commercialisation driven by broadcast rights, and sponsorship revenues and prize money. And I haven't mentioned the extraordinary revolution in stadium and venue designs, sportswear and equipment, sports institutes and of course the politics and astonishing entertainment magnetism arising from all of this.

Of course there have been some 'forward' thinkers and 'risk-takers' along the way; as I think of Juan Antonio Samaranch, Joao Havelange and Bernie Ecclestone in this respect. But much of my experience with athletes, coaches, administrators and the majority of people in the sport industry is that, at best, they are necessarily driven by their Olympic, World Cup, International and Regional Championship annual calendars. Most of those involved in the business focus on near-sighted agendas and timetables and give little thought to future change or innovation that may transform their product (think of, for example, Kerry Packer with one-day cricket).

Smith and Westerbeek argue that we – particularly as consumers within the sport business – are half a century behind the times. Their approach is highly academic, extensively researched, speculative and elaborates on opportunity, but is not without risk. They talk of the so-called 'Fourth Place' – the human space beyond home and work: 'in fact an extension of the social environment of pubs, coffee shops and clubs; a place which will be the centre of leisure activity, a virtual hub of entertainment, the nucleus of sport business; a media broadcasting interactive community nexus that will channel the distribution of sport, leisure and recreation experience'.

They claim that the possibilities that technology will offer future sport business are 'vastly underestimated' and throw the reader into the world of nanotechnology, technological singularity and artificial intelligence (AI). This is not exactly light reading: some might say, 'the ultimate in sports science fiction'!

The authors show respect for past achievements, and they offer up-front acknowledgement that, whilst their approach is entirely a futurist one, they admit their book is not about 'predicting the future correctly'. All planners and futurists in any field who are honest with themselves, accept that from day one there are forces at work counteracting them.

The authors thoughtfully include a guide for reading their book in the Introduction and the chapters, whilst naturally interrelated, have been constructed on a stand-alone basis. The subject-matter is wide-ranging. As well as the primary technology drive, the authors, always with the business of sport in the front of their minds, address corporate governance, sport citizenship, human rights and environmental issues. There is an abundance of philosophical and social thought in addition. If you think the book is about advanced methods in arranging sponsorship deals or negotiating broadcasting rights, you will be disappointed.

If you are ready to have your mind really opened, see cornerstones for the rules of athlete development and sports performance enhancement challenged, contemplate the technology of the future of sports competition itself, virtually having you sitting inside a Formula One car alongside the driver, on a football field with the player, or in the pool alongside the swimmers, you are in for an exciting read.

KEVAN GOSPER
Vice President
International Olympic Committee

Acknowledgements

This book could not have been written without the vast knowledge, eloquence and critical review skills of our Manage to Manage colleague, Colin Smith. Although he was too modest to allow his name to appear on the front cover, we would nevertheless like to acknowledge him here as the third author.

We are also indebted to another colleague, Clare Humphries, for her research efforts and uncompromising commitment to quality in helping us draft sections of the book.

Obvious thanks go to our publishers, Palgrave Macmillan, and in particular to Stephen Rutt, for his ongoing support and trust in us as an author team, and for his belief in the value of sport and its business future.

It is important to us to also thank Kevin Roberts, Editorial Director of *Sport Business International* magazine, who continues to help all of us to remain at the cutting edge of sport business.

Finally, thank you to our wives and families for their unconditional support and encouragement, and for patiently tolerating our obsession with the sport business future.

AARON SMITH
HANS WESTERBEEK

AFL   Australian Football League
AI   artificial intelligence
CE   Corporate Engagement
CEOs   Chief Executive Officers
CPU   central processing unit
DNA   deoxyribonucleic acid
EPO   erythropoietin
FIFA   Federation of International Football Associations
GAA   Gaelic Athletic Association
GDP   gross domestic product
IGF-1   insulin-like growth factor 1
IOC   International Olympic Committee
LCD   liquid crystal display
MIT   Massachusetts Institute of Technology
MLB   Major League Baseball
NBA   National Basketball Association
NFL   National Football League
NHL   National Hockey League
SETI   Search for Extraterrestrial Intelligence
UEFA   Union Européenne de Football Associations
UN   United Nations
UNEP   United Nations Environment Program
WWE   World Wrestling Entertainment
XFL   Extreme Football League

This is a book about the future. We care about the future because we have to live in it, as will our children and their children. It is important to us that they have the opportunity to experience and enjoy sport if they choose to, which requires a healthy global sport industry. In turn, we are obliged to make sound and thoughtful decisions about the sport business future.

As consulting professionals, we depend on the industry for our daily bread, and as academics we increasingly feel the urge to actively contribute to the direction of the industry by thinking, philosophising, researching and writing about it. From the professional and academic perspective we therefore feel the imperative to satisfy the needs of two quite disparate reading audiences (or, at least, the audiences of this book will judge its usefulness and correctness of reasoning differently). Managers in the business of sport will be looking for new perspectives and new ideas that will enable them to do 'more and better sport business'. The majority of academics, on the other hand, will judge the contents of this book on the appropriateness of data sources, method(s) of data collection and interpretation, and how the information we have drawn together stands the test of meticulous scrutiny. In other words, does the picture we paint of the possible future add value to academic debate and progress of research and, ultimately, to an increasing body of knowledge?

We hope to offer something of value to both groups of readers. For the practitioner, we have attempted to be speculative with the intention of highlighting opportunity. For the academic, we have attempted to ground our commentary in sound evidence and reasoned argument. It is, however, impossible to be 'right' about the future. For us, this has not been the point; rather, we consider it important to stimulate debate about the future of the sport business, and in order to do that we cannot 'play it safe' with watery observations. We have chosen not to be conservative.

The 'model' that underpins the book is really quite simple. At the centre of it lies the sport consumer. All the questions we pose and attempt to answer relate directly to those who are passionate about sport. In other words, the future of sport business depends on those who have made it into a business; without sport consumers there is no marketplace, and hence no business. The question that can be asked at the start of each chapter

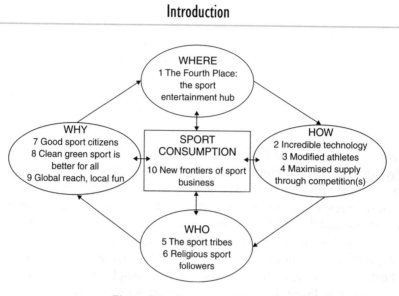

Figure I.1   Structure of this book

therefore is: what does this mean in relation to the consumption of sport? To further specify this meaning we have identified four principal areas of concern. They are the future of *where* to consume sport; *how* to consume sport; *why* consume sport; and *who* consumes sport. Although the content of the chapters does not perfectly reflect this structure – we can never exclusively deal with only one of these questions in a particular chapter as they are all interrelated – the four questions may well be the best tool to integrate the issues that are important to both 'professional' and 'academic' readers.

Readers may wish to keep in mind that we have written the chapters in such a way that they can be read independently. For 'quick scan' readers who know which topics they would like to read first, the individual chapters will provide them with specific insights and ideas. As a result, it is not necessary to read the book in order. Of course, reading the whole book will be more beneficial because we feel that the information we present adds to a more comprehensive appreciation of future issues. Figure 1.1, with the numbers corresponding to the different chapters, provides a 'road map' to reading the book.

In the first chapter we will more specifically introduce the contents and structure of the book. We have also provided a 'snap shot' at the start of each chapter. This overview is essential reading because it provides the reader with the broad-brush picture of the chapter and its context.

We hope you will enjoy *The Sport Business Future*, but this book will only serve its purpose if it makes you look at the future of sport business differently. It is not that being 'different' is important; it is because 'it can be different' that it is important. We look forward to receiving your feedback!

Aaron Smith at smith@manage-to-manage.com
Hans Westerbeek at westerbeek@manage-to-manage.com

CHAPTER I

The Sport Business Solution: The Fourth Place

People will spend most of their living days in the first and second place. The family and workplace are important hubs of connection and interaction with others. Until recently the 'third' places were (and for most of us still are) the locations where people gather outside the family home and office or factory to satisfy their leisure needs. The sporting meeting place, be it the clubhouse or the football stadium, has always been one of the most important third places in contemporary society. In this chapter we discuss the changing nature of the 'sportplace' and 'sportspace'. We argue that a 'fourth place' is emerging in which sport plays a vital part.

In the past and present, humans have always experienced their leisure activity in 'real' time and 'real' space. However, the Sony PlayStation 2 already fore-shadows the changing nature of leisure space. Like the slogan of the game console, the third place is increasingly a virtual leisure space. We are only at the start of our journey towards a leisure environment, and maybe even a daily life environment that will be mediated and manipulated by possibilities offered by *super*technology. Developments in artificial intelligence and nan-otechnology will offer the opportunity to design 'unreal' worlds that will feel like the 'real' thing. The fourth place will become as important as the first, second and third places of the past. Accelerating levels of technological advancement will lead to integration and convergence of our communication and socialisation in this 'unreality' that paradoxically will become our new reality: a living and breathing entertainment hub with sport as its cultural glue.

After we have painted this science fiction picture that many of us find difficult to imagine, we aim in this first chapter to provide the context for these pos-sible developments. We argue that exponential technological developments and an emerging global consciousness that is mainly expressed in a renewed appreciation of cultural diversity and sustainable natural environments will be the main foundations of the fourth place's construction. We show the differ-ent perspectives of futures studies, and explain our own approach to 'gazing in the crystal sport business ball'. This first chapter sets the scene for a radical future!

The Third Place

Since the first television transmission in 1950s humans have inadvertently created radio waves powerful enough to enter space. These waves carried information-bearing signals away from Earth at the speed of light. Any alien civilisation listening as intently as we are to space (via a range of search for extraterrestrial (SETI) programs using radio telescopes), would come to know us through these broadcasts. What might they surmise about human civilisation based on our transmissions? Satellite studies have shown that by far the strongest and most easily detected message from Earth is the action at the Super Bowl, which is broadcast from more transmitters than any other signal from this planet. Sport is not merely of global importance; it is our message to the universe.

Sport business may be global, but human experience is local. Humans need one another, and irrespective of any technological developments that will encourage independent sport and entertainment experiences, they will always seek a place (somewhere other than home and work) where they can nourish relationships, establish a sense of belonging, promote companionship and explore a sense of community. Ray Oldenburg, in his 1989 book *The Great Good Place*, called these locations of social condensation 'third places'. He noted that coffee shops, bars, hair salons, beer gardens, pool halls, clubs, and other recreational areas are as vital as factories, schools and apartments. Indeed, sporting organisations have always served as powerful and popular third places.

However, the nature of third places is changing. Perhaps best exemplified by its use as a marketing slogan for the Sony PlayStation 2 gaming console, the third place can also be created in a digital environment, where surreal spaces are the context of simulated adventure, combat and play. Similarly, physically or emotionally isolated but technologically empowered individuals flock to online communities and chat rooms to source human interaction: the third place of the new millennium.

This trend foreshadows the displacement of our conventional ideas of space. Technology has the potential to fundamentally re-engineer our perceptions of the third place. It will, we believe, inexorably change the way leisure is experienced, driven away from direct human contact in the third place to a more personal exploration of social and psychological needs through an artificial platform: the fourth place. The fourth place will be the centre of leisure activity. It will be a virtual hub of entertainment, the nucleus of sport business: a media, broadcasting, interactive community nexus that will channel the distribution of sport, leisure and recreation experience. The future of sport business lies in the fourth place, and this book is about such a future and the variables that will influence our decisions about how it might be managed. We are more interested in choice than prediction.

Ironically, we also believe that the very nature of sport offers an alternative to a world where the fourth place is pervasive. If humanity is to survive technological escalation, it will be because we have kept in touch with the aspects of life that make us uniquely human. Sport personifies much of what humanity is about: community, the pursuit of physical excellence and the full range of emotions. As technological forces drive sport-entertainment into extreme change, sport might just preserve our humanity, and help us to temper the revolution. If we wish to play a guiding role in the way sport business unfolds, we are obliged to consider the future that we want.

A Radical Future?

Speculations concerning the future of the sport business are slowly moving from the realms of science fiction and fantasy into the practical world of organisational need. A critical assessment of future scenarios, in order to establish pragmatic policies and strategies, is essential for the long-term prosperity of the industry and its sporting constituents. Although futures research cannot demonstrate statistically predictive solutions, it is capable of developing measured and justified forecasts for the future. These forecasts can help sport managers to move more confidently during times of uncertainty. This book seeks to broadly map a future for the sport business industry and suggests the veracity of long-term strategic thinking and scenario planning.

Over the next few decades new technologies spurred by increased computing power will change the way we live. Robotic automation within factories, and ultimately in service industries, will double or triple output. Cheap and almost limitless power generation will underpin vast improvements in manufacturing and mass-distribution industries, and will underwrite new trade and sporting relations. Genetic engineering will transform agriculture and medicine and will lead to a new generation of healthier older citizens. The working week will be reduced significantly, and with the additional time available individuals will increasingly connect with advanced versions of the Internet to play, watch and interact with their favourite sport. Technology will play a significant role in the future of both sport business and sport entertainment. But the possibilities that technology will offer are vastly underestimated, and sport will be amongst the first to embrace them. In the more distant future, of all the technological improvements which will most radically affect sport will be the twin concepts of artificial intelligence (AI) and nanotechnology.

AI can best be described as developing and using computers to model and copy the behavioural aspects of human reasoning, learning and perception. Effectively, this could allow a computer to operate as a human mind. In simple terms the computer has the capability to improve its performance of a task on the basis of a programmed application until it gets to the stage where it can generate its own programming. Given sufficient processing power and memory it is widely accepted that computers will, in the not too distant future, be able to 'think' for themselves, to become essentially 'self-aware'. To a certain degree, AI is already with us in the form of game technology.

Nanotechnology is also with us. Its genesis goes back some 20 or more years, to an IBM laboratory in Zurich, when scientists developed the first scanning tunnelling microscope (STM). This device made it possible to identify individual atoms by scanning a small probe over the surface of a silicon crystal. Robert L. Park, professor of physics at the University of Maryland, suggests that this ability to 'see' individual atoms was the first of the two essentials of nanotechnology. The second essential, that of 'manipulating' the individual atoms, came (he says) in 1990, when another team of IBM scientists, this time in California, found that they could use an STM to drag individual atoms of xenon over the surface of a crystal of nickel. This team managed to spell 'IBM' in block letters using 35 atoms of xenon. Park says that, in this scale, it would be possible to write the entire *Encyclopaedia Britannica* on the head of a pin.[1] While nanotechnology remains, in the views of some, a little bit science fiction, it has become, Park tells us, the highest priority in the US science and technology budget, and is the subject of major nanotechnology programs in five government agencies.

At a point in time that is best described as a technological 'singularity', trends in computer science and artificial intelligence will converge simultaneously to stimulate spectacular change. The choices will range from global catastrophe to the real possibility of intellectual immortality; from a mental immersion in cyber-space to vicious levels of overpopulation. Every conceivable aspect of sport, from broadcasting to drug testing, and performance enhancement to spectating, could become unrecognisable. Experiencing the thoughts and feelings of a favourite athlete is within the means of technology within three decades. By 2030 researchers are hoping to capture the 'data' from electrical activity in the nervous system. This will essentially preserve an individual's thoughts and feelings. An athlete's elation at scoring a World Cup goal might soon be recorded for all to experience.

Technology enabling nanobots to be released into the body could further revolutionise the sports-watching experience. Medical scientists have already successfully embedded computer chips in the body designed to feed back information. If positioned at every nerve junction, nanobots could shut down real sensory experiences and replace them with pre-programmed ones. Virtual reality would be indistinguishable from 'real' reality. Nanobots could create the sensory pressure of kicking a virtual ball. The step between computer games and reality would have disappeared completely. The release of nanobots into the body would also revolutionise the monitoring and performance capacities of athletes. Millions of nanobots released into the bloodstream could render it impossible for athletes to conceal drug use. With the ability to identify and use genetic information doubling every 12–24 months, future nanobots might re-write deoxyribonucleic acid (DNA), allowing a spectator to morph into a champion athletic specimen. Images of cloned sports champions are already high on the list of fears for some, while for others they represent a kind of sporting renaissance. These issues are considered in the first section of this book, examining the technical implications of scientific progress, comprising Chapters 2, 3 and 4.

The breaking down of nations, cultural barriers and religious belief systems leads humans to search for identity in other places. We have already seen this in the rise of phenomena such as 'new age' thinking which prospers in the Western world despite the abundance of scientific evidence and methodologies available to us. People have also sought refuge in subcultures, perhaps replacing the sense of identity through community once experienced in the villages and tribes of our distant past. In other words, there is an irrational, human drive towards building an identity in relation to others. In the future we will seek new contexts of belonging to achieve this, including 'virtual clans' – geographically disparate, placeless fans – clustered around sporting hubs. We address the undeniable power of sport to arouse the human spirit in the second section of this book, encompassing Chapters 5 and 6.

Future sport business will also provide opportunities for corporate enterprises to recognise and deliver their local and global community obligations. This will mark a change in the deployment of some corporate resources. Community sport and social sport programmes will be amongst the beneficiaries of this corporate citizenship. In other words, corporations will begin to realise that sport offers powerful social structures for the disadvantaged and disenfranchised to gain a firmer foothold in a ruthlessly commercial world that the corporations have been instrumental in constructing. Furthermore, new physical sport developments will provide leadership in sustainable environmental management. Chapters 7 and 8 focus on the power of sport in the future as a vehicle of social and community responsibility while Chapter 9 examines the power of culture as a variable in the future of sport business and as a mitigator of technological progression.

Chapter 10, 'The New Frontiers of Sport Business', returns to the theme of technological developments in sport business and entertainment by reviewing imminent and embryonic technologies. The chapter culminates in a speculative commentary on some important issues for the future management and marketing of sport enterprises. This final section attempts to ground our final remarks in present reality, both cultural and technological. While we accept that some of this book presents startling forecasts, a certain amount (in our view) should be considered inescapable even if the timing is impossible to pin down.

Thus, this book begins with the more distant future before returning to less distant future issues and culminating in a review of imminent technologies and their impact on the sport business. To that end, the remainder of this chapter lays the foundation for our exposition of the future by acknowledging the dangers and advantages of 'futures thinking'. We note some weaknesses, concede the fact that the content cannot be everything to everyone and try to give readers a feel for where this book fits into other attempts at distant strategic thinking. While in some disciplines futures thinking is commonplace, it has been limited in management and marketing and, notwithstanding creative pieces in the popular press, non-existent in sport business. At the risk of self-promotion, we would also suggest that it might be advantageous to read this book as a sister volume to our previous book, *Sport Business in the Global Marketplace*, in order to gain a more comprehensive view of the macro variables we consider pivotal to the future of the industry.

Pace, Change and Futures Thinking

At the heart of this book lie the dual threads of change and strategy. Of course, all change is relative, to both time and intention. In this book we are dealing with changes that might occur within the next 50 years. For some, there is evidence that they are manifesting already, while others are more speculative. Nevertheless, the introduction and timing of these changes will depend upon the pace of technological progress and the willingness of people to embrace them. Although it must be conceded that it is impossible to be specific about timing, we do believe that the issues highlighted in this book will play a role in the future at some point.

For individuals, a single lifetime is their eternity; the future is as distant as it can be conceived because the future without them is no future at all.

We can only contemplate what the future must be like by imagining ourselves to be living in it. But for the universe itself, our lives, and even the entire history of human civilisation, represent nothing but a short breath towards its inevitable demise, when all the stars have disappeared and nothing but the cold, lifeless dark remains. And yet despite the context of a universe 14 billion years old, and a home planet four billion years old, we still have the greatest difficulty in future thinking. Sometimes it is hard enough to plan to do the shopping later in the week, let alone how we wish an entire industry to develop over a half-century.

Mathematical modelling has shown that natural selection – the process that governs evolution – can work relatively quickly, when considered from universal or Earth time. For instance, if a 'mutant' version of a species produces only 1 per cent more offspring than its rivals as a benefit of its chance mutation, it can increase its representation in the population from 0.1 per cent to 99.9 per cent in around 4,000 generations. In the words of the evolutionary psychologist, Steven Pinker: 'A hypothetical mouse subjected to a selection pressure for increased size that is so weak it cannot be measured could nonetheless evolve to the size of an elephant in only twelve thousand generations.'[2] But do we want an elephant or a mouse for our future?

A futurist is someone who speculates about the future and gets its wrong. As Steven Pinker noted: 'The one prediction coming out of futurology that is undoubtedly correct is that in the future today's futurologists will look silly.'[3] This book is not about predicting the future correctly; it is about thinking towards the future and about how we wish to direct our energies to create it. If this book were to be correct about every aspect concerned with the future of sport and business, we would probably be thinking about retraining to seek alternative professions. But the purpose is not to pontificate and predict for the sake of it: the future of sport is important to us. There is always choice. In the words of Bussey:

> Mystery is as much an empirical as a spiritual reality. Scientists still grapple with the big questions about the origin of life, the mechanisms of evolution and the function of consciousness. Futures Studies is also centrally concerned with the mystery because the future is so closely enmeshed with one of the most mysterious of entities: the human consciousness and its powerful capacity to create the world in its own image.[4]

Although it has no predictive power, futures thinking is a prospecting skill which can shape the future in vision and collective purpose.

A Comment on Method

In addition to reading other material and environmental scanning, the contents of this book employed four methods of data collection and interpretation. First, trend extrapolation was used to examine phenomena over a period of time. Trend extrapolation assumes that present conditions will remain stable and that present behaviour will persist into the future.[5] This is an invalid assumption, of course, but it is still a useful starting point for thinking about future possibilities.

Second, cross-impact analysis supplemented the trend extrapolation by analysing a series of pivotal trends in the light of the occurrence or non-occurrence of additional related events.[6] We did this in matrix form. Cross-impact analysis enabled us to systematically examine the interactions among events. For example, we considered the trend known as Moore's Law, which holds that computer processing power doubles roughly every 18–24 months, in light of the success or otherwise of artificial intelligence software. Nevertheless, hardware must be software capable, and it shortly will be. As a result, we created matrices that reflect the outcomes of predetermined pairings. However, these events were limited to pairs, and the world is rarely so convenient that it allows only two variables to interact. Again, however, the technique was useful in conceiving the effect of combinations that would have less impact in isolation.

Third, the Delphi Method was used to solicit consensus from a panel of sport management, marketing, technology and other relevant experts. As consensus is difficult to achieve even amongst a small group, the final technique involved the development of future scenarios.[7] These scenarios represented the culmination of the research process and encapsulated the alternatives corroborated through triangulation with the results from the other methods of data collection and interpretation. The scenarios also allowed our panel of experts to agree to disagree. While they could see a common set of variables, they could not envisage a common set of outcomes. We have, however, decided not to reproduce all the scenarios in this book, partly because it is designed to highlight the issues rather than predict the future, and partly because we have explored the scenarios in our previous book, *Sport Business in the Global Marketplace*.

We must be honest with our readers at this point and confess that we also incorporated a fifth method, though it would doubtless fail any test for academic rigour or legitimacy; we allowed ourselves the inclusion of imagination. We considered sport, as we know it, and incorporated the ideas and beliefs we could imagine in sport within a generation or two.

We have chosen not to present in this book the raw data we collected. Aside from the limitations of space, it is not an exclusively academic book, and has been written with an audience of sport management and marketing practitioners in mind as well as academics and students. We have intended the book to be a lively discussion of the future of sport business and entertainment, not a reproduction of our method and results. Lastly, bringing together a mass of ideas about the future is a little like unscrambling an egg. We have done our best to present the possibilities in a format that makes sense, but the chronology is impossible to pin down, and we concede up front that we have no simple model that captures how the sport business will unfold.

Setting the Future Scene

Sohail Inayatullah, the United Nations Educational, Scientific, and Cultural Organization Chair at the University of Trier, suggests that there are three decisive factors to consider when thinking about the future. First there is the map of the future; second there are those structures that are difficult to alter (e.g., culture and deep power structures such as patriarchy, imperialism, and the military), and third there is our collective vision for the future. He draws on the work of Fred Polak (*Image of the Future*) who argues that the vigour of a civilisation's vision will determine its rise and fall. Once the vision of a group (corporation, nation, civilisation) disappears or loses significance, then either that group will decline or a new leadership with a fresh vision will emerge.

Inayatullah suggests that beyond changes to business, government and household wealth, there are three trends that are likely to transform our future beyond recognition. These are nanotechnologies/artificial intelligence, smart market technology and multiculturalism. He suggests these forces will challenge industrialism, capitalism and Westernisation. Similarly, Peter Schwartz and Peter Leydon[8] suggest two mega-trends in terms of future scenarios. The first, fundamental technological change, encompasses the benefits to be realised through developments in telecommunications, nanotechnology, biotechnology, personal computers and alternative energy sources. The second mega-trend, they suggest, is a new spirit of openness in geo-politics, with multiculturalism embraced and environmental stewardship assumed.

We agree with some of these assessments, although we suspect that they do not go far enough. For instance, Inayatullah focuses on the market impact of nanotechnology/artificial intelligence, suggesting that they will allow production on a scale never before possible, and may indeed allow the eradication of poverty. While our focus is more concerned with entertainment than survival and poverty, the full range of possibilities concerning nanotechnology and artificial intelligence is probably beyond our present imagination. Inayatullah also suggests that smart market technology will provide greater information to consumers about products, allowing them to vote with their feet. Bar-coded products will provide complete pricing details, including how much workers were paid to produce the product, how many trees were cut down and how much wholesalers made. This type of information overload will have serious implications for sport managers and marketers, but will also offer some opportunities for prescient corporations prepared to deliver upon their social responsibilities.

On the other hand, Inayatullah suggests that information available via the Internet could equalise the inequalities created by capitalism, creating a people's market. We do not agree. As yet, there is little trend evidence to suggest that this will come about. Human workers are unlikely to be producing products as we believe that this task will increasingly be taken over by machines, so how much workers are paid to produce products will become less relevant. The Internet will need to be subject to regulation if it is ever going to provide objective information to equalise capitalism's inequalities (compared to the propaganda machine it is at present). And further regulation of the Internet implies a global government/regulation body, which would be a more influential trend than the 'smart markets' he is suggesting.

We might take a moment to pause in our discussion and point out that neither Inayatullah nor Schwartz and Leydon include in their trends what has traditionally been called the X Factor: that is, something unforeseen and unexpected occurring which may have a profound influence on daily life. For example, the X Factor in the past saw a huge meteorite hitting the Earth leading to the extinction of dinosaurs. At one end of the continuum in the future it might be something as prosaic as a total breakdown of the world's major financial systems, while at the other extreme it might be the occurrence of a major epidemic. History is quite specific on this point. Periodically the X Factor will interfere with the way in which life is unfolding and may bring great joy, great sorrow or simply great change. It is always something to bear in mind when discussing the future.

The idea of multiculturalism challenges suggestions of homogenisation in terms of culture, nation-states and knowledge systems, and raises questions about the ability of nation-states to organise for differences in culture and worldviews. Inayatullah imagines a world government with representatives from 1,000 associations including corporate organisations, non-government organisations (such as Amnesty International and Greenpeace), traditional nation-state representatives and representatives voted in through cyberspace. Although this may seem impossible from our present location, the Federation of International Football Associations (FIFA) and the International Olympic Committee (IOC) already demonstrate steps towards a global 'government'. They are not perfect, but neither is the United Nations (UN).

There is, however, an opposing view to that of Inayatullah. This view suggests that while Europe, the Americas and Asia may be moving towards greater internal economic, political, financial and military integration, the move towards regionalism and devolution within other countries may continue. Thus, for example, while Britain surrenders power to the European Parliament in Brussels, it also devolves power to regional entities such as Scotland, Wales, the North, the Midlands and the South West of England. Already we see distinct signs that where power used to reside overwhelmingly in central governments, it is now dispersed through regional governments, business and other non-government organisations.

Professional sport, because of its association with the business of sport, is likely to be caught up in the move towards greater integration. Rules for the conduct of professional sport need to be standardised across nations. The higher the authority, the easier it is to accomplish this. Amateur sport, however, may well be devolved to the regional entities and be subject to the whims of the local electorate. Wales may choose to cap salaries for part-time players, while Scotland may seek to put all of its funding into specific, indigenous sports.

Such a schism between amateur and professional sport could herald significant changes to the way in which sport is both viewed and undertaken. It is quite possible that under the scenario suggested some regional entities may mandate that only regional, amateur sports are shown on local television with commentaries in the local language. Transfer between amateur and professional levels might be precluded, through design or unintended effect. Similarly, television rights and sponsorship might differ from region to region.

Under Inayatullah's proposal there are three potential future scenarios. First, the globalist scenario suggests the breaking-down of all national and religious barriers and an end to our feudal history, although he does not explain what feudal structures exist and why they will end. Perhaps we need to consider whether corporations will continue to monopolise the means of production, and what control empowered employees might have. Second, the organic scenario emphasises community and relationships wherein self-reliant communities will be linked electronically and spiritually.

The potential disadvantage of this scenario includes the stripping of individual freedom. Finally, the collapse scenario lists catastrophic events that may herald the dawn of a new age, including natural disasters, biological and digital viruses. Inayatullah suggests these events could promote the end of capitalism and encourage a new moral order.

The path to this new moral order involves a process of phases. The first phase, globalisation of capital, is occurring presently, whilst the second is likely to be the globalisation of labour. Inayatullah counsels that this will involve the realisation of the Marxist dream, with labour travelling freely with standardised conditions. This, however, might be a reinvention of the Marxist vision that is usually expressed in terms of the workers owning the means of production. He claims the third phase of globalisation will be multiculturalism, where an authentic acceptance of difference will exist, rather than cultural assimilation.

The fact is, however, none of us actually knows what will happen. This example neatly illustrates the inherent dangers of futures thinking. Predictions are more useful when they are used as examples of possible futures, rather than as definitive forecasts. That is why scenarios are a popular way of tackling futures thinking. So it is almost impossible to agree with all forecasts provided by a 'futurist', but we would argue that work like that undertaken by Inayatullah is worthwhile because it makes us think about the possibilities. It is these possibilities that we hope to entice you to create as a consequence of reading this book. You may well agree or disagree on various points but, more importantly, we hope that you will air your views in due course.

A Critical View of Futures Studies

Richard Slaughter[9] suggests that a deeper analysis of problems is required in futures studies. He criticises *pop-futurism* as offering only media-friendly, superficial observations about the future impact of science and technology; these observations are bereft of theory or true insight. He suggests that ultimately pop-futurism is compromised by marketing and the pursuit of mystification. On the other hand, *problem-oriented futures* work offers a more serious and well-grounded approach. Problem-oriented futures evaluates the ways in which organisations and societies should and do respond to the challenges of the near-term future, providing insight into business innovations, environmental legislation, regulations and other practical matters. However, Slaughter suggests that the problem-oriented approach is limited by the empirical paradigm it uses, and that it misses other aspects of reality such as how people derive meanings (such as 'growth is good' and 'nature is a set of resources').

The final approach Slaughter outlines is the *critical and epistemological* approach, which offers deep-level observations into the impact of meaning and paradigms. He suggests that successful futures work encompasses elements of each level of these three levels of inquiry. Elements of pop-futurism can offer accessibility and appeal, aspects of a problem-oriented approach can ground observations in current thinking, whilst epistemological work (the science of science) can help to provide rich and more innovative understandings.

We have attempted to heed Slaughter's warnings and marry some of the three approaches he outlines. For the most part, we have taken a popularist approach to the written style of the book. The research upon which the content is based is problem-oriented, while our approach to discussion and interpretation is also critical. However, it was more important to us to provide accessible content rather than overwhelm the reader with specialised academic jargon, and thus the balance is weighted towards practice rather than theory. A summary of Slaughter's overview of approaches appears in Table 1.1.

Naturally, we are concerned with the sport business but, keeping in mind the counsel of Richard Slaughter, we also consider the socio-cultural contexts in which it operates where they help explain possible future circumstances. We also attempt to bring each chapter back from the future in order to consider the practice of sport management and marketing now.

A cursory look at the table of contents shows that we discuss a range of future circumstances under themes. This does not constitute an exhaustive set of commentaries, but rather one which we consider relevant to the future practice of the management and marketing of sport. Inevitably there is a skew to our observations. As we are interested in sport business, we focus on the sport activities that are directly associated with economic imperatives. That is not to suggest that other aspects of sport are less important; they are simply not the focus of this book. To be blunt, the business side of sport – where the money is made or not to be made – is our principal interest. Although rightly criticised at times as 'pop-futurism', the consideration of technological developments is, in our view, of sufficient importance to warrant detailed discussion. The development of technology is therefore a key theme in this book and is the topic of the following chapter. However, the next chapter leaps ahead to discuss some of the implications of technologies that are still speculative or in their developmental stage, but which could have a revolutionary impact on the delivery and experience of sport in the future.

Table 1.1 Structural mapping matrix

	Pop-futurism (the litany)	Problem-oriented (social sciences)	Critical and epistemological (discourse, metaphor, myth and worldview)
What stays the same?	Seldom asked. Social relations not in picture.	Existing social relations institutions, rules, etc.	Nothing; all structures are provisional and can be problematised.
What are the key trends?	Main dynamic created by obvious external trends, strong emphasis on technology.	Empirical and social dimensions, laws, rules, regulations, responses.	Empirical, social, etc., all depend on deeper cultural commitments, values, metaphors and presuppositions.
Change processes?	Restricted overviews, snapshots of change, ahistorical.	Appreciation of complexity of social change. Insights into specific areas.	Highly contested. Revealing of social interests, power and civilisational factors. A major area of interest.
Problems?	Outrageous, shock value. Or restricted to litany. Naively optimistic.	Major focus of inquiry. Detailed analysis of problems and possible solutions, social innovations.	Problems are problematic without a deeper view. All such socio-cultural constructions can be deconstructed and renegotiated.
Items in pipeline?	Mainly new gadgets.	Use of environmental scanning and foresight methods to anticipate developments.	Highly problematic. Questions notions of inevitability. Vastly more choices than ever seriously explored.
Sources of inspiration and hope?	Wealth, power, technical development. Continued 'progress'.	Creating well-grounded social and institutional responses. New agendas, taking charge, etc.	Cultural critique, reconstruction and renewal of worldviews. Civilisational concerns. New stages of civilised life envisaged. Transpersonal energies engaged.

Source: R. Slaughter (2002), 'Beyond the mundane: reconciling breadth and depth in futures enquiry', *Futures*, 34(6), p. 494. Reproduced with permission.

Notes and References

1   Park, R. (2003). 'Tiny Terrors'. *New Scientist*, 179 (2402), p. 22.
2   Pinker, S. (1997). *How the Mind Works*. New York: W.W. Norton, p. 164.
3   Pinker, S. (1997). *How the Mind Works*, p. 83.
4   Bussey, M. (2002). 'From Change to Progress: Critical Spirituality and the Futures of Futures studies'. *Futures*, 34, p. 307.
5   Ramos, J. (2001). *Global Challenges for Humanity: From Instrumentality to Emancipation*. Melbourne: Australian Foresight Institute.
6   Eichler, M. (1982). *Science Fiction as Desirable Feminist Scenarios. Women in Futures Research*. Oxford: Pergamon Press.
7   Slaughter, R. (2001). 'The Flight of American Super-Ego'. *Futures*, 33 (10), pp. 891–6.
8   Schwartz, P. and Leydon, P. (1997). 'The Long Boom'. *Wired*, 5 (7), pp. 115–73.
9   Slaughter, R. (2002). 'Beyond the Mundane: Reconciling Breadth and Depth in Futures Enquiry'. *Futures*, 34, pp. 493–507.

CHAPTER 2

Sport Business Singularity: Real Virtuality

Within the next 20–30 years advancements in the development of artificial intelligence combined with molecular engineering will lead to a technological singularity. This technological singularity – an exponential technological progression – will come about when computers take control of their own development and become capable of processing trillions of times more information than humans. This power will be enhanced through immense information-sharing and the parallel processing of a global Supernet. The Supernet represents the combined sentient power of millions or even billions of machines, each with superhuman intelligence.

Scary thought? Nonsense? The end of the world? Or just the end of humanity? Moore's Law, named after Intel's boss in the 1970s, states that the processing power of computers will double every 18–24 months. It is a prediction that has so far proved resilient for 30 years. If the Law holds up for another decade and a half, then individual computers will reach levels of processing power that are equal to the capacity and capability of the human brain. Computers may ultimately consider themselves alive, and this may lead to computers programming themselves to meet their own 'needs'. Humans may lose control.

Where does sport business fit into all of this? Does sport have a place in a world that is technologically so advanced that 'real' sport no longer needs to be played because reality can be simulated? With infinite options to choose from, and with no limits to technological capacity, why would we bother endangering ourselves in the socially, mentally and physically damaging world of imperfect sport?

Sport may symbolise all that it means to be human, and the experience of being human in the future will be tied inextricably to technology. A lesser-known Law called Monsanto's Law predicts that our ability to identify and use genetic information doubles every 12–24 months. In other words, we may witness the performances of cloned sporting champions within four or five Olympics from now.

In all probability sport will offer an abundance of opportunities for technological application. Sport will be a great Petri dish, a testing ground for new technology, and an arena for exploring the 'most preferred vicarious experience'. In the context of all this, we need to determine whether a world of 'virtually real sport', which through technological perfection cannot be distinguished from the real sport experience, is for the better or worse for humanity. Do we want big corporations (that still sponsor sport) to know the exact time when we opened the fridge on our yacht in the Caribbean and when we grabbed the last beer, so they can customise their virtual advertising during the sport event we are watching on holovision, allowing the local nano-distributor of our preferred brand to deliver our next supply within the next fifteen minutes? Will we stay in control or will we be controlled? Does the word 'we' include the humble sport consumer or does it really mean only big business? Welcome to the sport business singularity!

Spectacular Change

The world as we understand it is always ending and beginning. It is a part of the natural order of events. A way of life ends; a new way of life begins. The beginning that we accept most readily started with the formation of Earth, perhaps four-and-a-half to five thousand million years ago. Though many endings and beginnings continued, the beginnings which influenced us the most occurred some 200,000–400,000 years ago when *Homo erectus* populations evolved into *Homo sapiens*, and then, around 100,000 years ago, when they evolved into Neanderthals and Cro-Magnons towards common humans.

The advent of religion gave us yet another beginning, as did the discoveries of fire, the wheel, language, mathematics, science and technology. Now we are faced with yet a further beginning, and one that has the potential to overwhelm us unless we learn to fully understand and use its capabilities.

Some speculate that we are on the cusp of a change comparable to the evolution of human life on this planet. If this is true, in the space of a century, the human race would progress in relative terms more than it has in the past twenty millennia (20,000 years). Some time in the next two or three decades we will have the capacity to create superhuman AI; computers, if not smarter than we are, will most certainly be infinitely more capable. Once this occurs, the world will be changed irrevocably. The direction humanity takes following this radical upheaval will determine our fate as a species. At a point in time that is best described as a technological 'singularity', trends in computer science and artificial intelligence will initiate spectacular change.

The way in which that change will affect us depends upon factors both within and outside our control. Within our control is the speed with which we accept, embrace and learn to coexist and live with the new environment. Regretfully, for many of the world's population the difficulties in understanding and acceptance may well be overwhelming. The ritual and religious movements of the last century will give way to the belief in 'supernatural' technology.

Outside our control will be the limits to growth imposed by science. At least we can understand this limitation. What we may not be able to control, or even understand, is the way in which AI may develop under its own initiative. It is quite possible that AI may 'think' differently from humans: logic rather than reason, evolution rather than revolution and the development of theory rather than practice. Yet, for all anyone knows, human quirkiness of thought, our 'gut feelings' and 'intuition' may have AI counterparts.

What we do know is that the way in which AI and humans interrelate will impose a set of possible choices never before faced by the human race. The choices will range from inherent catastrophe to the real possibility of living forever; from a mental immersion in cyber-space to vicious levels of overpopulation.

While our aim is to explore the 'singularity', we need to keep in mind that this book is primarily about sport and sport business. Surprisingly, perhaps, for two ostensibly contradictory reasons, sport will be one of the few global socio-cultural institutions that will play a role in how our relationship with AI unravels. First, sports, sport organisations and the sport media will be amongst the foremost to embrace the technology that the singularity delivers. Second, if society succumbs to the fear of the new AI technology, the prospects for humankind dim perceptibly. In such a situation sport may prove to be our saviour by offering us a reminder of those aspects of humanity that we do not wish to lose in the microscopic bowels of a computer chip or the billions of lines of code in some software program. Put another way, when all hell breaks loose, and humanity teeters on the edge of chaos, it might be sport that offers us a reminder of that which we wish to cling to, and what it means to inhabit a body.

We have described the point in time when we believe this new beginning will be upon us as a technological 'singularity'. We owe our use of the term to the mathematics professor and science fiction novelist, Vernor Vinge, who popularised the concept of the technological singularity. He used the term as a way of defining a model where physical reality fails. In mathematics, singularities represent the infinite. In a science fiction context, just as in cosmology, the term reflects a physical version of this unimaginable infinite, such as the threshold of a black hole. In the last eight years, however, Vinge's singularity has transgressed theoretical and science fiction supposition. It has been conceived as a point in time where technology leaps ahead of human ingenuity. It is at this point where the exponential curve of development accelerates beyond its human beginnings and where imagination fails because change is driven at thousands of times the customary rate. It is a time where human-level machines can take control of their own development, and where the future of humanity dangles in the balance. Scientists who accept its arrival speculate that immortality or catastrophe are the extreme stakes possible in this game: a game that is likely to be played this century.

The singularity, or what Damien Broderick calls the Spike,[1] implies that AI is a kind of black hole of the future, created by a continued exponential increase in technology that is likely to culminate in artificial intelligence. A further supporter of the singularity concept is Ray Kurzweil, one of the world leaders in the development of AI. Kurzweil wields the language of the singularity with unhesitating certainty. He speaks of near immortality, genetic engineering, nanotechnology and artificial intelligence vastly exceeding human capacities. It is knowing the potential that science offers but not yet knowing how to harness it that will cause intense anxiety among the general population. It is a hazard already foreseen by the chief scientist and co-founder of Sun Microsystems, Bill Joy. He suggested with some anxiety that with such advances come great power and danger.[2]

The strongest historical evidence for a coming singularity has emerged in the historical accuracy of Moore's Law, labelled as a consequence of the observations of Intel's chief in the 1970s. Moore noted that improvements in computer hardware were following a remarkably steady progress curve. In fact, processing power, he predicted, would double every 18–24 months. Not only was this prediction correct, but technology has ensured that the time is diminishing between evolutions.

The key to appreciating the impact of a potential singularity, however, lies in the very nature of artificial intelligence. AI practitioners such as Ray Kurzweil,[3] such as nanotechnology scientists Ralph Merkle as well as theoretical physicists such as Michio Kaku[4] have argued that the development of computer hardware capable of human-level tasks and able to pass tests for consciousness will be available within two decades. Such machines will play a fundamental role in the next evolution of technology. Instead of 18 months to double levels of processing power, 'conscious' machines will increase this output exponentially. Merkle, for example, argues that if Moore's Law holds up as it has for the past few decades, then by 2020 manufacturing technology will be sufficiently advanced to arrange individual atoms in pre-arranged sequences, effectively duplicating the structures of the human brain. While they disagree on timing, they all agree on the outcomes: once human-like intelligence is achieved, anything is possible. Vinge has suggested, perhaps only as a Hugo award-winning science fiction novelist and mathematics professor can, that it will mark the end of humanity itself. Others have claimed that it will bring everything from the elimination of bad weather to effortless interstellar travel.

The implications do not end with independent computers capable of outthinking us in all our endeavours. After all, IBM's Deep Blue showed that given computational boundaries such as those associated with the rules of chess and the potential permutations of moves, any human (including Kasparov) could be defeated.

IBM's current project, Blue Gene (designed to explore protein folding), will run at a quadrillion operations per second. This system will unravel the immensely complex protein sequences that accompany gene recipes. The mind-boggling implications come when artificial intelligence is used en masse, or to supplement organic intelligence. In other words, what happens when millions of computers thousands of times more capable than a brain are linked together in an Internet-style network, and what happens when these same computers tell us how to safely connect ourselves to this 'Supernet'? This is the singularity.

It is the dangers that Bill Joy alludes to and the beliefs of individuals such as Vinge that make predicting the future problematical. Nonetheless, if we were to be confident optimists, we might argue that humankind's inherent faith and ingenuity will overcome the obstacles ahead. And so, while this book is concerned with the future and with charting the sport business path, it does not ignore the technological progress that will inevitably occur. If Vinge is correct, we need not concern ourselves with the lot of sport. But, as optimists, we come out firmly against Vinge's cataclysmic future. However, we believe sport needs to be considered in a role far wider than that of a grateful receiver or of a casualty of technology.

If humanity is to survive an almost unimaginable technological escalation, it will be because we have been able to keep hold of those aspects of life that make us human. Sport personifies much of what humanity is about. It is our view that sport, and importantly, the business of sport, is worth discussing beyond the redesign it will assume in the face of radical techno-logical change. We believe it is also worth discussing as an agent of human-ity. While sport and the sport business will change drastically, they will also provide a fundamental socio-cultural link to our humanity. This book recog-nises that technological forces will drive the future of sport-entertainment to extreme change, but sport is also a reminder of the humanity we all share and that we should be seeking to maintain. The global phenomenon of sport and the prodigious entertainment industry it drives provides a vital clue to how rampant change can be tempered.

This chapter continues by charting the implications of the singularity for the future of the sport business by considering the impact of powerful tech-nological convergence on the industry. It maps the pre- and post-singularity sport future, and demonstrates how sport will be irrevocably affected by human–computer interfaces, the Supernet, nanotechnology, gene therapy and super-intelligence. It also provides an overview of how sport will pro-vide a powerful socio-cultural glue capable of maintaining one of the only buffers against revolutionary change.

Artificial Intelligence and the Human Brain

More than any others, a series of books in the late 1980s and early 1990s began to distil the possibilities associated with rapidly advancing technology. Marvin Minsky (*Society of Mind*, 1985), Erik Drexler (*Engines of Creation*, 1986),

Hans Moravec (*Mind Children*, 1988) and Ray Kurzweil (*The Age of Intelligent Machines*, 1990) each placed a piece of the puzzle on the table. Together, they sketched out a sort of theory of mind in the future. Although they each went about it in their own way (the mind as an emergent computational system, the progression of miniaturisation, the implications of robotics within a broader framework of humanity and the inevitability of self-aware computers), collectively they outlined the pathway for a singularity to occur.

More recently, critics have correctly pointed out that some of the predictions made in the books have yet to occur. The critical issue as we see it is not temporal. If AI can be developed, it will be, irrespective of when. It is true that some predictions have been overzealous, but in order to understand the possibilities, it is necessary to explore the hardware and software sides of the AI equation. We are more concerned with the development of software that possesses human-level decision-making capabilities rather than the more abstract notion of a hardware–software system becoming 'sentient', and even a new form of consciousness or life itself.

Obviously, there is a relationship between the realisation of AI and the ongoing progression of computer hardware. In contrast, the human brain – our hardware – has been virtually unchanged over the last 100,000 years or so. Our software, on the other hand, is the culmination of millions of years of ongoing evolution and adaptation. The human brain contains an investment of millions of years in addition to the vast complexity of the neural system that contains 100 billion neurons and 100 trillion synapses. But what is the difference between the capacities of a human brain compared to those of a computer?

In the simplest possible terms, both brains and computers are far from the theoretical limits of computational power. To compare for a moment, brain neurons fire approximately 200 times per second, stimulated by impulses that travel at around 100 metres per second at best. This seems slow in comparison to the raw power of a modern computer. Most relatively new personal computer central processing units (CPUs) can operate at around 1,000 million cycles per second, at a minimum. They do this far closer to the 300 million metres per second theoretical limit of light speed than does the brain. But despite this clear differential, the human brain has a hundred million times the computing power of such a machine. This is an outcome of the sheer volume of neurons and synapses. It is this parallel processing power which allows the brain to control and regulate the prodigious sums of information that arise as a consequence of managing a body. While we might be incapable of personally processing a mathematical equation as quickly as a computer, if a brain was able to focus on such a task virtually exclusively and ignored the homoeostasis of the body, then it would outperform the computer easily (but we would, of course, perish).

Artificial, or as it is sometimes called, autonomous intelligence is the software that would effectively mimic the behaviours of a human brain; but software of such prodigious complexity cannot be run on an ordinary computer. In fact, a computer capable of human-level intelligence must be capable of performing some 1,000,000,000,000,000,000 (10^{17}) operations per second. IBM's Blue Gene, when ready, will be capable of around 10^{15} operations. If Moore's Law continues to hold, let alone decrease between cycles, this level of computing power will be ubiquitous by 2010. We are, even now, extremely close to the hardware requirements for artificial intelligence.

Once there is human-level AI, there will be super-intelligence shortly afterwards. It is likely that once a computer is able to design its own upgrade, the progress of computational power will increase massively, without necessarily more parallel processing power being needed. If we accept that AI will not be restricted by the availability of computational power, it would seem as though it is the software side of the equation that will determine its realisation. The industry adage might hold true: whatever Intel gives us Microsoft takes away.

Trans-humanity

The impact of a single computer with superhuman level intelligence will revolutionise human experience. Super-smart computers will inevitably design even smarter software. They will rewrite the source codes so quickly that the evolution of hardware cannot keep up. That is probably where nanotechnology will play a major role.

Nanotechnology, or molecular engineering, is the science of manipulating the very building blocks of matter. Erik Drexler's book, *The Engines of Creation*, exposes this science and its future admirably. Assuming that this science continues down its current path, it is anticipated that nanotechnological manufacturing will eventually be able to build anything from the bottom up, from the very atoms of which it is constructed. As well as the incredible implications of technology that can construct everything from food to precious gems, it is also expected that nanotechnology will be responsible for the development of computer hardware to keep up with AI software should this be necessary.

Nanotechnology, as a science that could yield significant practical benefits, has been taken seriously by the military as well as the scientific community. The Institute for Soldier Nanotechnologies (ISN), a joint research collaboration between the US Army and Massachusetts Institute of Technology (MIT), was established recently with a US$50 million grant from the Army. They are undertaking research in the areas of protection, performance improvement and injury intervention and cure. Examples cited include dynamic armour systems, biological warfare protectors, and artificial muscles.[5] Similarly, the Lawrence Berkeley National Laboratory in California reported in the prestigious scientific journal *Nature* that they had developed a nanomotor 250 times smaller than a human hair, small enough to ride on the back of a virus. The nano-rotor, as they have named it, comprises a gold blade attached to an axle made from a carbon nanotube, anchored by two silicon dioxide electrodes. The rotor is powered by voltage which flows down the nanotube.

The singularity will presumably arrive when AI computers can control nanotechnological engineering to include a proliferation of AI-capable computers, all of which can produce others. Some have speculated that from the moment AI machines can control the building blocks of matter, it will take only days before the world is completely changed. Whether this means an eradication of poverty, famine and suffering or the annihilation of the human race is anyone's guess. Drexler imagines a computer constructed through nanotechnology that will undertake 10^{26} operations per second. We can scarcely imagine what a computer that can operate at this level and is self-aware will actually do.

The optimists, among whom we count ourselves, suggest that they will take over the manufacture of food and material goods, will reverse ageing, eliminate disease and generally protect and uplift the human experience. The more pessimistic consider this a trans-human scenario, or the end of the human race. We foresee trans-humanity and sport being affected in another way.

Trans-human Sport

To follow the progression of post-singularity technology, it should be possible to 'upgrade' human neurons and improve brain functioning in one of two ways. First, consider the effects of upgrading the neural capacities of the brain through nanotechnology, just as we do with a computer CPU. Imagine for a moment that your brain can be upgraded or enhanced using artificial means.

For example, let us assume that your neurons can now fire 200 million times per second, and your synapses can send signals at 100 million metres per second. Thus, somehow your brain is wired into a computer and you can access that level of 'thinking' speed. What would this mean from a practical viewpoint? The result would be the capacity to think at a million times your current speed. Consider what that actually means. You could do a year's worth of thinking in under a minute, or experience subjectively a millennium's passing in a single day. Is sport in its current form suddenly less appealing? The argument that it would be gets stronger when the second aspect of the computer–brain interface is considered.

The second approach would involve the linking of a human mind directly to a computer. In a sense, this is the movement of a human mind into a computer consisting of programmable neuronal equivalents, only far more powerful. In theory, this process equates to the uploading of a mind into a computer. Within this context – a completely programmable and pliable universe – the uploaded individual would assume the same level of computation power as a computer. Thus, some see this approach as a kind of pathway to immortality. It is little wonder that the ramifications of such interactivity with computers and AI systems are almost unimaginable, and have hitherto tended to be the domain of science fiction novels.

By 2030 it might be possible to capture the data associated with a human nervous system's electrical activity. In essence, researchers are already working out how to preserve an individual's thoughts and feelings. This means that every goal scored at the World Cup or every Olympic gold medal performance might soon be recorded. Sooner or later the technology will also be available not to just observe these events and emotions, but also to experience them personally. Researchers working for the BT laboratories of British Telecommunications have ominously named this concept 'the soul catcher'.

Soul Catchers and Virtual Immortality

The seeds of the soul catcher are already sown. Researchers at Carnegie Mellon University in the USA, for example, demonstrated what it might be like to speak to Einstein about his theories, or even just to shoot the breeze. It is like a live videoconference. You ask a question, which is subsequently translated into the backend database through voice recognition software, the sort we use to pay our bills, and the most suitable answers are chosen from the bank of 500 video recordings using pattern recognition software similar to those employed in Internet search engines. A marvel of modern computer simulation? That was five years ago, and it was only just a beginning.

The hardware for unsophisticated versions of 'virtual immortality' is already available. The technology exists for anyone to document their daily life through inconspicuous cameras embedded in glasses, which could be fed into a computer hard disk roughly the size of a coin. On the best of these we could easily store a month's worth of visual recordings. IBM is working on disks of a similar size that could fit a year's worth of memory, or around 3,600 megabytes of data. Other researchers are working on contact-lens style cameras that fit over the retina. Sport is an obvious area of application. With athletes wearing such devices, the data could be transmitted directly to viewers who could choose an athlete to follow, just as they have a choice of angles and replays currently through select digital transmissions. The lack of bandwidth may presently be a problem for uptake, but it is unlikely to remain an obstacle for much longer. Progressions such as these will pave the way for the soul catcher. The supercomputer is likely to be wired directly to athletes, or even at first in a wearable form such as a wristwatch or sweatband. This chip will interface wirelessly with the microsensors under the athlete's scalp and at the nerve junctions that carry sensory signals. These steps will occur well before the singularity. While the technology for soul catching and virtual immortality might be another 30 or more years away, sport is likely to be a testing ground for new ways of vicariously experiencing elite athletic performance.

Professor Kevin Warwick of the University of Reading is at the forefront of man–machine interactivity. He has implanted himself with microchips to remotely monitor his body's movements and functions. On the last page of his book, *I Cyborg*, Warwick states that he intends to become the first genuine human cyborg.[6]

Sport, Super-intelligence and the Supernet

This is just the beginning. Computer power today in the form of commonly available personal computers, in biological terms is roughly analogous to the brain-power of insects when compared to the human brain. If this gap can be bridged in a decade or less in a pre-singularity period without the help of nanotechnology and AI, we have absolutely no idea what thousands of years of exponential increases would deliver. Most scientists agree that there must be a theoretical limit. For example, the impulse speed of computer signals should not be able to exceed the speed of light as a matter of physical law. However, we have already described what impact massive parallel processing can achieve. What about the entire human race networked together in one omniscient Supernet, all fully integrated into an immortal collective that makes *Star Trek*'s Borg (a race which functions as a collective mind) look positively simplistic?

Once human thought processes can be contained within a non-biological medium, the evolution of super-intelligence will be remarkably swift, and will soar past human levels effortlessly. Because one computer can share information almost instantly with millions of other networked computers, all will share the knowledge of one immediately. Within a decade, the Internet will also see a new incarnation. We can expect a global wireless Supernet to possess the capability to connect virtually every device containing a computer chip in the world.

It has become quite boring to talk about virtual reality and sport. We have all imagined the possibilities: putting on a helmet or glasses and watching your game of choice from the sidelines, or from the perspective of a favourite player, or even the coach/manager. Holograms are also a regular vision in this future version of sport spectatorship. Perhaps we will all sit around a small-scale version of the venue – as big as can comfortably fit into our lounge rooms – and watch the game as if it were a fusball table. Alternatively, we might even travel to specific venues where we can watch the life-size holographic versions of the players, but be closer to the virtual action than those lucky few who are attending the real game. The companies at the cutting edge of this technology have these concepts carefully mapped. For example, California-based IDEO is all about cutting-edge technology. IDEO is known for its products such as Palm, but it has its future pinned on the success of a new generation of apparatus that incorporate flexible and tubular scrolling liquid crystal display (LCD) screens for the large-screen mobile television, computer notebook or mobile phone. The company is pursuing holography, rapid and practical speech recognition and versions of artificial intelligence.

Although we may not expect computers to become self-aware with the next generation of artificial intelligence software, they will be useful for helping us deal with the information overload of the twenty-first century. Even two weeks out of the office means hundreds of unanswered emails and communications, many of which are of no interest, or at least are not urgent to us. AI software will help to filter, prioritise and even respond to some of these communications. The technology has already been developed for earring mobile phones, thumb and retina print identification and completely integrated wireless connectivity.

All the available evidence suggests that these are perfectly realistic expectations for the future of sport spectating. In many ways, we find these examples well within the bounds of acceptable reality. Certainly for some they are welcome possibilities, but for most sport fans they are not just anticipated, they are the inevitable extensions of a hyper-commercialised, sport-media-entertainment triumvirate that is constantly on the lookout for further opportunities to maximise revenue.

The pioneering AI researcher and author, Ray Kurzweil, has no doubt as to the inevitability of physical human–computer collaboration. He envisages a nano-world where computing can be undertaken at a molecular level billions of times the processing power of the human brain. Like his counterpart, Drexler, whose vision of the surprisingly near future is also packed with nanotechnological gizmos, Kurzweil anticipates methods of scanning a body and the brain using nanobots that can be released into the bloodstream. Billions of them could forage through every brain capillary. It will no longer be possible to hide anything as an athlete, from drug use to a covert greasy snack. Before we discard the notion of these nanobots as another imaginative but implausible *Star Trek* into the future, it is worth considering why some of the world's leading researchers are so certain that such a future is inevitable.

They point out, for instance, that we already have the capacity to electronically scan neurons and neurotransmitter concentrations in the brain. Some medical scientists have experimented successfully with computer chips that are embedded in the body and that relay information back to a central computer, while others have developed miniature cameras that can reveal the intimate workings of patients who swallow them, providing a kind of incredible voyage inside the body. Once technology allows for the creation of a database of every human neuron – a map of the human brain – the possibilities for duplicating consciousness itself are real.

A map of the human brain is effectively a blueprint of intelligence. This means that not only will we be capable of reproducing intelligence, but also the genetic sequences required for extraordinary physical performance. If we accept, as do scientists, the theoretical veracity of nanotechnology in the first instance, it may not be such a large step to contemplate a medium-term future where nanobots can rewrite DNA to allow an armchair spectator to literally morph into a spectacular athletic specimen.

Stewart Brand, in his book *The Clock of the Long Now*,[7] highlights a little-known axiom similar to Moore's, called Monsanto's Law. It states that the ability to identify and use genetic information doubles every 12–24 months. The practical implications are significant in areas such as agriculture and health sciences. The latter has, of course, been the topic of heated debate, particularly when it comes to cloning. Images of cloned sports champions coming to life again are high on the list of fears for some but for others it represents a kind of sporting renaissance where the greats, or at least their progeny of sorts, can all play together.

The introduction of artificial, rather than biological, 'tampering' adds another, more complicating, dimension. The merging of technology and biology has already produced some controversial outcomes. For example, human embryos have been transplanted and grown in artificial wombs. The experiments, although successful, were terminated after a few days to avoid breaking the law.

Other scientists have constructed what they call bio-computers out of DNA that are capable of crunching a billion operations a second. Compared to what is expected to be the most powerful computer ever developed, IBM's Deep Gene (mentioned earlier), this is actually rather slow. Deep Gene is expected to handle a million billion operations in a second. However, it is claimed that these DNA calculators are so small that a trillion of them could fit into a test tube. Since Deep Gene itself is largely based on the principle of parallel power (lots of powerful computers strung together instead of one), a parallel arranged DNA system with trillions of replications could clearly forge a part in the future of computing.

A little more alarming are the machines US scientists have built which, when released into the environment, can power themselves by feeding on snails and other creatures. Then there is the robotic fish that is guided by the brain of an eel. In counterpoint to these 'new' artificial-biological life forms is the unprecedented decline of the world's range of species. It has been estimated that up to one-fifth of all living species will have disappeared within the next three decades. According to Ervin Laszlo in his book, *Macroshift: Navigating the Transformation to a Sustainable World*,[8] our civilisation is simply not sustainable given the rapid technological and economic progress it is undergoing. We revisit the significant implications of this fact in Chapter 8, 'Green Sport'.

For some scientists, such as Kurzweil,[9] we can expect billions of microscopic nanobots to profile each of our brains, communicating with each other via wireless networks, all linked to a global Supernet. If such a capability were created, and nanobots were positioned at every nerve fibre that emanates from our five senses, they could shut down the impulses coming from our real senses and replace them with artificially simulated, pre-programmed impulses. Virtual reality would then be indistinguishable from 'real' reality. It would be as if you were actually in that virtual environment. If you wanted to, say, kick a ball, the nanobots would create the sensory pressure against your foot as you made contact. Even a normal amount of errors, such as mis-kicks, could be programmed to interrelate with your senses. Even the hairs on the back of your neck could stand when you are introduced to the crowd for that Wimbledon Final you always wanted to play in. Anything that can be done in reality can be done in this virtual environment, although participants need not be confined by the realities of their talent. We are not talking about computer games or simulations; rather, we are talking about an environment that is every bit as real as it gets.

Through the connectivity of the Supernet, we could even interact with real people if we wanted to, whether by snowboarding in New Zealand or surfing in California. Various Supernet sites will have different environments available. The 'holodeck' of the ubiquitous Enterprise could be effectively duplicated within 50 years. Most importantly, we would have the ability to enter and leave such a site at will. The salient question, at this point, is to what extent will traditional, physically real sports remain interesting to us as spectators?

Some AI researchers suspect that computer super-intelligence will emerge before nanotechnology takes hold. Others believe that it will take computer super-intelligence to develop nanotechnology to the levels we have just discussed. Their conclusions tend to be the same, however; machines that design new machines.

I Robot

Lord of the Robots[10] Rodney Brooks, Director of MIT's Artificial Intelligence Laboratory (the largest AI research institution in the world), points out that autonomous, intelligent machines will soon become a fixed feature of our everyday lives. Beyond the existing robots that have been first to market, such as the Electrolux home cleaning robot in Sweden and those which perform remote oil or mine drilling, we can expect the next generation of robotic technology to be founded upon what Brooks calls pervasive computing. Offices, for example, will be packed with what are effectively fully integrated working environments, where wireless connectivity is not just a feature but also an essential requirement.

Third-generation mobile phones already offer two-way video calls, high-speed content downloads and fast Internet access. Companies such as Sony have teamed up with others such as IBM and Butterfly.net to develop network services using grid computing to connect thousands of PlayStation 2 users simultaneously. Darren Kelly has developed 'Drancing', a form of digitally synthesised light and music controlled by body movements. These applications are not futuristic but can be seen in almost any information technology page in the local newspaper.[11] Thirty million Japanese already browse the web on their mobile phones, and Nokia provides a service in Finland where a soft drink machine will charge a drink to a mobile phone. Similar services are reasonably common in many cities for paying parking meters without using pocket change. MIT's AI laboratory has developed a prototype phone that can be used by anyone who picks it up, automatically customising its accounts and interface based on the recognition of the user's facial features. The challenge now is to integrate existing equipment and computers with wireless technologies that interact seamlessly anywhere a user travels, in what will be the precursor to a roaming Internet that the laboratory is currently working on. These imminent technologies are considered in the final chapter of this book, 'The New Frontiers'.

The benefits for sport and its commercial partners are significant. Genuinely wireless connectivity and full integration of computing and broadcasting resources means that sporting events can be watched from anywhere in the world at any time. Regulatory and privacy legislation notwithstanding, intelligent software can track the products that consumers purchase – given that all purchases will be made without the use of cash – and the appropriate products or services can be added to that individual's sporting telecasts.

Sponsorship itself can be a rotating and completely customised undertaking. Thousands of companies and millions of products or services could be allied with each sporting event or organisation. When you watch the Super Bowl from your yacht in the Caribbean, the virtual advertising and sponsorship messages will be tailored specifically to your needs. They will be real-time aware and linked to the satellite global roaming systems embedded in your mobile display. Every time you switch on to watch a sporting broadcast, your mobile transceiver will send a message to the broadcaster including an inventory of the products or services you have purchased over the previous few weeks. These in turn will be matched against the list of sponsors' products and services and a customised sponsorship will be transmitted to your mobile viewing station. From one game to the next, and from naming rights to virtual advertising, the sponsorships displayed are likely to change depending upon your location in the world and your recent consumption behaviour. These messages can remind you that it may be prudent to stop in at the next port to top up your supply of beer, or that the chip in your toaster has been registering some anomalous power surges and may soon be in need of replacement.

Sponsorship placement technology will revolutionise the sport sponsorship industry. Sponsors will pay when they register sales against those to whom their messages were targeted. It will also make the sponsorship equation even more complex than it currently is. Some sponsors will seek to continue with the broader mass marketing strategy associated with raising awareness, while others will be delighted to finally use a razor instead of a shot gun approach.

The ongoing evolution of AI also holds some influence over the future of sport and entertainment. It is a misunderstanding of the technology to assume that AI has not yet arrived; what has not yet arrived is computer sentience. Rudimentary AI, however, is a common feature in modern software. It is found in the fuel injection systems of modern cars and chooses the most efficient gate to which arriving aircraft are directed when they land at busy terminals. Stealth fighters have their movement trimmed literally a thousand times a second as they fly. In addition, AI systems also determine what you are doing when word processing and display help when they think you might be stuck or whey they recognise the beginning of an incorrect sequence of letters. AI also sits behind the wheel of that car children race against in the latest video game, and directs the activities of whatever monster or villain chases them in first-person shoot-'em-ups. They may not be self-aware, but they are advanced, pattern-recognising, learning systems.

As AI becomes more advanced and mimics with greater precision the behaviours of humans, the impact on the entertainment industry will become even more pronounced. Research in Australia, for example, has shown that the emerging generation of Australian Rules Football players, now aged between six and thirteen, find the option of playing an official Australian Football League (AFL) video game just as appealing as kicking the ball around with friends in the real world. It is easier to be a hero indoors, which requires less time and commitment for skill development, in the warm and dry and against the increasingly realistic play of an AI-driven computer opponent. The 'PlayStation Effect', as the researchers called it, is set to become more pronounced when video games provide a realistic option to actual activity, and particularly where those activities are impractical, such as flying through space or driving a racing car.

The question is to what extent AI-driven entertainment will supplant more conventional entertainment options such as sport spectatorship. The answer to that lies in the extent to which AI can provide the experiences that match the needs and motivations of sports fans. This issue is revisited in several later chapters.

Rodney Brooks' new book, *Flesh and Machines: How Robots Will Change Us*,[12] argues that the differences between humans and their machine creations will ultimately be impossible to distinguish. He points out that technologies are already in use where the machines interact directly with the human body or, as he puts it, where nerves and silicon work together. Thousands of people, for example, have cochlear implants so that electrical signals can stimulate neurons and allow them to hear where they previously could not.

Brooks' AI researchers are experimenting with nervous system interfaces to support advanced prosthetics and even to bypass diseased parts of the brain. The possibilities for sport performance are evident for both able-bodied and disabled athletes in the future. Augmenting the physical structures of the human body may, however, be a clumsy way of improving athletic performance, and certainly would be an easily detectable advantage. The possibilities with genetic engineering and gene therapy probably offer athletes more subtle opportunities. We discuss athletes of the future in detail in the following chapter.

It is the longer-term post-singularity future that presents the greatest challenges to sports and sport business in general. Brooks and his MIT team are amongst the scientists that accept nanotechnological devices as inevitable elements in the future. In a sense, this future involves 'hijacking' biology. One of the senior research scientists at the MIT AI laboratory, Tom Knight, has already engineered *E. coli* bacteria to do simple computations and produce different proteins as a result. The ultimate ambition is to have digital control over cells themselves, the consequence of which is quite startling. Instead of, say, growing a tree, cutting it down and building a bookcase, manufacturers could simply grow a bookcase from scratch. Just as nanotechnologists believe that they will eventually be able to build anything simply by constructing it atom by atom, the MIT AI laboratory believes that the interaction between artificial devices and biological structures, such as humans, will be smoothed by cellular engineering.

AI is not without its critics. Roger Penrose and John Searle, for example, are often held up as representatives of the anti-AI camp. Both tend to object to AI in its pure form as a potential source of new consciousness, although they object for different reasons. Penrose, a mathematics professor from Oxford, believes that the machinations of consciousness are too complex to be modelled artificially, while Searle considers the duplication of consciousness objectionable on philosophical grounds. Searle may well be correct in that human consciousness can never be duplicated by software. On the other hand, we may well be the products of machines ourselves already, built by a distant or omnipresent super-intelligent species that we, as primitive human beings are simply not aware of. But our focus has not been about making human consciousness out of computers. Instead, we are more interested in the possibilities of engineering software functionality that operates in a human-like way, with comparable decision-making capabilities. We cannot duplicate consciousness but, with enough time, it is likely that it can be simulated. Thus AI is a complete unknown, but to expect human characteristics may be presumptuous given the opportunity for computers to write code for themselves. Whether AI will bring genuine sentience – and subsequently give birth to a new form of life – is another matter, and one which is perhaps as much philosophical as technological. What is important for us to remember is that super-intelligent computers can provide a 'fourth' place for the experience of life in general, and sport in particular.

Who amongst us is not prone to fantasy, sport or otherwise? For every Beckham or Tiger want-to-be, there will be a facility to make it real. What remains unclear is the role of athletes in this fantasy-reality world, and the prior mechanisms of sporting experience that will lead to it. If genetic engineering manifests before the singularity, which would seem likely, the sport business is on a definitive path to unreality. The place of the athlete in the future of the sport business is examined in the following chapter, while the role of sport to the consumer or fan is discussed in Chapter 6, 'Worship in the Sport Cathedral'. Thus we begin to work our way back from the more distant, unknowable and potentially radical future, ultimately concluding in the final chapter with a review of imminent technologies and their impact on current sport business practice.

Notes and References

1   Broderick, D. (2002). *The Spike: How Our Lives are Being Transformed by Rapidly Advancing Technologies*. New York: St Martin's Press.
2   Joy, B. (2000). 'Why the future doesn't need us'. *Wired Magazine*, 8 (4), *http://www.wired.com/wired/archive/8.04/joy.html*, accessed 3 November 2003.
3   Kurzweil, R. (1999). *The Age of Spiritual Machines: When Computers Exceed Human Intelligence*. Sydney: Allen & Unwin.
4   Kaku, M. (1997). *Visions: How Science Will Revolutionize the 21st Century*. New York: Anchor Books Doubleday.
5   See *Jane's International Defense Review*. Available at *http://idr.janes.com*, accessed 11 July 2003.
6   Warwick, K. (2002). *I Cyborg*. London, UK: Century.
7   Brand, S. (2000). *The Clock of the Long Now: Time and Responsibility: The Ideas Behind the World's Slowest Computer*. New York: Basic Books.
8   Laszlo, E. (2002). *Macroshift: Navigating the Transformation to a Sustainable World*. San Francisco: Berrett-Koehler.
9   Kurzweil, R. (2001). *The Singularity is Near*. New York: Viking.
10 With due reference to the interview with Rodney Brooks of the same name published in *Technology Review*, April 2002, pp. 78–83.
11 See *The Australian* newspaper, 4 March 2003.
12 Rodney Brooks (2002). *Flesh and Machines: How Robots Will Change Us*. New York: Pantheon Books.

CHAPTER 3

Athletes of the Future: Cyborgs, Mutants and Clones

Homo technicus, the next incarnation of human evolution, will be a 'merger' of biomaterials and inanimate materials. It will be an assemblage of ceramics, metals and fluids, thinking and feeling as we do, but boasting unparalleled self-sustaining capabilities such as automatic injury repair protein structures and energy-generating micro engines. There will even be the capacity to replace body parts with those that were grown from *Homo technicus*' own genetic materials. Advancements in genetic technology, such as this, may offer the ultimate performance-enhancing tools for sporting brilliance.

What are the current limits of athletic performance? Are we record-hungry sport spectators or can we live without records, continuing our consumption of sport on the basis of sheer sporting participation? Maybe there is an opportunity to amplify and intensify the enjoyment of the sporting experience by using increasingly sophisticated means of performance measurement and umpiring/refereeing control. Microchips attached or implanted into athletes already allow us to track their performance in real time and deliver vital biological and performance statistics to optimise and judge performance. Are sport consumers willing to pay for these experiences? And to whom will they pay the bulk of this money?

Sport performers have, since the start of recorded sport history, attempted to boost their performance levels by using a wide range of enhancing tools. These 'tools' can include the most sophisticated methods to train the human body and are certainly not limited to 'natural' means. Performance-enhancing drugs have been around since the ancient Olympics and are unlikely to disappear in the future of sport business. The 'what' and 'how' of future doping, however, remains unclear. Scientists are on the verge of mapping the human genome, or the complete map of all our genes, and this will allow the same scientists to detect and treat disease, or indeed, to create new structures or even beings. Sheep are only the beginning.

We need to ask ourselves the hard questions in relation to the literal 'building' of super-athletes. Should we build them, and what impact will they have on sport business? Do we as sport consumers have a choice? The probable reality is that there will always be a few who will make the available choices and this will ultimately lead to successful and unsuccessful genetic experiments. Will the natural distance runners from African countries be surpassed by the genetic freaks from the West, simply because the West will have the resources and technology to build 'freaks'? Or do we not need to bother because virtual athletes – 12-year-old children in virtual reality – will rule the world of professional cyber-sport? In this chapter we will survey the technological developments that will probably deliver this range of potential scenarios.

Crystal Ball Gazing

The athletes of the future most certainly have their genesis in the past: to be precise, 25 April 1953. It was on this date that the scientific journal *Nature* published an article by James Watson and Francis Crick that transformed the scientific world, detailing the structure of DNA. Watson and Crick determined that each DNA molecule – a long, two-stranded chain made up of sub-units called nucleotides, containing a sugar (deoxyribose), a phosphate group, and one of four nitrogenous bases: adenine (A), guanine (G), thymine (T), and cytosine (C) – was connected by hydrogen bonds between the bases and was coiled in a double helix. Watson and Crick noted that adenine bonded only with thymine (A-T or T-A) while guanine bonded only with cytosine (G-C or C-G). The complementarity of this bonding ensured that DNA could be replicated, thus allowing identical copies to be made in order to transmit genetic information to the next generation.

With this paper as a foundation, researchers began to understand the true science of genetics and finally were able to sequence the human genome. This, in turn, has allowed humankind to improve quickly and effectively on nature. Cloning, still primarily confined to the laboratory, is moving at amazing speed towards daily implementation. Starting with the creation of mouse eggs and embryos from stem cells, progression will be made initially to the production of healthy replacement parts for a sick person's tissue or organs until finally it will be possible to develop designer body parts.

Professor Alan Goldstein, Director of the Biomedical Engineering Science Program at Alfred University in New York, already talks of *Homo technicus*, a sentient being combining engineer metals and ceramics with biological materials. According to Goldstein, replacement parts for human bodies will become commonplace as new materials are developed. In the future, he suggests, biotechnology will merge with materials science so that engineered biomaterials will enhance the function of medical devices and implants.[1]

Now the possibilities that are rapidly becoming part of our common future allow us to conceive the athlete of the future. What does this mean for athletes? What it means is an athlete totally different from the ones we are used to. Bear with us as we describe the athlete of the future. He has a surgically reinforced skeleton, calcium replaced by titanium shells bolstered by diamond composites. His hands have been genetically engineered to grow an additional opposable thumb. Thick and dextrous, his fingers can now clutch a basketball like an acorn. He can run at 80 per cent of maximal speed for several hours, his muscle fibres genetically programmed to regenerate and mobilise glycogen reserves twice as fast as normal. The bothersome cruciate ligaments in his knees have been armoured with strands of

kevlar; he can turn on the spot without fear of trauma. He has been skele-
tally designed with extra ribs, added posteriorly and attached to the muscles
of the lower back with tendons. The added strength and stability has
improved his clean and jerk by 12 per cent, at the cost of mobility and tor-
sion. He has been engineered with enhanced myoglobin levels and red
blood cells to carry more oxygen to the musculature. He has had his
immune system redesigned and is one of the first humans to be capable of
manufacturing his own vitamin C, improving recovery time and retarding
ageing through its qualities as an anti-oxidant. He has been designed with
reflexive skin pigmentation that adapts to sun brightness by darkening the
skin. He has been designed with larger intracranial blood vessels that can
better withstand the brain jolts he receives when boxing. He will never be
bald unless he shaves his head as a fashion choice. He has a surgically
inserted timed-release capsule of melanin that allows him to sleep one-third
less than usual. He has been engineered with better innervation in eroge-
nous zones, which has not added to any public athletic performance but was
worth the money anyway.

Thus, when asked 'Who is the athlete of the future?' the image of a
highly-paid freak of genetic engineering is readily cultivated. But is this a
valid prediction, or the product of media hype and science-fiction fantasy?
Who is the athlete of the future? What does she look like? How much is she
paid? How many millions or billions of spectators know her face, her name?

Speculation about whether we have reached the limits of human potential
is perhaps the most compelling question concerning the future athlete. Will
we know a three-minute mile, a 400 kilo (895 lb) clean and jerk? Studying
the lessons from history might lead us to respond with a resounding 'yes',
aware that athletes have consistently capitalised on advancements in medical science and technology to enhance their performances, although the
exponential improvements over the past three decades are tapering off in
many sports. Dietary supplements, stimulants, steroids and diuretics are
amongst the mass of substances that have been ingested by athletes as they
aspire to excellence. With the ongoing and exponential acceleration of technological advancements in developed countries, the bar is likely to be continually raised.

This chapter considers the future of the athlete from a number of perspectives. First, we review the physical aspects of athletic performance, and
the likely avenues for improved performance. Second, we highlight the
relevance of technological improvements in measuring sport. Third, we
debate the economic dimensions that will decide the future of athletes
within the context of the sport business and, finally, we will consider the
interrelationship between athlete and spectator.

Medal-winning Mutations

Medal-winning mutations are not new to elite sport. Notable (and apparently natural) examples include the Finnish sportsman, Eero Mantyranta, who won two cross-country gold medals at the 1964 Winter Olympics, and the Australian swimmer, Kieren Perkins, who won back-to-back Olympic gold medals in the 1500 metres at Barcelona and Atlanta (and a silver in Sydney). Mantyranta was born with a genetic abnormality that infused his blood with 20–50 per cent more red blood cells than the average person. His body was able to provide additional food (oxygen) to the muscles for longer, giving him a powerful competitive advantage in distance events. Australia's Kieren Perkins was blessed with an oversized heart muscle capable of pumping oxygenated blood around his body with extraordinary vigour. The remarkable performances of these athletes are sanctioned because their genetic make-up is inherited. However, the introduction of foreign genetic material into an athlete's cells remains a highly contentious, but very real, issue. The latest offerings of medical science come in the form of 'genetic doping', otherwise known as gene therapy.

Gene Doping

Allegations of doping have tainted the elite sport world for decades. Scarcely anyone in the Western world has avoided hearing the saga of sprinter Ben Johnson's Olympics drug scandal in 1988, when he was stripped of his gold medal and world record after testing positive for anabolic steroids. Less interest was taken in the entire team banned from competing in the Tour de France after their cyclists were discovered to be taking erythropoietin (EPO). A naturally occurring hormone, epo instructs the body to produce new red blood cells in order to raise oxygen levels in the blood. Typically the kidneys will release epo in response to a drop in the oxygen levels in the body's tissues. Once equilibrium has been attained, epo production halts. Medical research in the late 1980s produced an injectable form of epo as a treatment for severe anaemia, a condition characterised by inadequate red blood cells. Of course, the advantages of injectable epo for athletes, especially from endurance sports, were immediately evident. A boost of red blood cells, which carry with them precious oxygen, could be achieved by injecting more epo into the bloodstream. Fatiguing muscles would then receive more of the oxygen demanded by aerobic exertion, allowing athletes to perform faster and longer. Epo has revolutionised distance sport, but it does not even come close to the impact that gene doping will have.

Shortly, the doping stakes will be forever changed with the introduction of gene therapy. The technique involves inserting a gene into the body which subsequently replicates itself. At present this technology is in the experimental stage, and is primarily aimed at curing diseases including muscular dystrophy, cancer and anaemia. However, as with many medical advances before it, gene therapy also offers the contemporary athlete the alluring chance to gain a competitive edge.

Blood-boosting and muscle growth are the two areas in which most gene therapy research has concentrated to date. 'Blood-boosting' is the colloquial term that describes the process of increasing red blood cell count in the body through the stimulation (rather than the injection) of epo. Medical researchers have been developing gene-therapy techniques to deliver the epo gene directly into the body's cells, stimulating those cells to produce the protein in patients with anaemia. Currently the use of viruses to transport the epo gene is being investigated, with the disease-causing components of the virus removed.

Two medical trials in the late 1990s tested the use of certain viruses to carry the EPO gene into animals including mice, monkey and baboons.[2] The increase in the proportion of red blood cells in the mice, for instance, was 32 per cent, with a single injection elevating red blood cell production in the mammal for over a year.[3] Superior to the benefits of injecting epo, this kind of gene therapy can provide athletes with added stamina.

Mapping of the human genome and creating a detailed map of all our genes is expected imminently, and it should only be a few more years before commercial applications are tested. This will allow doctors and medical scientists to trace and treat genetic abnormalities.[4] On the other hand, it will also allow the same practitioners to *create* genetic abnormalities. Unless prevented by legal means – which never excludes everything – parents will have available to them the technology to affect the genetic configuration of their children. Naturally, this is a double-edged sword, fraught with ethical implications that are well beyond the focus of this book. For example, while parents are checking to ensure that their child is not genetically programmed to contract a fatal or even inconvenient disease, why should they not also make them more handsome, strong or smart? After all, social research has proven that taller, better-looking people experience fewer social difficulties and get better jobs than their equally intelligent but undersized, fatter, uglier contemporaries. Would not any parent want a better life for their child? And would it not be better for their child to be good at sport, that powerful social determinant, than poor at it? For every parent that simply wants their child to fit in better by being a good athlete, the bar will escalate, until the genetic profile of children born to ambitious parents will be unrecognisable and the sporting freak will be normal. It will simply be a matter of whether your parents decided you were to be a sprinter, football player, violinist, dancer, artist or surgeon. Each will have their own unique set of genetic characteristics, which we might expect to be available to any parent who is prepared to pay the right amount of money. Even if parents avoid such genetic tampering, there may soon be nothing to prevent the athlete from self-gene therapy.

There are millions of athletes who have tried performance-enhancing drugs. If we were to be honest with ourselves, would we not personally find attractive the possibility of taking a harmless pill that produces a 'six-pack' overnight? Would you not even think about undergoing some gene therapy to eliminate that cellulite, grow back a thick head of hair or just never have to shave again?

Of course, the use of such gene therapy is not necessary risk-free, at least not at the moment. Increasing the levels of red blood cells also thickens the blood, leading to complications such as high blood pressure, atherosclerosis and stroke. However, in the competitive and lucrative world of sport, many athletes are prepared to risk their health to win. Several surveys over the past two decades have revealed that elite athletes are prepared to incur permanent injury and damage to themselves in order to be successful.

Recently, a team of Australian scientists published their research indicating that athletic performance could be the result of the presence of a certain gene.[5] Their results are perhaps another step towards the inevitable profiling of genetic ideals for sporting performance.

The team discovered that the gene in question, ACTN3, comes in either a sprint or endurance variation. One makes a protein found only in muscle fibres responsible for fast movement, known as fast twitch; these are essential to sprint and explosive performance. The other does not produce this protein and therefore allows for the default slow twitch fibres to develop.

The researchers examined the genetic profiles of 300 athletes, 50 of whom had participated in the Olympic Games. They discovered that 95 per cent of elite sprinters possessed at least one copy of the essential sprint protein, while half had two, one from each parent. On the other hand, 76 per cent of endurance athletes have the gene, and 31 per cent have both the sprint and endurance genes.

Although some commentators have counselled that the influence of the gene is only one variant in athletic performance, and therefore not an exclusive predictor of performance, the discovery of 'performance' genes is suggestive of screening methods for talent identification and for gene therapy or doping interventions in the future. A suite of screening tools could be employed to quantify athletes' size and mechanical leverage, muscle fibre type, metabolic processes, oxygen utilisation and psychological disposition.

Data from a combination of genetic and anthropomorphic tests could be fed into analytical software to match individual athletes against idealised equations. Each athlete could subsequently be given a score or rating, which they could carry around as a badge of potential. We will lament the individuals who had high scores but chose not to become involved in sport, and perhaps some of the crowd favourites of the future will be the athletes who defied the statistics to become more prominent performers than they 'should' have been. Contracts from talent farms could be issued to expectant couples on the basis of post-natal potential. Clones of the same horses or dogs will race in control events. We may see an event of the future a little like control series motor car racing where all jockeys ride the same horse in a genuine test of riders' and trainers' skills. Perhaps one day we might even see an all Ben Johnson 100 metres Olympic final.

Insulin-like Growth Factor I (IGF-I)

Whilst epo gene therapy promises added staying power for endurance athletes, gene therapy that uses the protein IGF-1 (insulin-like growth factor 1) promises muscle growth and power. Research on this protein is primarily concerned with the treatment of debilitating diseases such as muscular dystrophy, where muscle atrophy has a devastating impact. However, where research may promise decreased suffering for patients, it also conjures images of bulkier athletes.

Research into IGF-1 genes has caught the attention of body-builders and power athletes. It suggests a possible growth in muscle bulk of up to 20 per cent. For the 'average' male that means around 35 lb (16 kg) of added lean muscle mass. Imagine that weight of beef steak distributed around a body. Gains in muscular size of this proportion are only possible in the early years of training for the lucky few who are genetically suited to easily adding muscle in the first place. The gene, which again occurs naturally in the body, stimulates muscle repair and growth following hard exercise such as resistance training. Injected directly into the muscle, IGF-1 does not appear to circulate in the bloodstream, reducing both the potential risks and its ability to be detected as a foreign substance.

Measuring Conventional Sport with Technology

As one of the most powerful solicitors of human passion, sporting events have a habit of making just as many people unhappy as happy. This is not always exclusively about winning, for the average fan experiences the full gamut of emotions by the time he leaves a closely contested event. As often as not, when anger flares, it is because the fan has witnessed what he perceives to be an injustice, and the most frequent perpetrator is the referee, umpire or official. But technology is not just a vehicle for objectivity; it is a tool to bolster the weaknesses of sporting measurement. It might even reinvent a number of sports altogether.

It is standard technology in large field distance events such as marathons and triathlons for electronic race monitoring systems to be employed. In addition to simple microchips attached to every participant to track their movements from start to finish automatically, the monitoring systems also link into the vital statistics of athletes, including heart rates and blood pressure. In addition to the health management dimensions, it also offers race spectators new insights into the performance of athletes during the event.

Timex, for example, retails a watch that can be used for global positioning systems via satellites to beam information about the precise location of the wearer to secondary systems monitored by officials or coaches. Coaches and team managers of Tour de France cyclists are able to monitor the power output of each of their riders. Chicago marathon participants wear a tiny accelerometer clipped to their shoelaces. It transmits data concerning their speed and distance covered by radio signal to a wristwatch, which in turn sends the data to a server over a wireless network. Officials and spectators on a website can view the data.

The next generation of this performance measurement technology will enable officials, players and coaches/managers to track the location, movement and actions of every player during every moment of performance. Performances have demanded increasingly precise time-keeping technology, to measure hundredths of a second and fractions of a millimetre. Photo-finish results are now standard in sports ranging from Formula One to the 100 metres backstroke, whilst 'third-eye' video camera technology is evident in team competitions such as cricket and rugby. In the future, electronic sensors and high-speed cameras will be able to detect whether a tennis shot is in or out anywhere in the court, and determine whether a let, net or out was played based on the speed and direction of the ball.

Aside from the performance management dimensions, such technologies will revolutionise the way players approach the game. Advances in scoring technology, 'third-eye' umpiring, sporting equipment and training techniques are also destined to change the face of sport as we know it. For example, what if intelligent software was acting as the referee of a water polo match? With ubiquitous cameras including access to underwater vision, nothing would escape the eagle eye of the referee. Surely the game would evolve differently, with players seeking new ways to stay ahead of their opponents, and the intelligent learning software inventing new ways of keeping unpredictable human behaviour in check.

Preceding complete computer control of sporting events, technology is being used to augment human decisions. Disk-based recording has facilitated instant replays where real match footage is generated into three-dimensional animations, allowing the analyst to view it from an infinite number of angles. Interactivity allows viewers to select replays at will, view action from a number of different camera locations, and track the movement of individual players ('Playercam').[6]

'Navicam' is the latest sport-camera technology to be used in coverage of British touring car championships. It controls the motion of robotised television cameras with unparalleled precision and reaction time. This enables motor racing coverage to zoom in on fast moving action, providing an enhanced experience for television watchers and, most importantly, improved visibility for sponsors. The technology is touted to increase sponsor footage from 100 to 300 seconds per hour.[7]

Similarly, 'Hawk-eye' technology is being targeted at sports such as baseball, tennis and cricket. It enables the user, the broadcaster in the first instance (and shortly the digital Internet user), to compare pitchers, servers and bowlers and examine the difference between their techniques. Like most cutting-edge sport broadcasting technology, it encourages greater 'interactivity' between the spectator and the player, which in turn creates greater spectator 'expertise'.[8] As any marketer will argue, educating a customer is one of the first stages of fostering brand loyalty.

Computer technology is being used to design sports equipment from Formula-One cars to golf clubs and training shoes. The athletes of today appear as lycra-clad 'torpedos' with sleek, space-age helmets, each accessory potentially slashing minute (but precious) hundredths of a second off their performance. In the future, sporting equipment will be designed so that it can be integrated with the athlete herself through computer chips and wireless connectivity. Just as power and speed data is sent to professional cyclists' support crews, the next generation of equipment will relay everything from the stroke volume of oars in water to the number of motor units and muscle fibres recruited during a weightlifting snatch.

The information technology revolution has also elevated training regimes to increasingly sophisticated levels. Improvements in software, processing speed and graphics capabilities have enabled coaches and athletes to construct three-dimensional simulations of how the athlete's body moves. Jumping, running, hurdling, shot-putting, and even complex gymnastic movements can be evaluated in this way. Actual athlete movement patterns can then be compared against optimal movement configurations that have been electronically modelled.

In a related vein, virtual reality technologies are currently being used by bobsleigh teams to practise when snow levels are inadequate. Whilst, again, the resulting improvements in performance that such training techniques promote may be slight, it is also true that increasingly smaller margins are separating winners from losers. In fact, the distinction between the first and last across the line is already so infinitesimal in some sports that the human eye has difficulty determining it.

Computer management of sport will be welcomed by sponsors and other commercial sport stakeholders. Precision in timing and management is important for broadcasters, sponsors and advertisers, each of whom have carefully targeted their products towards specific segments of the market-place, and do not want to miss opportunities because the referee decided it was more important to start the game than wait for a carefully positioned commercial to finish. It is already commonplace, of course, for spectators attending professional sport to be subservient to television audiences. Umpires and referees are bound to commence play when a signal indicates that the commercial break has concluded. Time-outs, breaks in play, drinks and injury time are all carefully choreographed around the needs of the broadcasting rights' holder.

Notwithstanding the simmering legal issues associated with virtual advertising, the technologies that allow the superposition of sponsorship and promotional images over a venue, we can expect that eventually all signage will be computer controlled. Venues will be forced to negotiate the broadcast of their local images with event owners and broadcasters. The intricacy of broadcasting sponsor images will become so complex that only sophisticated software will be capable of undertaking it smoothly. Through technological convergence, incorporating wireless connection with the Internet, each individual's viewing choices will be relayed to the broadcaster and suitably customised sponsorship images will be shown. Complete connectivity may even lead to intelligent decision-making by the software in selecting appropriate sponsorship images at any given time. For example, the refrigerator, which contains a laser scanning eye beneath the seals of the door to identify product bar codes, might report that you removed the last beer at half time. It will be no coincidence that the virtual advertising for the third quarter will be beer related, or is for that distribution company that can deliver inside 15 minutes. How long before privacy legislation prevents this technological convergence and connectivity from getting out of hand is unclear; perhaps it will be when the refrigerator instructs the central heating to turn itself up because you are drinking too slowly. On the other hand, consumers love a deal, and many of us might well be prepared to relinquish even our most intimate consumption details if the offer is attractive enough. Discounts, loyalty programmes and frequent flyer points have a strong history of convincing consumers that their purchases are worth sharing.

The question remains, however, as to whether the athlete of the future will slice only minute slivers off records. With no significant improvement in some athletic events over the last few decades and the general slowing of record-breaking, do science and technology have anything further to offer a record-hungry society? Will it take a genetic mutant to take our collective breath away again? The answer is almost certainly yes. Improved drugs, gene therapy and genetic engineering will provide a generation of athletes so potent that present records will be smashed and left as the last contributions of mainly natural athletes. Even strict regulations that force athletes to provide genetic profiles of their parents to ensure they have not undergone manipulation will be inadequate to prevent the first generation of super-athletes taking over the sporting world. In this world, there will be infinite angles to view their freakish performances and perfect resolution at any magnification for replays. Although there will still be angry fans, there will scarcely be an argument to be made as the 'grey area' of human decisions is melted within the boundaries of software precision.

A side effect, though probably unwelcome, of genetic enhancement is that we might expect the bulk of the new breed of sports stars to come from those countries most able to deal with advanced technology. This means that the Western World is likely to profit at the expense of the emerging world and the Third World. In turn, this will arguably strengthen those businesses connected with sport in the West. If the sports stars are Western, then we might rightly expect the television syndicates and sponsors to also be Western. We might similarly expect the sport culture to be Western. The 'natural' runners of Ethiopia will soon lose dominance to the rising genetic stars of America, Europe, China, and Japan.

We must admit to a very large 'hold on a second' factor in this last comment, which is connected to the concept of 'regulation'. To date there appears to be a growing concern in the West relating to the use of genetic manipulation. While there are comparatively few formal laws or regulations governing the use of what we might term 'ultra-technology', certain aspects of it do appear of concern to many people. If such technology is perceived in the public eye to be a menace to the future of mankind or in fundamental opposition to what some might consider the 'word of God', then it is equally likely that a public backlash against the use of ultra-technology might cause the imposition of laws preventing its full potential. If such laws applied only to certain countries or cultures then we might expect other countries or cultures to step in and fill the potential gap. Conceivably, the politics of a President or the religion of a Supreme Court judge could derail US supremacy in sport or US hegemony in business. But, as we have previously stated, we remain optimists, although what we are optimistic about we have, in this instance, yet to decide.

Virtual Athletes

In our post-, or at least near-singularity scenario, where sporting hubs will be the virtual (fourth) place of our entertainment futures, we will not need to worry about venues and genetic engineering. Athletes post-singularity will perform in cyber-space. The sporting heroes of the future will be those of us capable of creating the best virtual athletes, and their performances will have to be strictly regulated like Formula One cars or else any form of competition will be nonsensical. Virtual sporting performance will have to be controlled and monitored with far more limitations and intricate rules than physical sport requires. Without tight regimentation, cyber-sport will become like a game between two people where the winner is the one who can name the highest number. In the next chapter, we expand our examination of future athletes by looking at the competitions in which they will participate and the economic nature of their athletic contributions.

Notes and References

1   Interviewed by Peter Thompson on ABC Radio National Breakfast, 1 October 2003, Australian Broadcasting Corporation.
2   Svensson, E.C., Black, H.B., Dugger, D.L., Tripathy, S.K., Goldwasser, E., Hao, Z., Chu, L. and Leiden, J.M. (1997). 'Long-Term Erythropoietin Expression in Rodents and Non-Human Primates Following IM Injection of a Replication-Defective Adenovirus Vector'. *Human Gene Therapy*, 8 (15), p. 1797; Aschwanden, C. (2000). 'Gene Cheats'. *New Scientist Magazine*, 15 January 2000.
3   Svensson *et al.*, 'Long-Term Erythropoietin Expression', p. 1797.
4   The Herald Sun (2002). 'The Human Body Liftout: Forward with medical science into the future. Part Ten'. *The Herald Sun Newspaper*, Melbourne.
5   Yang, N., MacArthur, D.G., Gulbin, J.P., Hahn, A.G., Beggs, A.H., Easteal, S. and North, K. (2003). 'ACTN3 Genotype is Associated with Human Elite Athletic Performance'. *The American Journal of Human Genetics*, 73, pp. 627–32.
6   Wallace, T. (2003). 'Coverage enhanced by regular analysis'. *Sport Business International*, 77, p. 41.
7   Hytten, M. (2002). 'Putting sponsors into sharper focus'. *Sport Business International*, 74, p. 48.
8   Gillis, R. (2002). 'Hawk-Eye sees new markets'. *Sport Business International*, 74, p. 49.

CHAPTER 4

Sport Competitions of the Future: Free Markets and Freak Markets

At the heart of all sport is competition. Without 'us' against 'them', or even 'me' against 'you', there is no sport. The greater the uncertainty of outcome of this confrontation, the greater the potential for entertainment spectacle. From an economic point of view sport marketers are always striving to maximise the supply of the number of confrontations, combined with generating the highest level of outcome uncertainty. However, what will happen to sporting confrontations in a world of genetically enhanced athletes? How can supply be maximised, given the radically changed nature of the athletes making up that supply?

In this chapter we will present ten dimensions of league or competition structure. Overall, these dimensions will provide a framework for considering the structural choices that sport competitions are facing in the future. We will look at the *format* of competition. Are knock-out competitions or league-based structures best, and do they apply to virtual sporting competitions? What will be the *hierarchy* of competition? How will the best athletes become involved in the best competitions? How will they be recruited; advancement through the ranks or through parallel feeder systems, such as athlete farms? How many leagues will there be? Can there be *multiple* top leagues coexisting, or will they compete against each other until one becomes the preferred supplier? Which teams or athletes can be '*members*' of the competition? Do the old relegation and promotion rules apply, or are US-based structures of continued and secure league membership more likely? Who will be the *governors* of the competitions: independent boards of professionals who will try to maximise income for the league as a whole, or fiercely parochial club presidents who are out for the best deal for their own teams? And who will control the supply of *labour* and *finance*? Power to the players or the owners? What about the *distribution* of sport? Will we continue to go to the stadium or will there be new ways for the stadium to come to us? Can we play where we are or do we need to travel to an arena? And who will own sport and its spin-off products? If the present trends continue, the mega-media companies will have absorbed most professional sport entities (*integration*) as part of their empires. It almost seems certain that the level of *professionalism* will only increase, both on and off the field of play.

From the perspective of future sporting competition structures, the athletes who perform in them will remain important components of the value chain of sport. In other words, the talent of athletes will continue to determine the attractiveness of the end-product. We will finish this chapter with a discussion of how these athletes are 'produced', nurtured and, ultimately, sold and traded. Will the athletes improve their bargaining position as they currently are doing, negotiating with their preferred employers and controlling their image equity, or will sport competitions and leagues devise ways of protecting their long-term investments by committing athletes to them for the duration of their productive athletic lives? Who will get shown the money?

Introduction

Does a different kind of athlete require a different kind of competition? After all, in the previous chapter we noted that in the future there is likely to be greater opportunity to identify high-potential athletes based on pre-natal tests that assess genetic make-up, as well as the real possibility of 'freak' athletes who have undergone self-gene therapy. Even further athletic specialisation can be expected at younger ages. Some athletes may have been prescribed genetic manipulation pre-natally as part of an official pro-gramme in some countries which are prepared to employ unscrupulous means to gain an advantage. Of course, this assumes that sport will remain the bastion of the naturally gifted athlete, whereas gene therapy may even-tually become so commonplace that it will effectively level the playing field to a point where, although performances are remarkable, they will also be closer and more uncertain than ever before. In addition, success may be determined more by mental discipline and training than by parental genetics. However, in the previous chapter, we expressed our suspicion that in the end money will drive success, irrespective of the circumstances.

The first genetically manipulated athletes will have the greatest advantages, and the use of gene therapy will probably be outlawed by governing bodies until its use can no longer be avoided or policed. As the only method of catching gene-cheats is by comparing a recent genetic profile with one from birth, it will be some time before testing can possibly catch up with infringements. It will be another generation or two before genetic records can inexpensively and quickly be produced from a DNA sample. However, parents who consider sporting activity important for their children will submit to the tests in order to provide them with every opportunity they can. Most prospective parents would probably be happy to initiate genetic profiling in order to ensure that their children would be free from disease or perhaps even imperfection and, given the option, to correct any defect with pre-natal gene therapy.

It is difficult to imagine a deep future where genetic manipulation is not an option for parents, and as a consequence becomes a technology available for anyone. With this in mind, it is hard to suggest that sport will remain untouched. Thus, at first, we can expect sporting competitions to become gene-regulated. However, whether governing bodies eventually relax such regulation will revolve around the health consequences of genetic tampering. Perhaps then only official, medically sanctioned, genetic interventions might be allowed. Pharmaceutical companies will only be permitted to produce genetic drug stimulators within tightly controlled, government-endorsed guidelines. Gene therapies will have to be structured so that the effects are not cumulative. The great danger of current performance-enhancing drugs lies in the massive overdoses athletes take. If gene therapies work in a similar way, professional sport will become a platform for athletes to outdo each other in physical capability until many kill themselves in the process. Some middle ground might emerge where genetic modification is tolerated provided it meets certain criteria (height and weight ceilings for sports or greater use of divisions). Alternatively, unlike drugs, genetic changes may be more rigidly regulated through accredited medical practitioners who will monitor usage and after-effects.

While many will practise forms of gene therapy to prolong or enhance their lives, there will remain some who prefer a 'natural' condition. Divisions of competition might be developed for these individuals, providing they can verify their unchanged genetic status since birth. Despite the opportunities for enhanced injury recovery, the sheer volume of athletes in the future will ensure that longevity in elite sport is a rare achievement. It is possible that sporting competitions might divide into those conducted in cyber-space and those in reality, or even those between humans and those between or against machines or computers.

These possibilities raise some important questions about the future structure of sport and the economic consequences of the performance of athletes. While it is not the intention of this chapter to venture deeply into the theory of labour or industrial economics, it does seek to continue our examination of the impact of changes to athletes on the structure and execution of sporting competitions.

The Future of Sporting Competitions

Team sports have typically been organised into league structures. According to Roger Noll, leagues must make choices concerning at least five dimensions of structure.[1] To these dimensions we have added five of our own and broadened the context to sporting competitions rather than looking exclusively at leagues. These dimensions are outlined below:

1   Format: the method for scheduling matches or tournaments to determine the champion.
2   Hierarchy: the relationships between leagues or competitions of lesser and greater quality.
3   Multiplicity: the number of leagues or competitions at the same level of the hierarchy.

4   Membership: the conditions under which a team or athlete enters and exits a league or competition.
5   Governance: the methods for deciding and enforcing rules and policies, ownership and legal structure.
6   Labour: the methods employed to enhance competitive balance and outcome uncertainty by manipulating the labour market.
7   Finance: the methods employed to manipulate the financial dividends of the league or competition.
8   Distribution: the methods of distributing and timing the game to markets.
9   Integration: decisions concerning activity horizontally and vertically in the value chain.
10 Professionalism: the nature and level of compensation to players and managers.

Although there are some overlaps between dimensions, they do collectively provide a useful framework for considering the structural choices that leagues and competitions face. In the following sections, these dimensions are used to discuss the future of sporting competitions.

Format

Leagues and competitions are normally formed so that structure is given to the resolution of the best teams, to facilitate scheduling and to enhance the financial circumstances of participants. Pivotal to the acquisition of these features are the structural choices associated with formatting. In essence, the key issue is about the control of supply and the elusive goal is to increase supply without eroding demand. Event-based competitions tackle this problem with series of, or individual, tournaments, which can utilise a range of systems to determine a champion or an ongoing series leader. Horse, dog and motor racing are good examples, as are athletics, tennis, golf and equestrian sports. Leagues have the luxury of more activity and therefore greater supply to manipulate. As a result, they have choices to make about balance (whether all teams play each other) and evenness (whether the teams play the same number of games). Generally speaking, event-based competitions are more likely to be imbalanced than league structures. For example, the English Football Association (FA) Cup typically has more than 500 entries, so a round robin would be impractical and could not be completed inside one season.

Most leagues employ a mix between a round robin during the season and a knockout finals system. From an economic viewpoint, winning the league by finishing on top of the ladder does not maximise the competitive uncertainty and revenue opportunities. More exciting knockout-style finals or playoffs are therefore added to determine championship positions, which artificially increase supply while simultaneously enhancing attractiveness. Cups and other tournaments can occur simultaneously with regular season activities, such as the Champions League. Interestingly, the Champions League and World Cup are organised with round robins for qualification to participate in elimination finals. These are the best approaches to balance the number of games being played (supply) and the importance of the games (demand). It might reasonably be expected in the future that this is a popular avenue to improve and enhance the importance of the overall competition (European Champions League to a World Champions League). A world club championship does exist, but not in a league-style format. This would typically demand an expansion in geographical territory, and has been practised in Europe by the International Basketball Federation and to a lesser extent holds potential in South America and Asia (but for lack of organisation), because the distances are not as troublesome.

Perhaps the greatest challenge to formatting in the future will come from the need to develop new avenues of supply. Some of this force will be a consequence of new forms of sport entertainment, where virtual and real elite competitions emerge as separate entities, although it is unlikely that the cyber-dimensions of sport will be owned or administered by the bodies responsible for its physical version. It remains unclear, however, who owns the rights to cyber-sport experiences. In addition, if genetic manipulation of athletes becomes a reality, there may be a need for new divisions of sport to cater for their performances. More high-quality athletes will also provide leagues and competitions with the opportunity to increase supply without diminishing quality. Control events might be introduced in horse and dog racing, where owners of the same cloned animal can put their training and jockeys to the test.

Hierarchy

The relationships between other leagues or competitions of lesser and greater quality provide the structural pathways for players and teams to progress and regress. Lower levels are often viewed as feeder systems that provide better players and teams with the opportunity to move to a pinnacle competition. Depth often varies enormously but, in general, the taller the hierarchy the stronger the quality of competition. For instance, there are

10 levels in the English Football Association, which culminates in the Premier League. The US college system is the feeder system for the lower minor professional leagues, although it is not common for a college player to progress to the lowest of the feeder leagues and move through each one in turn to reach the highest level. College systems are also hierarchical in nature, being divisions of the National Collegiate Athletic Association (NCAA). Major League Baseball (MLB) has five levels, which is the most in the USA. Basketball and football have only one minor league, while soccer and (ice) hockey have two.

In the future, we might expect the current trend, where the distance between the peak and the lower divisions, will continue to expand. This is likely to develop to the point where movement between minor leagues or feeder structures is possible, but entry into the top league is not possible by simply being the best of the next level down. Recruitment into the highest professional level will occur earlier and will more frequently come about through talent farms than through scouting. In the USA, more top athletes will make their way to the big four leagues directly from high school, having been identified early in their teens. Similarly, in structured sporting systems with sport institutes and development programmes such as those in Australia, the Netherlands, France and Japan, more gifted athletes will bypass the need for outstanding club performance for regional and national representation, instead having been cultivated and selected through talent squads.

Multiplicity

In some circumstances, more than one league has competed for the same hierarchical space, but generally this has not been a viable position and has tended to be met with market failure. However, leagues and competitions do sometimes try to enhance demand by creating numerous championships within the one. As a result, the division of leagues into conferences or regions is common, particularly in large competitions covering a substantial regional area. The World Cup, for example, requires success within a regional zone before a country qualifies for the final tournament. The use of divisions or conferences also has the advantage of adding uncertainty to the championship showdown, as the teams that reach the finals have had few if any opportunities to recently play each other to determine the better side, which in turn adds to speculation.

European and Australian leagues tend to employ single, unified league structures, while many in the USA have several distinct divisions. MLB, in fact, has two actual leagues, and is differentiated by three divisions.

The National Basketball Association (NBA), National Football League (NFL) and National Hockey League (NHL) have conferences, which are in turn comprised of a number of divisions. In addition, it is possible to find a number of somewhat independent leagues, which do not clearly fit within feeder structures. NFL Europe and basketball in the USA, which has several minor leagues, are good examples.

The failure of the Extreme Football League (XFL) to rival the entrenched NFL in the USA augurs poorly for new competitions seeking to establish alternative peak leagues. If a well-resourced and established sport entertainment company such as the World Wrestling Entertainment (WWE) in partnership with a media distributor cannot crack the market, then the opportunities are genuinely limited. Nevertheless, if the force for a new competition were to come from some of the key teams or franchises involved in the existing one, then the chances are radically improved. The possibility of break-away groups is high in the future in a number of sports including motor racing and soccer, particularly in Europe. A European super-league format orchestrated by the leading soccer clubs who make up the G14 group has been a possibility for many years, for example, and, if the financial equation deems it more lucrative, then the teams will make their move. There is also the possibility that there will be more multiple membership in leagues in the future in a similar manner to the way the best European clubs participate in their domestic competitions as well as the Champions League. Again, the opportunity for clubs to increase their supply is compelling.

Membership

The conditions under which a team or player enters and exits a league or competition can either be extremely rigid to the point of exclusivity, or can be relatively open and performance-linked. Promotion and relegation systems are the distinguishing feature of open leagues, which are a feature of many European structures. In the USA and Australasia most leagues are closed, with effectively no opportunity for additional teams to join. The great advantage of closed league structures is the geographic monopolies held by participating teams who have the opportunity to command the undistracted loyalty of a market in a catchment area. Sometimes, as in Melbourne, Australia, rigid geographical identity can be extremely competitive, with nine Australian Football League (AFL) clubs (out of 16 in the league) being located in suburban regions of the city. However, mostly this situation is found in promotion and relegation systems such as

English football, where theoretically any team in the system can eventually make its way to the Premier League, however unlikely. Relegation and promotion systems work well when there are not evenly spread and populated metropolitan regions that are equally interested in the sport. In addition, they can bolster competitive balance, unless the 'lack of parity' tools such as salary caps makes the gap between the top and bottom of the league impossible to close. Event competitions tend to be less rigid in their barriers to entry. Some, such as golf and tennis, allow qualification based on performance in lower levels, while others, such as Formula One motor racing, are essentially a function of money and lobbying. Still other systems, such as boxing, rely on rankings and negotiation, while test cricket is played in series between countries.

One of the biggest difficulties concerns the contraction or expansion of leagues which are not geographically imbalanced, which possess members that are not as attractive as others, or which hold the prospect of consolidations or mergers. Also, the relocation of teams has been a source of some controversy, mainly because reasons for relocation have tended to revolve around financial opportunities. This relocation is essentially limited to professional leagues, and has occurred in the USA more than any other country, usually motivated by highly attractive tenancy agreements in other cities. If anything, rather than consolidation, leagues and competitions are likely to expand the number of teams or participants they allow. However, a simultaneous expansion and fragmentation is possible. While more teams gain entry to leagues and more players enter events, the best method of maximising the added supply is to create further divisionalisation, where it is possible for success to be achieved in conferences or divisions before playoffs and finals are staged to determine the overall champion. We can therefore expect more fragmentation within competitions.

Governance

The relationship between sport governing bodies and leagues is often ambiguous. Some governing bodies organise their own events or leagues, such as the IOC (Olympic Games), FIFA (World Cup) and the Union Européenne de Football Associations, or UEFA (Champions League), while others have only loose liaisons with their league or competition counterparts. Many professional leagues are autonomous and are not responsible for the participation development and infrastructure of the sport. Thus, the big four US leagues (NFL, NBA, MLB, NHL) are independent, as are the college systems that feed them. The European and Australasian systems, being more club-based, are more likely to have responsibility for non-elite development of the sport, or at least are more likely to have formal relationships with the organisations that do. The English Football Association is, for example, responsible for the management of the Premier League as well as the growth and maturity of English football in general. Similarly, the Australian Football League is the custodian of the grassroots of the game. Although the development of the participation side of sport is fundamental to its business future, it is unlikely that elite leagues and competitions will be capable of dividing their attention. Despite relationships that foster cross-subsidisation, the management and development of the participation side of sport will continue to stray from the management interest of the games' elite competitions.

Part of the reason for this trend is associated with the imperatives that go along with the ownership structure of event competitions, leagues and their constituent teams. There are two common legal structures from which to govern sporting competitions: joint ventures and single entities. In the former, independently owned clubs get together to form a joint venture, where the club owners or Chairmen/Presidents or their representatives constitute the directors of the league. Some governing bodies which administer events operate in this fashion. The latter structure, the single entity, is one wherein the league owns the teams and either allows shares in the league to be sold or appoints management of their own for each team, such as in Major League Soccer in the USA. Unfortunately, although the league is well structured for competitive parity, it has not been a success with sport fans.

Joint ventures tend to be more efficient as potential team operators want to own the team, not a share of the league. Conversely, joint ventures are more often lop-sided competitions, because the teams do not cooperate as they would in a single entity to maximise uncertainty. However, sport followers are reluctant to appreciate collusion between teams, which they view as natural adversaries. Better joint ventures get around the problems of parochial decision-making by developing an independent and external governance system. Nevertheless, the single entity approach is highly appealing to new entrants in sporting competitions and events. It diminishes accusations of anti-competitive behaviour and centralises financial control and therefore profitability. In joint venture structures, courts will play an ongoing role in rulings on anti-trust cases. In the future, fewer differences will be discernable between corporate entities and leagues and competitions.

Labour and finance

There are two dimensions to the regulation of a league or competition: the labour market and the financial market, both discussed in this section. The first focuses on what is called the labour market, in which player movements

Highly Regulated	**Quadrant 2** Equity	**Quadrant 3** Command
Finance Market **Unregulated**	**Quadrant 1** Free Market	**Quadrant 4** Distributive

Unregulated　　**Labour Market**　　**Highly Regulated**

Figure 4.1　Stewart structural typology for sport leagues

can be tightly regulated, at one end, or unregulated at the other. Players may be free to locate to any club, subject to previous contractual obligations, or (once contracted) are tied to the club in perpetuity.

The second dimension of league or competition regulation focuses on the revenue or finance market, in which revenues are collected and spent either collectively or independently. For instance, the central administrative body can collect revenue, and then redistribute it equally amongst the participating teams. On the other hand, it can be collected by the competing teams, or even only the home team, and retained without any redistribution.

It is possible to construct a two-dimensional model of regulatory structures, which provides for four distinct administrative and regulatory possibilities. These possibilities are revealed in Figure 4.1, developed by Bob Stewart of Victoria University, Melbourne.

Quadrant 1 comprises an unregulated finance market with an unregulated labour market, which is labelled the free market model. In this model, for instance, home teams collect all game revenue, television rights can be negotiated by the individual clubs, and players are bound to clubs only in so far as they have a formal employment contract. Quadrant 2 comprises a regulated finance market with an unregulated labour market, which is labelled the equity model. Revenues from games, television rights and merchandise are redistributed to assist poorly resourced teams, but players can choose the club they wish to play for. Revenue flows are partly controlled by the central administration, but players are not. Quadrant 3 comprises a regulated finance market with a regulated labour market, which is labelled the command model. This is the most tightly controlled structure, since both revenue and player movements are controlled by the central administration. Quadrant 4 comprises a regulated labour market and an unregulated finance market, which is labelled the distributive model. That is, the movement of players is regulated to ensure that playing talent is distributed evenly between teams. Revenue streams, though, are retained by the teams that generate them. There is no scheme to ensure an equitable income for clubs.

Drafts and salary caps severely constrain the free movement of players between clubs and teams. Drafting systems are focused on controlling the physical reallocation of playing talent. The NFL draft is typical in that it rations the order in which teams can select available new players. This order is determined by the reversing of championship results from the previous season, with the worst-performing team receiving the best choices of new talent. Salary caps are used as a ceiling on the amount of money that can be spent on players, in theory preventing the wealthy clubs from out-buying their competition and monopolising all the talent. The big four US leagues employ salary caps, although MLB employs a luxury tax that is imposed upon payments over a certain threshold. In 2004, the luxury tax threshold was set at US$120.5 million. In 2003, the threshold was US$117 million, with a 17.5 per cent penalty on every dollar over. The New York Yankees exceeded the cap by US$54.1 million and paid US$9.47 million in tax. Despite the increase in penalty to 22.5 per cent in 2004, the team seems to consider the tax a necessary burden for the player list they want, which provides them with not just playing talent, but marketability.

Caps are also common in Australia and in some parts of Asia, but have not been embraced by European soccer. They are, however, used in Rugby League and Union in the UK. Reserve option clauses in US baseball and retain and transfer systems in European soccer are further examples of labour market clauses designed to restrict free agency. However, although labour market restrictions have applied to player salaries and mobility in Europe and the USA, free agency is likely to increase in the future, particularly after the Bosman Ruling made by the European Court of Justice declaring that no fee could be expected by clubs upon the transfer of an out-of-contract player, and the pressures in the USA for free agency and restricted free agency. Interestingly, in the USA, research on the impact of the draft or free agency has provided little compelling evidence that either affects competitive balance.[2]

Revenue sharing and cross-subsidisation is common in sport leagues, but they vary substantially. In the USA, for example, NFL teams share gate receipts, media rights and licensing almost evenly. However, the NBA allows for shared media but the home team keeps all the gate receipts. In MLB, gate receipts are heavily skewed to the home side, but both share evenly in licensed merchandise and media rights. In several of the top European soccer leagues, in contrast, revenues from national television deals are redistributed on the basis of performance.

Stewart's typology therefore identifies a number of structural possibilities for a sport league to consider when deciding upon the organisational form it will take. It enables a league to succinctly compare and contrast its structures with other leagues, and to make sense of what often amounts to an apparently unrelated clutter of policies, rules and regulations. It also shows what may need to be done in order to move from one structure to another or, alternatively, to ensure that a league retains its current structure. In short, the typology highlights the variety of ways that a sport league or competition can be organised, and hints at the different outcomes that may follow from adopting new policies and rules.

The future may hold a mix of changes to regulatory policy. Events have the luxury of taking a far more straightforward approach, where prize money is paid out from available revenue, but with few imperatives for percentages, and no labour market restrictions applying to individual performers. On the other hand, revenue-sharing policies vary across leagues, even within countries, and are likely to continue to be individual. However, there is increasing pressure for European soccer competitions to embrace salary caps, while managing the push for free agency. A salary cap will have to be uniform across Europe if it is to work, however, because a cap will place a severe competitive disadvantage upon any team competing against a club from a country with no such impositions. As more high-quality athletes become available, free agency will pose fewer problems for clubs, but players will find themselves increasingly 'owned' nevertheless.

Distribution

Distribution policies reflect a structural decision in the management of competitions and leagues. In the future, if more people can watch the same matches through forms of virtual spectatorship, the Internet or conventional broadcasting, then there is less pressure to play more games during a regular season in order to maximise attendances and viewership. In this sense, the relationships competitions and leagues develop with venues, the media and promoters are pivotal to their success, as are attempts at international positioning.

Technology can facilitate the distribution of sport events in both high-profile and modest ways. For example, it is possible for smaller sports to conduct interregional or international events using Internet and digital platforms as an integrator. For example, imagine a national ten-pin bowling tournament staged simultaneously in each state in the USA, with real-time results from each location uploaded to the Internet allowing for a genuinely national competition. Swimmers might soon be able to attend their local accredited pool to participate in a national 'swim-off', where they can register their best times for any distance, event or age, to be posted on the Internet in the form of a national ranking. As attempts to increase supply and availability are an overriding concern for some competitions, the possibilities accompanying virtual seating and other opportunities for remote but sensory-rich spectator experiences will be highly valued.

The short-term future of sport at venues is probably secure despite technological options which facilitate the distribution of sport through new channels. While new venues and stadia will be constructed as broadcasting studios housing live audiences, there will remain demand for the live spectatorship experience. Some of this demand will tend to fall away as virtual spectatorship begins to rival live attendance as a sensory experience; but this will only improve the value of broadcasting rights and is unlikely to disappoint leagues and competitions. It will also afford smaller competitions the opportunity to sell their virtual experiences to more diverse markets.

Integration

The financial pressures placed upon sport businesses and competitions are immense. As a result, they are seeking alternative avenues for revenue creation, which will increasingly include horizontal and vertical integration activities. Horizontal integration refers to a form of product differentiation. For example, a sporting event organisation might venture into staging concerts. Vertical integration, on the other hand, relates to an involvement in activities up or down the supply channel. A sporting league that decides to manufacture its own merchandise, produce its own sporting equipment or develop a marketing company would constitute a step towards vertical integration. It is not uncommon presently for governing bodies to create a corporate subsidiary responsible for the marketing and profit-making aspects of the sport, but hold no assets as legal protection.

More integration can be expected in the future of both kinds, as the spin-off sectors to the sporting industry become more lucrative and governing leagues and competitions decide that they do not want to sell all their licensing rights for spin-off commodities produced by other companies. This integration is likely to take the form of joint ventures, with partner companies providing the core business skills. Sport businesses can expect spin-off products and services, or those further up or down the supply chain, to grow, using sport as the vehicle. Some of these spin-offs will constitute an opportunity for enterprising sport business competitions.

Professionalism

Levels of professionalism have steadily increased across sport business competitions and leagues, and sport management and marketing professionals. This trend is likely to continue with the inflow of more higher-quality players. Although the industry is experiencing a downturn in sponsorship and rights fees, the more robust competitions will emerge from this phase with more streamlined and professional systems that more closely resemble conventional businesses than ever before. The possibility of parallel competitions in cyber-space may also bolster the professionalism of the virtual dimensions of sport in the future.

The role of volunteers in sport in the future remains critical to the success of sporting clubs, athletes and competitions, but their future activities in an increasingly professional and legalised context are unclear. The importance of volunteer labour is unquestioned, but competitions and leagues will have less interest in their involvement, preferring professional employees, and encouraging volunteers to remain involved in club activities. Fewer volunteers will engage in sport business activities in the future, marginalised by money and the demand for accountability. A summary of the 10 dimensions discussed appears in Table 4.1.

Future Billionaires?

Although the professional athletes of the future will undoubtedly be stronger and possess greater endurance, there might be some question as to whether they will be richer. There are two ways of looking at this question. On the one hand, it might be observed that athlete salaries, while higher in absolute terms than ever before, represent a disproportionately greater component of sport enterprises' revenues. In other words, player salaries have increased more than the revenues of the organisations they represent. While we might expect a correction in the short to medium term, on the other hand it can be argued that those same sport organisations are playing in larger and larger markets, capable of returning significantly higher revenues in the long term. It is worth exploring these two viewpoints to help unravel the role that the professional athlete will play in the future of sport business.

Phil VanFossen[3] is one who has made the argument that some professional athletes are actually, from an economic viewpoint, underpaid. He draws on the experiences of MLB. In MLB, drafting relationships are heavily restricted so that young players must be drafted by individual clubs and subsequently must sign with that club. Also, the owners of MLB franchises adhere to strict regulations concerning both the number of teams in the

Table 4.1   Structural dimensions of sporting competitions

Dimension	Current	Future
1 Format	Most leagues use playoffs and finals. Events employ cumulative series or tournament structures	More aggregate matches across geographic regions such as Champions League. More seeding to ensure most powerful teams have greatest chance of reaching the money rounds. More imbalanced because it maximises uncertainty and revenue. More uneven because certain teams have more demand to play
2 Hierarchy	Depth in larger competitions with feeder structures	Larger gaps between pinnacle and lower levels, with recruiting occurring earlier and bypassing second level leagues and competitions. Greater distance between top and bottom of premier leagues, leading to champions levels or competitions in addition
3 Multiplicity	Divisions and conferences used mainly in the USA. Little if any competition for highest level of sport	Increased use of divisionalisation to provide more opportunities for staged success in larger competitions. Possibilities of break-away leagues and competitions formed by strongest clubs. New levels of competition for genetically enhanced athletes. Media and broadcasters to become more involved in ownership of single entity leagues and private events
4 Membership	European soccer employs promotion and relegation systems. Most leagues are fixed in membership with huge entry barriers. Performance standards for events for qualification	Membership of fixed competitions to expand to include more geographical regions. Ongoing migration of teams. Multiple membership for the powerful clubs to champions-style leagues in addition to domestic competition
5 Governance	Joint venture more robust than single entity. Governing bodies and private business run some events and series	Greater interest in single entity structures driven by business opportunities, particularly from broadcasters. Joint ventures remain the standard for the stalwart sports, but single entities created in unexpectedly popular sports. Greater importance of companies in delivering events and competitions
6 Labour	Generally restrictive practices including drafts, salary caps and transfer contracts	Restrictive player movements and payments to continue, but strong push to free agency not necessarily to the benefit of players with increased quality options for clubs

Table 4.1 Continued

Dimension	Current	Future
7 Finance	Mix of cross-subsidisation practices and uneven revenue sharing	Fragmentation to continue, but growing gap between the wealthy and poor clubs/athletes
8 Distribution	Fixed live supply, but broadcasting increasing geographical spread	Unfixed live supply through virtual spectatorship at the top end and coordinated activities across disparate geographical zones at the bottom end
9 Integration	Limited horizontal diversification, based on outsourcing and focus on core business. Vertical integration with event ownership	Further use of independent corporate structures owned by governing bodies to administer profit-making dimensions of sport. Vertical integration taken up by broadcasting and other companies with independent events
10 Professionalism	Business structures and systems the norm	Increased levels of professionalism resembling corporate structures

competition and the number of players belonging to each of those teams. Underpinning these two factors is the implication that MLB players will be continually exploited and paid well below their economic productivity where possible. The players probably hold this view, as evidenced by the 1994 strike.

If indeed this is true and sport organisations are enforcing tighter controls on salary payments, then we might conclude that the economic future of professional athletes does not hold the exponential increases in salary that have been observed during the past few decades. Notwithstanding the fact that athlete salaries in some sports leagues have increased too fast for clubs to keep up with, this is at least partly because the regulatory control held by leagues and clubs has diminished, supplanted by more power to player unions and agents. Salary caps have almost universally increased, and in some leagues they must be paid out. For example, in the Australian Football League, 95 per cent of a team's salary cap must be paid out in player salaries. In general, clubs tend to believe that the leagues that govern them have given away too much to players, which constricts their freedom to realise their full revenue potentials.

Although (the rich) clubs are probably right in that they could generate more money selling their rights independently and that players have advanced their relative power through collective bargaining, the regulatory argument often fails in the middle of the market. For example, studies have been done to determine the actual productivity that a player contributes: that is, what is effectively their percentage contribution to the overall revenue of the team. What the studies tend to reveal is that rookie players are underpaid because they do not have bargaining leverage yet, and the star players, believe it or not, are also underpaid because they attract revenue beyond that which is acquired directly as a result of their playing performances. As a result, both unproven and mega-star athletes tend to be underpaid. This probably holds true for teams and individual performers, the latter group being vulnerable to the predilections of promoters and event organisers. This does not of course reconcile the fact that in elite sport broadly, star athletes are demanding more than event organisers and teams can afford.

Part of the problem is that the clubs prepared to go into the red for a win sometimes circumvent the usually ruthless forces of supply and demand. They have artificially and disproportionately elevated the importance of athletes beyond their contribution to the bottom line. Clearly, this cannot continue indefinitely. There will be a correction, particularly in European football leagues, but the value of athletes in the future will continue to increase for one simple reason: the value of sport will increase.

What is an Athlete Worth?

Alex Rodriguez signed with the Texas Rangers for 10 years for US$252 million and Tiger Woods has a US$100 million sponsorship contract with Nike. Will they and other mega-stars of the future command commensurate incomes? With seven-figure incomes and endorsements of titanic proportions, it may seem absurd for the 'average' person to consider a future where athletes' incomes continue to grow. However, with more and more of us 'average' people spectating via broadband and pay television, and viewing replays on mobile phones, the future bank balances of our elite athletes seem secure. For example, there might be some debate as to whether Lennox Lewis is worth US$20 million per fight, but few boxing fans would argue that he (in concert with a sound undercard) supplies 20 dollars' worth of pay-per-view entertainment for an individual. The fact then remains that Lewis's salary will always be an equation relating to the proportion of the number of spectators through all distribution methods multiplied by how far they reach into their collective pockets.

Remuneration for athletes is principally determined by the number of people prepared to watch them. This will be as true in the future as it is today. Before broadcasting technology, sport events could only hope to reach the 50,000 spectators or so that constituted the stadium's capacity.

The introduction of radio in the 1930s, television in the 1950s, cable in the 1970s and (most recently) satellite has exponentially expanded the number of potential and actual spectators. This radically enlarged population has, in turn, elicited substantial investment by media conglomerates into the sporting organisations and athletes providing the content. This feedback loop is sure to continue well into the foreseeable future as technology enables increasing numbers to consume sport in diverse formats. The professional athlete of the future is sure to be well paid.

Whether it seems absurd or not, the issue is quite clear: Tiger Woods is a millionaire because he is the most entertaining golf player in the world. But he will be a billionaire because the market to which golf is commercially viable is extremely large. Some professional athletes are wealthy because they are in high demand within their league or playing contexts. Professional athletes are absurdly wealthy because the world is 'getting bigger'. We can expect that the salaries of professional athletes will continue to increase along with the revenues of the organisations that 'own' them.

Athletes as Assets

More than any other sport 'entertainment' organisation in the world, WWE (formerly the World Wrestling Federation) has controlled the earning potential of its stars admirably. Each wrestler's identity is trademarked and owned exclusively by WWE. This means that the massive revenues that come from merchandise and other related sales of those identities (including films – WWE produced *The Scorpion King* – computer games and food) are exclusively owned by the company. The approach by the company's President, Vince McMahon, may be the blueprint for the future.

Imagine, for example, that every player in a professional sport club is trademarked as an athlete. All merchandise and rights associated with that player in their association with the club may be owned by the club. The freedom that athletes have gained over the past 10 years just might be overturned in the next 10 by clubs trying hard to regain some control over their own rights, which have traditionally been held stringently by leagues. The fight over players as 'trademarkable' identities is likely to be inevitable, and may even be determined ultimately outside league regulatory mechanisms. More astute athletes competing in individual sports such as tennis may approach athlete licensing brokers, which will become as ubiquitous as player agents.

The problem for professional athletes is the control over rights that they might have always assumed was rightfully theirs. In league situations, players and agents on their behalf have always sought the opportunity for free agency. Anything less, in their opinion, was considered a restraint of trade that would be unacceptable in other non-sporting situations.

Free agency is a major issue in the US National Football League. Simply put, the players want it, while the owners are opposed. Perhaps the real issue is the philosophical one that Jerome Ellig highlights cogently: what lover of liberty, he claims, can oppose a concept as 'American' as free agency? In the end, players only want a free market. Teams should bid for their services just as they would for any other employee. The market should be the resolution of supply and demand. In the last 25 years, free agency has emerged in the US major sport leagues from a history of rigid reserve arrangements. In Europe, moves towards free agency have been encouraged by the Bosman Ruling.

Market freedom is not as simple a concept as it might appear, however. At one level it is a matter of principle; on another, it is just another scrap over who is going to pocket more of the loot. To continue the US example, players in professional team sports (such as baseball and football) generally negotiate their own salaries with their respective clubs through their agents. Player unions help the players by forming league agreements that govern the basics, such as minimum salaries and conditions. Free agency, has, however, encouraged longer-term contracts as players seek to gain as much employment security as they can within their short careers.

The future therefore promises the meeting of two contradictory forces. On the one hand, the teams striving to control the identities and contract conditions of their players will meet the players and player unions who will be seeking the right to solicit a better deal from as many other clubs as possible. A free market for players' services will inevitably lead to a more expensive market. On the other hand, the rights that athletes have over their images, athletic identities and choice of employer would seem to be fundamental. What will the future deliver?

Perhaps the key to predicting the future of 'athletes as assets' might lie in understanding the role that leagues and organising and governing bodies might play, in conjunction with the lessons contained in commercial business practice. In the first instance, official governing sport organisations are tending towards marginalisation. Nowhere can be seen a sharper example of the power of super clubs over the activities of their governing body than in Champions League and UEFA football. The successful, and often wealthiest, clubs will go their own way if they ultimately believe it to be in their best interests. Currently, the G14 are demanding somewhere around 20 per cent of World Cup (of soccer) revenues. Moreover, the G14 has been continually predicted to become the G20 or G24. These additional clubs might not just be European, but might include South American and Asian teams, opening up several new and lucrative markets to the owners of the television and other rights. Although less than triumphant, a number of European basketball 'super-clubs' did form their own super-league several years ago. The power of official governing sport bodies is decreasing. Clubs are on the move.

Furthermore, the role of commercial enterprises to the future of athletes is likely to be significant. It is particularly appealing to media and entertainment companies, for example, to move into ownership of sport without investing heavily in its infrastructure. The list of networks that own sport franchises is growing in the USA, Canada, Europe and Asia-Pacific. Although the XFL (designed to rival the NFL) was a failure, the concept may have been ahead of its time as a joint venture between an entertainment company and a network. Perhaps the only change to the formula would be the involvement of existing teams in the pre-eminent competition. Leagues setting up in competition with the existing monopoly might find it better to poach clubs rather than to go head to head with them. Rupert Murdoch grabbed a piece of the Australian rugby league competition as fodder for his pay television broadcasts this way.

On the surface it may seem appealing for clubs to defect to such break-away competitions and haul in the biggest short-term pay day imaginable, but the G14 has the right idea: better to have control than to give it away for a short-term windfall. If clubs lament the draconian decisions of their league masters, they will be in for a shock if they sell their souls to commercial businesses. Just as these companies covet the intellectual property created by their employees, so too will they squeeze their athletic minions with contractual loopholes that will end the concept of free agency once and for all.

The ultimate demonstration of athletes as assets will be seen in the proliferation of athlete farms for producing and developing athletes to be sold off like cattle to clubs, or even as competitors in events. Of course, such sports academies are not new: almost every professional soccer team has an academy for its juniors. Indeed, the modern sports academy is just a continuation of the old Roman gladiatorial schools. What will make the future athlete farm so important will be both their number and their financial clout. Money will come in from everywhere for these institutions. Sponsors will seek an early opportunity to pick from the range of imminently marketable talent. Parents will send their children to attend, as a concession to their offspring's dreams of fame and fortune, as well as to realise their own dreams of vicarious fame and fortune. These commercial facilities will become the talent centres of the future. They will overshadow government institutes for elite sport development, and in some cases will become essential tenants of their facilities. Free agency will become less of an issue because players will be snapped up by clubs earlier and tied up with immense long-term contracts.

In the USA, the institutions will become parallel feeder structures to high school sport, spilling into the college and professional systems. Entertainment and media companies will be heavy investors in these programmes, eager to acquire first bidding rights to graduating athletes who can be drafted directly by a franchise owned by the company. Alternatively, the athletes can become company sponsees, committed to wearing monitors and cameras during events such as the Olympics, not to mention their obligations in front of the camera.

The flip side of this will be twofold. First, the cost will be enormous and will need to be recouped from somewhere or somebody. Accepting that there are only a limited number of multibillionaires prepared to stake such institutions for nought but the philanthropic thrill and glamour of aiding humanity, we may assume that the cost will be borne by the advertiser and the spectator. Either way, it is your pocket that will suffer. Second, and infinitely more harmful, there is the expectation that as the dreams of some youngsters fail to be realised, increasing numbers of failed, or less successful, athletes will seek recourse to drugs, to litigation and depression.

The Sport Business of Athletes

Professional athletes are always going to be well paid by virtue of the simple economics of limited supply and exaggerated exposure. Their battle for freedom of market conditions is a difficult one, however. Even the courts are unlikely to grant complete freedom within regulated sporting leagues. That is not to say that athletes are likely to be paid less in the future. They will undoubtedly be paid far more as a consequence of one simple fact: the market is getting bigger. So, while their identities and market availability is likely to be restricted, as sports and clubs gain greater exposure throughout the 'globalised' world the wealthier they will become. This money will flow down to the players in salaries and, by consequence of their exposure, through endorsements.

Some athletes in individual sports – the Tiger Woods of their time – will have the greatest salaries, but will also have the most stringent obligations to clubs, the media and sponsors. It is also worth remembering that even the best-paid athletes are poor cousins of the media barons who 'own' them. Tiger Woods and Michael Schumacher might be multimillionaires, but Philip Knight and Bernie Eccelstone are multibillionaires.

In the greater scheme of things, athletes are probably worth it considering what they contribute to the economic and social networks that surround sport. However, just as business executives who command vast salaries and options packages are feeling the pressure to commit their companies to corporate citizenship programmes and give something back to the communities that have driven their profits, professional athletes will increasingly feel the pressure to give something back to their fans beyond the feeble efforts they make to fulfil contractual obligations. This is discussed further in Chapter 7 on corporate sport citizenship. What is yet to be explored is the response of sport followers to the changes we have noted. In the next chapter, the marketing issues that arise from these groups are discussed.

Notes and References

1   Noll, R. (2003). 'The Organization of Sports Leagues'. *Stanford Institute for Economic Policy Research, Discussion Paper No. 02–43.* Stanford University, pp. 1–51.
2   Kahn, L. (2000). 'The sports business as a labour market laboratory'. *Journal of Economic Perspectives,* 14 (3), pp. 75–94.
3   VanFossen, P.J. (1995). 'Underpaid millionaires?' *The Senior Economist.*

CHAPTER 5

Tribal Sport Business: Caveman, Fan and Clan

It can be argued that in our post-modern society, nothing is more tribal than sport, except perhaps warfare. It is part of human nature to seek the comfort and safety of a group of people that we feel close to. This closeness is achieved through sharing important experiences with the other group members. The higher the number, importance and intensity of joint experiences, the more likely it is that group members will 'act as one', as a tribe. Through shared experience and belonging tribal members build their individual identities. Sport offers a tribal arena for collective identification and community expression.

In this chapter we explore sport consumption within a cultural context. Whereas in Chapter 9 we look at cultural sport business from the perspective of globalisation and internationalisation – or the macro level – in this chapter we deal with the micro components of culture such as tribes and clans. These are the groups of people that we meet face-to-face, in and around the stadium. In the context of globalisation it is important to consider 'tribal belonging' because it offers a basis of common meaning in a world of mass communication and consumption that is increasingly faceless and isolating.

We argue that future sport business should consider the application of tribographics as well as the more common segmentation criteria such as demographics and psychographics. We discuss this concept of tribographics as a means of recognising that marketing attention should be shifted from the object of belonging (the club, the team or even the sport), to focus on delivering 'belonging' as the core service. More than any other leisure product, sport offers the benefits of belonging to young and old, male and female, black and white, rich and poor. What draws people to the sport product is a desire to 'be part of', to belong. Tribographics are underpinned by tribal needs.

The process of educating the young about which tribe they belong to, which other tribes to be wary of and which to despise, further underpins the importance of using tribographics. Tribes constitute all generations and require constant education of the younger tribal members to make sure that the bonds remain strong. This will ultimately lead to 'high context communication', high levels of unspoken understanding further facilitated by symbols (colours and logos), heroes (star players) and rituals (terrace songs in football), understood by all, irrespective of psycho-demographics.

If we tentatively accept the concept of tribographics, can sport then offer tribal security in an increasingly unsafe and insecure world? How can the business of sport cater for the universal need of 'belonging'? We are in no way implying that the sport tribe itself is a new concept, or even that seeking 'to belong' is a newly emerging consumer need. However, we do believe that understanding and mapping tribographics is a key to success in future sport business.

The Tribal Experience

The original idea of sport has changed. Early modern sport was designed by 'educated' gentlemen as an alternative reality to work and commerce, and was controlled rigidly by strict, enforceable laws. Either participants played according to the rules and laws, or they did not play at all. In some circumstances, this may have involved the expulsion of cheaters. However, the reality of the present situation is that sport has spread, multiplied and been modified beyond recognition. Like all living cultures, sport is constantly changing, dynamic in nature and subject to constant reinterpretation by its participants. The only apparent consistencies in sporting culture are the pursuit of competition, the love of winning, the ability to summon strong emotional responses in both victory and defeat and the desire to belong to a group.

The previous chapters have described a changing sport landscape, potentially including virtual sport, genomic engineering and larger, more complex competitive structures. The opportunities to experience sport in new ways will facilitate the emergence of the virtual fan, interested in clustering with like-minded individuals and groups located anywhere in the world, but connected intimately through technology. However, we would foreshadow another type of sport follower, one uninterested in technology and disillusioned by the 'progress' of the sport business. These individuals will also cluster together and will ensure the survival of the conventional live delivery of sport experiences. Despite the emergence of these disparate groups, in one pivotal way the future experiences of sport followers will be similar: they will be less interested in the objects of consumption than in the social links and identities that come with them. More than ever before, tribal marketing will need to be amongst the tools of those involved in sport business.

This chapter ventures into this tribal sport marketing of the future, exploring sport consumers as a tribal force and the relevance of social identity as a determinant of sport tribalism in the future. The chapter culminates in speculation about the nature of tribal identity and marketing in a technologically advanced sport business context.

The Tribal Bond

All religions are conceived as the result of one individual having an experience she defines as mystical, an experience where she perceives a direct understanding of ultimate reality and which is beyond the realm of the five senses.[1] (We tackle this phenomenon in the following chapter.) Groff suggests that the individual then attempts to share this direct experience of spirit or God with others (in sport, these are the fans/tribes), hoping to impart a sense of life's purpose.[2] He argues that it is usually others who champion the eventual formation of a system of teachings that pivot around the 'founder'. The teachings later become scripture passed down through generations as part of social learning and culture. Religions, according to Groff, are labelled as fundamentalist or extremist when the teachings are dogmatically interpreted or violent behaviour ensues, an outcome that can occur in any religion and in any sport.

Debate continues as to whether the mystical experiences of the founders of the world's diverse religions were the same phenomenon, or whether their experience was mediated through cultural learning, values and a sense of belonging to a particular group.[3] There is little doubt, however, that the cultural and tribal phenomenon of sport has been the tool of religious and political propaganda. In 1972, for example, Palestinian terrorists seized and killed eleven Israeli athletes at the Olympic Games. They explained their choice of venue: 'We recognize that sport is the religion of the western world ... So we decided to use the Olympics, the most sacred ceremony of this religion, to make the world pay attention to us.'[4] Although an extreme example, tribal belonging is powerful enough to command death and devotion. Death might be a little extreme, but sport marketers are always after more devotion for their products, and sport has traditionally demanded more than its fair share of 'brand' loyalty. The key difference in the future will be that smart sport marketers change the nature of their communications away from the object of devotion (the club or sport) and concentrate on facilitating the belonging to it.

Humans have a need to come together in order to share common meaning in life. This may be through sport, religion, work or hobbies. These socially proximate groups or communities – they need not be necessarily geographically proximate, although they tended to be before modern communications technology – are more effective and influential on members' behaviour than either conventional marketing messages or other formal cultural or social authorities.

Globalisation pressures have encouraged the development of what is sometimes called the global village; a world system that is economically, technologically and culturally linked. In a strange way, the expansion of the sport market has not necessarily meant that sport followers have found greater meaning. In fact, larger markets, competitions and choices tend to have the opposite effect. Instead of making people feel like part of a global village, they tend to make people feel more alone, an anonymous fan, just a membership number or a pay television subscriber. Worse, some sport fans feel like nothing more than faceless consumers, and end up feeling isolated in a world of social dissolution.

While many sport fans conduct their supporting activities in small groups, many others are unable to acquire tickets or do not enjoy the club/pub atmosphere where groups can congregate. Some therefore meet socially at each other's homes, and others still find themselves watching alone. However large the marketplace, it is still subject to fragmentation, and this means that there are more fans seeking to use sport as a vehicle for social recomposition. Meaning is found in membership of small groups with strong, common values. This is the foundation of tribalism.

We believe that tribalism will be more important than ever before to the sport business for two reasons. First, if even some of the likely technological developments described in the earlier chapters find their way to a sport application, then sport markets will become even larger, and more homogeneous. Those elements which make them uniquely local to a region will be watered down to make their supply more palatable to a broader market. There will be sport followers who will use technology to find comrades amidst the masses. Through virtual attendance they will be able to sit with their tribe on a weekly basis, irrespective of their actual location. They will also be able to interact via the virtual hubs of their particular clan. These clan fans will constitute a new sector of the market, embracing technological innovation, new experiences and the opportunity to find companionship in a cold, distant social and professional world. There will be countless of these clans even within the same club's supportership, each one with slightly different values and judgements about their place in the sport world and the relevance of their club or favourite athlete.

The second reason reflects the reactions of another group. Their response will be a rejection of the hyper-commercialisation that the sport business has undergone. To them, the more radical technological developments for the distribution of sport will represent all they despise about the world. However real, there will be no virtual attendance, or Supernet visits to clan 'hubrooms'. Watching replays on the phone and playing director with Internet digital views will not be appealing either. The circumstances will encourage these fans to become affiliated with others like them in an attempt to meet their needs for social identity. Sport and commercialism will reinforce the attractiveness of niche clan groups.

Fragmentation will accompany globalisation and the development of the sport business. In turn, the tribal movements within sport will grow. For the marketer of the future, this will mean a decreased interest in cultivating the relationships between the sport brand and the consumer, a process which emphasises cause (brand) and effect (consumption), and an increased focus on facilitating the relationships between tribal consumers. In sport tribal marketing, the brand becomes the glue for consumers, rather than their direction of aspiration. It will be the sport brand that holds the consumers together.

Traditional demographic or psychographic market segmentation is in danger of losing its magic. In a highly fragmented, information overloaded society, sport consumers are not as easily pigeon-holed into conventional market segments. Sport consumer behaviour transcends traditional segmentation boundaries. Typical lifestyles of the 'young' are adopted by the 'older' fans, and young people unashamedly go 'retro'. Sport consumers will increasingly belong to tribal groupings, held together by sets of principles and values. They will belong to a family of like-minded people, cutting across a range of traditional segmentation barriers such as age, gender, profession, income and motivation. In this way, tribes are heterogeneous, made up of people from a diverse range of demographics, but linked by a common passion or value set. It is tribographics, rather than demographics, that promise the most rich sport marketing data. The key to segmentation in the future of sport business is to identify the core tribal values and behaviours that unleash members' undying support, passion and, perhaps most important of all, their cash. Tribal values are more relevant than product differentiation. Tribalism, or 'belonging', is the currency of future sport marketing. Tribalism is what brings small groups of people together, and glues them to each other through values and identity. Tribalism is the great differentiator. There is nothing in marketing more powerful than that which makes you and I think we are the same.

The Sports Tribe

It has been more than 20 years since Desmond Morris coined the term 'the soccer tribe'. Describing soccer fans as tribal beings may have appeared more popular rhetoric than social fact, but sport fans have proved they can be fiercely tribal. Tribal identity has been responsible for violence and vandalism as well as friendship and goodwill. From a sport business viewpoint, this very tribalism is the catalyst for billions of worldwide sales in merchandise, memorabilia, pay television subscriptions, sponsorships, tickets, newspapers, magazines and even sport business books. Sport's contribution to ethnic and social identity is so important that researchers such as Richard Giulianotti believe it to be a critical variable in the formation of social identity.[5] From the sport marketer's viewpoint, tapping into tribal identity represents a 'holy grail' of sorts. But it is also the greatest danger marketers face. When sport fans feel slighted, they can defect from a club with the same fervour with which they once supported it.

Coming to be an accepted member of a sporting tribe can involve lengthy trials demonstrating trust, loyalty, commitment and self-sacrifice. This can include various initiation rituals, such as pulling on the team jersey, joining senior tribe members on visits to the sacred ceremonial sites where violent clashes with the opposing tribes take place, and learning the tribal chants by heart to express allegiance openly. Once initiated, reciprocal loyalty between the tribe and individual will be expected and demanded. As sport marketers realise, once the club is accepted by a sporting tribe, that tribe will walk through fire for it. The tribe's children will wear the club's colours, shout its name, defend and protect its place and bail it out of trouble. But most importantly, they will passionately support the club to win on and off the field of battle.

We have argued that the traditional sport marketing segmentation approach, based on psycho-social divisions, will need to be augmented in the future with a more ethno-sociological flavour. This need will be further driven by the pervasiveness of technology, which will make all consumers potential gamers in the cyber-world of sport. Those people who never received tribal sport indoctrination may loathe sports for reasons that can be overcome when they can become champions themselves. There is nothing so liberating for sports-haters as sporting talent, just as art-loathers will find a new appreciation for painting when they can create works like the masters on cyber-canvas.

For example, some major strengths of the ethnic club clearly lie in the fact that there are high levels of unspoken understanding amongst organisational members or, in other words, there is high context communication. According to de Mooy, 'context, or the information surrounding an event, is inextricably bound up with meaning. If people have extensive information networks among family, friends, colleagues, and clients and are involved in close relationships with each other, communication generally is high context'.[6] High context communication is facilitated by symbols, organisational heroes and rituals, and in general is likely to lead to stronger loyalty and identification.

There can be little doubt that sport is a powerful social force. Guilianotti observed that: 'it is now a sociological truism that sport has a crucial impact upon the construction (and preservation) of particular senses of social identity'[7]. Akindutire views sport as having greater utility than merely the expression of prowess,[8] whilst Stevenson and Alaug maintain that, 'sport in many cases informs and refuels the popular memory of communities and offers a source of collective identification and community expression'.[9] From the perspective of marketing, sport develops and reinforces identity, which is a powerful determinant of brand loyalty. As noted by Boyle and Haynes, 'the subculture of international events like the World Cup, the European Championships and the African Nations Cup are reminders that the sport [soccer] is a global enthusiasm, of mass appeal and the builder of affective relationships between different nation groups'.[10] Sport has the potential to remind us that we all belong to a global mega-tribe.

Popular sporting competitions have segmented sport consumers for the marketer according to the team they support. Traditional demographic segmentation – age, gender, ethnicity, nationality and occupation – will not apply as neatly as it used to. The fact is, the market of the future is more complex than being limited to easy divisions on the basis of consumption levels or demographics. Tribal segmentation will prove itself useful in the next wave of sport marketing success.

In our post-modern society, nothing (apart from war) is more primal than sport. The key to success is to understand the factors that force tribal groups to form. In order to do this, future sport marketers need to find out what rituals and rules practised by tribal clans tell us about the values that cluster them around a collective identity. Sometimes this can be deceptive. It is not a matter of ascribing certain characteristics to all New York Yankees supporters, or all Asian baseball fans. Fragmentation is a pivotal feature of tribalism. It cannot be assumed, for example, that a single unified culture exists for all sports or clubs.

Take, for instance, the common incident in international cricket of ball tampering. According to the rules of the game, it is clearly illegal to deliberately damage the ball, but hand polishing the ball so that it 'swings' in the air when bowled is a standard and encouraged practice. Exactly what cheating encompasses in this context is therefore highly debatable. Indeed, the concept of cheating is one that varies enormously between different sports. While ball tampering is a contentious issue, there are certain behaviours in cricket that are generally accepted, but which are also not quite 'sportsmanlike'. For example, in the event that the batter edges a ball and is 'caught behind', he will invariably wait until the umpire makes a decision. It is not unusual for the batsman to stand his ground innocently following a close call, knowing full well that he is out. If this is an example of cheating, then many people sometimes cheat at cricket, and cheat even more frequently at football. However, many would rather figuratively die than cheat at golf. This is not a matter of selective morality; in fact, their moral positions are perfectly consistent. This is simply because their position is not a function of the rules or laws of the game, but directly reflects the game's prevailing values, which vary significantly. It is acceptable to sometimes cheat in cricket and football, but never in golf. In other words, it is the prevailing values, customs and beliefs that are the predominant influences on behaviour, not the rules of the game. These in turn are modified by supporters in ways that reflect their own group's needs. To some, incurring a foul deliberately in football is 'ungentlemanly', but for others it is a serious part of the game where failure to act can be seen as 'soft'.

Fighting and violence during a sporting contest is a further example of the variability of values. While in just about every ball game it is illegal to punch people, it is acceptable behaviour in many cases. The situation could not be clearer in terms of official rules and regulations. An overt punch in soccer is an immediate red-card, sending-off offence. In contrast, a punch in rugby union will only get the player a warning, and the opposition a penalty in their favour. In soccer, punching is unacceptable. In rugby, it is merely discouraged. The identical behaviours have quite different meanings to different tribal groups. Furthermore, in ice-hockey, fighting is virtually considered an inherent and accepted part of the game, and punching the pitcher is considered to be almost within the batter's moral right should they be struck deliberately by a pitch in baseball. Consider the ramifications of a tennis player at the Wimbledon Tennis Championships being struck by a particularly powerful passing shot, only to hurdle the net and punch his or her opponent. How would golf fans react if Vijay Singh wrapped his driver around another player's head on the eighteenth green at Augusta, in response to a racial comment? On the other hand, who bats an eyelid when a couple of ice-hockey players use each other's heads as golf balls?

Tribalism is not a simple matter within a single sport. Some tribal groups hold specific views about events and circumstances, and it is the job of the sports marketer to find out what these are. For example, some (particularly English) World Cup spectators were disgusted by Maradona's 'Hand of God' goal, and still talk about it with disdain all these years later. However, others were not upset with Maradona; rather, they believed that he was doing what he had to do. They were, however, disappointed with the officials, who did not. Others still would have condoned the behaviour if it came from one of their players, but never from Maradona. This variability of attitudes is symptomatic of a wider, and more troublesome area: the clash of tribes within sport. This is illustrated best at an international level, where players from different countries have been brought up with profoundly different ideologies of the game, and how it should be played. Cricket and rugby are illustrations of this culture clash, particularly with the prolonged length of tours and matches, in addition to the immense cultural significance inherent in the game. Subsequently, in the past Australians have defended verbal 'sledging' as an aspect of manly gamesmanship in cricket. Similarly, those few opposing players who have attempted to belittle the Maori 'Haka' performed at the beginning of New Zealand All Black rugby union matches have discovered that it is not a ritual to take lightly, as the players consider it the most serious of personal insults, and do not take personal insults well.

Thus, for marketing efforts to induce tribal groups to purchase sport-related goods, the identity and behaviour of tribal groups must be first be identified, differentiated and understood. The 'hot button' for one clan will be different from another. Determining this hot button is not as easy as conventional segmentation research in sport suggests. If not demographics, then consumption patterns or evident motivations guide segmentation criteria. For example, some sport consumers clearly attend or view more games than others. Equally, some are motivated by a desire for entertainment and others out of a sense of sporting aesthetics. These represent quite valid and essential information to guide segmentation. The troublesome issue is that they are not necessarily the best categories to represent tribal segments. The difference between tribes is rarely as convenient as the attendance rate. However, traditional segmentation criteria are essential for building tribal *profiles*. As a result, we are interested in describing how one clan is different from another or, perhaps as important, to describe why one clan thinks it is different from another. Values have to be operationalised in order to be expressed consistently, so tribal clans can have conventional criteria attached to them, but the approach does not work if marketers are looking for those criteria to be the reason for differentiation. They are merely descriptors at a superficial level. The real game demands the exposition of the values that glue a clan together. This is difficult for many reasons, not the least of which is because the composition of sport tribes is likely to become even more complex in the future with more inter- and cross-tribal allegiances.

Our view is that in the future we will see far more inter- and cross-tribalism. Inter-tribalism will come about because groups will come together more to support country rather than just club or team (with far more emphasis on country versus country sports with teams such as the USA, China, Russia, Germany, Japan, etc., continuing and increasing the use of sport and sport technology as a weapon of ideology and pseudo-warfare).

Cross-tribalism will occur because, with increased exposure via technology of sport, fans will support many different types of sport and thus teams. Fans who are maniacal supporters of one soccer side may be bonded together in their support for that team but may split apart in their support for different basketball teams. Tribes may ebb and flow, come together and fall apart dependent upon the sport and how effective marketing of that sport might be, keeping in mind that good marketing will cultivate the bond between tribes. The most effective sports and clubs will generate the most powerful tribal identities.

Tribal conflict is probably more likely to occur at a micro or clan level, because each tribe will have sub-groups or clans that hold slightly different perspectives. Even subtle variations in values can lead to conflict. For example, clans will form within the tribe that favour certain players in the team, or that share a passion for a sport such as tennis or golf, but support different athletes. More fragmentation of clans will be facilitated by technology which helps the like-minded find each other and celebrate their uniqueness.

Cultivating Clans

In attempting to understand the behaviour of a tribal target market, it is useful to consider how an individual develops into a fan in the first place. We are suggesting that in the future it will be useful to consider tribes of sport followers as essentially composed of 'clans', which in turn are made up of individual fans. Sport fans are typically defined as passionate, or at least enthusiastic devotees of some particular sports object, to which there is an attachment which manifests itself in a some related behaviour. Different types of clans and tribes exist because of variety in both the object of devotion, and the underlying motivation for sports-related behaviour.

It has been observed that the way people process information lies at the basis of how they develop a belonging to certain clubs or, in our jargon, how they are encouraged to join not just tribes but explicit clans within those tribes.[11] Essentially, the enthusiasm and passion of sports fans is fed by a pool of memories that connects them to a sports institution and/or other tribe members. For example, the colours of a certain club appealed to us from the moment we laid eyes on them as a child, or we remember games our parents took us to before we really understood what was going on. The processing or storage of this reservoir of memories, associated with either or both sport institutions and tribe/clan members, tends to form a commensurate set of expectations, beliefs, perceptions and ideas. Fragments of memories combine to form an instinctive representation of belonging to the tribe: your father shouting abuse at the referee, older siblings celebrating victory, endless stories around the dinner table, Saturday afternoon pizza and beer in front of the television, late nights huddled around a large screen in a crowded pub, yelling, waving, crying, hating and most of all, belonging. All of these experiences combine to form a 'schema' from which some understanding of the sport institution and tribe are derived. Accompanying it will also be an emotional reaction, positive or negative, that will lead an individual towards loving or loathing a sport, team or athlete. A positive response will almost always provide a sufficient platform from which to develop a strong tribal affiliation. Naturally, the younger this becomes concrete, the stronger it is likely to be. Taking that perspective, children (for example) can become 'fans' by first being exposed to the sport, then the league, then the team and then the player(s), the halo process starting to take effect from initial exposure to the sport. Of course, smart club marketers would seek to encourage that emotional bonding as soon as possible. Although it may be difficult to convert a child from a parent's club to another, there are plenty of children that are never encouraged to develop their tribal sport identity.

As the learning of tribal mental programmes is a socio-cultural process, most of it will take place in the early years of life, when the mind is still relatively undeveloped. The dependence of children on parents, friends, teachers and their extended family makes them 'learn' which behaviours are approved of and rewarded, especially when compared to behaviour that is clearly not 'valued'. The core values that lie at the heart of a tribe have intense relevance and potency. Tribal values, therefore, can be powerful expressions of behaviour that make individuals identify with larger groups of kindred spirits. Intense exposure early in life will strengthen the relevance of behaviour, and hence the value-instilling power of identity.

Bold sport marketers have attempted to tap into these values, sometimes through easily recognisable patterns of behaviour such as rituals. For example, the apparel manufacturer, Adidas, has tried to use the Haka from New Zealand rugby as a communication tool. Unfortunately, indigenous Maoris have taken the company to court for using culturally significant practices for mass communication purposes. Without condoning the commercial exploitation of important cultural practices, the idea was not wrong so much as clumsy. Tribal sport marketing is about getting to the bottom of values; understanding what makes clans hold together and what drives them to see themselves as a collective, and then encouraging and facilitating the process. Trying to employ the Haka for marketing purposes bludgeons the target market with their identity, instead of communicating an understanding of it. Tribal social identity is robust, but complex, with a number of overlaid characters making up a single individual who may be a member of several clans.

Sport and Social Identity

The process by which people develop their identities in the social sphere can shed some light on how and why they consume sport, and subsequently on which tribes they seek to join. One way of looking at the concept of identity is to assume that only one 'self'-identity exists. This is unhelpful given the complexities of tribal affiliation. Social identity theory provides a more complex scenario where the 'self' is composed of multiple selves, each of which is part of a social network.[12] Put another way, different social groups that people belong to contribute to their multiple social identities. One individual may occupy a 'Manchester United fan' identity in the context of a group of the club's supporters, as well as a 'father' identity in relation to his family. The local football club, the workplace and the family are just three examples of social networks where individuals may develop varying identities. If the identity is strong enough, then clan mentality can be formed.

It is also important to note that a sport-related identity can be more or less important to the individual than other identities they hold. This is known in social theory as 'identity salience' and relates to the importance of one identity relative to others. For example, if being a fan of a football club is more important than being a member of a family, the fan identity salience is higher. This is further expressed by engaging in identity-related social ties (fan clubs), and the consumption of identity-related products (club merchandise). Some clans will hold particular hierarchies of identity salience. For instance, when it comes down to it, there are few fans who treat all other identities as subservient to their tribal sport one. On the other hand, some clans might pretend this is the case through intricate rituals involving attendance, violence or overt relief at getting away from the family. Understanding the hierarchy of identity salience is essential for sport marketers of the future in getting to the bottom of tribal consumption.

Sport also provides the individual with a central point from which to express other, 'non-sport' selves. Complex identities based on political preference, religious orientation and ethnic backgrounds are not easily expressed in 'pure' identity-related behaviour. Often, shortcuts for expressing identity need to be found and sport offers many such shortcuts. For example, soccer clubs in Scotland and Australia offer fans the opportunity to express a part of their identity based on religious preference (Rangers: Protestant; Celtic: Catholic), and ethnic background (South Melbourne: Greek; Melbourne Knights: Croatian).

It is the fans' self-concept that determines what they believe they are allowed to think and how to behave.[13] This is based on assumptions, such as how a person of a particular age or gender is expected to act, and on idealised notions from the media and family. However, the expectations and assumptions can be specific and uniquely personalised to a clan. They may make little sense to sport marketers until they are able to understand the underpinning values that manifest in particular or apparently erratic behaviours. For example, what is a marketer supposed to make of 'bandwagon' fans? Are they really so simple and straightforward that they 'jump on' when a suitable team begins to be successful? Human beings, and fans in particular, are nowhere near as simplistic as we think they are. We are all 'bandwagon' consumers and we are all loyal consumers, in our own ways. Tribal affiliations simply put certain scripts in front of us that require our undivided interest in some things, including sporting teams, and contempt for others. The pattern of loyalties we each hold shifts all our lives, mitigated by subtle changes in self-identity.

In the context of the sport industry, views of self and others are aptly used to marketers' advantage. What people are (or ought to be), and how they should act in particular roles is often expressed by successful, high-profile athletes. Athletes feature in tightly scripted commercials and public relations programmes that convey overt and sometimes subliminal messages of what is valuable in society, countries, cultures, tribes and clans. Sport celebrities can be role models and, if they fit the profile of the marketer's target tribe, they are used to endorse a wide variety of products.

Belongers

The key message to sport marketers of the future is to become aware that being close to sport fans is not a proxy for intimacy with them. That is why higher levels of customer service are inadequate to appease the tribe member. They are not seeking an improved transaction (the sort they demand from retail shopping): they want to get closer to the focus of their passion and the source of their identity. And getting closer is achieved through tribal experiences, where the fan–fan relationship is just as important as the club–fan relationship. Furthermore, the club is there to provide 'clan places', where rituals and symbols are cultivated to enhance the shared experience. As a result, the place dimensions of marketing also need to help fans find their anchoring spaces, some of which will be physical in the future, while others will be provided through virtual hubrooms (what we have referred to as the fourth place).

In the future, it will be useful to pay more attention to relationships, rather than holding an exclusive concern with the transaction. The key unit then becomes the congregation of fans who share similar emotional connections and value perspectives, and who gather in physical or virtual clans and tribes. These tribes, along with future athletes and competitions, form the contents of the space in which sport exists, whether virtual or real: the sporting cathedral.

Notes and References

1 Carmody, D. and Carmody, J. (1996). *Mysticism: Holiness East and West*. New York: Oxford University Press.
2 Groff, L. (2002). 'Intercultural communication, interreligious dialogue, and peace'. *Futures*, 34, pp. 701–16.
3 Groff, 'Intercultural communication', pp. 701–16.
4 Houlihan, B. (1994). *Sport and International Politics*. New York: Harvester Wheatsheaf.
5 Guilianotti, R. (1996). 'Back to the future: An ethnography of Ireland's football fans at the 1994 World Cup finals in the USA'. *International Review for the Sociology of Sport*, 31 (3), pp. 323–43.
6 Mooy de, M. (1998). *Global Marketing and Advertising: Understanding Cultural Paradoxes*. Thousand Oaks, CA: Sage, p. 157.
7 Guilianotti, 'Back to the Future', p. 325.
8 Akindutire, I.O. (1992). 'Sport as a manifestation of cultural heritage in Nigeria'. *International Review for the Sociology of Sport*, 27 (1), p. 31.
9 Stevenson, T.B. and Alaug, A.B. (1997). 'Football in Yemen: Rituals of Resistance, Integration and Identity'. *International Review for the Sociology of Sport*, 32 (3), p. 262.
10 Boyle, R. and Haynes, R. (2000). *Power Play. Sport, the Media and Popular Culture*. Harlow, England: Pearson Education, p. 198.
11 Hunt, K. A., Bristol, T. and Bashaw, R. E. (1999). 'A conceptual approach to classifying sports fans'. *Journal of Services Marketing*, 13 (6), pp. 439–52.
12 Laverie, D.A. and Arnett, D.B. (2000). 'Factors affecting fan attendance: The influence of identity salience and satisfaction'. *Journal of Leisure Research*, 32 (2), pp. 225–46.
13 Usunier, J.C. (1996). *Marketing across Cultures* (2nd edn). Hertfordshire: Prentice Hall Europe.

CHAPTER 6

Worship in the Sport Cathedral: Keeping the Faith

> *That very moment of spectacular perfection washed away my tiredness and I became overwhelmed with joy. As my body was lifted up into a beam of light I touched the gates of heaven, I was one with the world and the world was one with me. It was magical, mystical and spiritual all at the same time.*

The above quotation could have been articulated by a devout Catholic visiting St Peter's Square during a religious address by the Pope, but at the same time could have been the words of a spectator, present on the night when Michael Jordan in spectacular fashion secured the sixth championship for the Chicago Bulls in the dying seconds of the game. Without being disrespectful to the Pope and the millions of Catholics around the world, Michael Jordan has elicited similar feelings of exultation amongst his legion of religiously fanatical followers.

Religion and sport are arguably comparable from the perspective of the feelings they elicit amongst followers. The case can be made that sport is *a kind of* religion that satisfies religious needs for both participants and spectators. We try to address these issues by first attempting to define what separates religion from sport, and what joins them. We argue that at the heart of an optimal religious and sporting experience is spiritual enlightenment. With this in mind we introduce some information on 'the flow state' or the experience that emanates from a perfect match between the skill of the participant and the challenge they are undertaking. Have you ever hit the perfect golf shot, scored that magical goal, or experienced a runner's high during a marathon? Were you there (or watching it on television) when your favourite team or athlete achieved seemingly superhuman perfection? How did you feel? What happened to your body, your mind, your sanity?

In regard to the future of sport business we propose a number of different perspectives. It is important to realise that business can destroy everything that makes sport suitable to be a 'religious substitute'. In other words, the 'specialness' of sport can be destroyed by big business if it fails to comprehend the spiritual components of the products that it is trying to sell. If you take away the rituals and stories — take the 'gods' out of the temple — you cut the spirit and soul from the sporting religion. If you replace the terraces with corporate boxes, clean up the image of the club, design some commercially viable logos and tell your (mostly foreign) stars to 'behave' when they enter the stadium, you may well commit sporting suicide.

The future of sport business will offer a multitude of opportunities to artificially strengthen the spiritual sport experience. Rather than being side-lined, new technology will offer us the opportunity to play and feel what it must be like to be the star, to be 'gods'. Having outlined the technological possibilities in previous chapters we can ask ourselves the question, 'How real can unreal be?' Ultimately we have to wonder if technology can replace the real challenge that sport presents us on the field of play and, if it can, will this deliver the same mystical experience? God only knows!

Nietzsche was a Sports Fan

Athletes, competitions and tribes are all subject to the same invisible force
or spirit that sport generates, each with their own interpretation depending
upon where they fit into the sport cathedral. Ironically, while this spirit has
been sufficiently powerful to develop sport into the immense global business that it is, it may also provide its salvation from overwhelming technology. Technology removes the focus of sport from its physical dimension,
or at least the ideology of making the best of one's personal circumstances
and, in the process, seeking spiritual fulfilment.

It may seem strange to some to equate religion with sport, as we appear
to have done in the title of this chapter. On the face of it, one is concerned
with God and one with humans. Yet, at the expense of appearing irreverent,
we are of the view that religion and sport have much in common and, in the
technologically rich future, will have far more. Considering sport analogous
to religion is not new. Both religion and sport maintain a system of thought
and feeling which, when shared by a group, gives members an object of
devotion. Usually, religion concerns that which transcends the known, an
acknowledgement if you will of the extraordinary. Sport understands the
known but elevates some individual athletes or teams to the stage of the
extraordinary. In both instances, in religion and sport, we congregate
together because our humanity requires us to seek a mystical union with
what we perceive as the supernatural.

The human condition is one of exquisite complexity. Such is our construction that we spend much of our lives searching for meaning, substance
and identity in a world that shows depressingly little evidence that life is
more than a chaotic concoction of events. Humans have always sought
enlightenment; liberation from their physicality and insight about their
place in the vastness of space, time and thought. It has always been the hope
for transcendence against the hopelessness of despair. Sport has played an
unexpected role in this spiritual tug-of-war.

The 'post-Christian' prophet, Friedrich Nietzsche, made philosophical
history when he proclaimed that God was dead. The observation, although
now well over 100 years old, remains a stalwart of atheism, although no one
can agree whether it was prescient or short-sighted. Nevertheless, the secu-
larisation of the Western world has underpinned Nietzsche's point, and the
rise in fundamentalism in the Middle East implies that God might be in need
of resuscitation in some cultures. Part of Nietzsche's point was that we had
killed God. If Nietzsche were around today, perhaps he would shift the
blame. It was not our fault; rather, it was Michael Jordan's. Indeed,
Nietzsche's rejection of the 'slave morality' of Christianity and his

championing of a new, heroic morality that would be led by a breed of supermen whose 'will to power' would set them apart from the common man seems strangely applicable to sport warriors such as Jordan.

It is easy to arrive at one of the most pervasive clichés in Western culture: sport is the new religion. This is nonsense of course. Sport is not *the* new religion: it is more correctly *a* new religion. It joins the ranks of animism, ancestor worship, totemism, spiritualism, monotheism, polytheism, dualism, supratheism, pantheism, and many others. Most properly it may be considered part of the polytheism school of religion in which there are many gods. In this religion, gods are revealed because they display a supernatural talent. The temple, mosque or cathedral of worship with which we are most familiar has simply given way to the temple of the media portrayed most emphatically with an endless run of flickering images from a television screen. The book of worship is the daily press, weekly magazine or Internet, gospels in which the deeds of the gods can be continually read. We repeat, we are not irreverent; it is not our intention to outrage or offend. We simply invite you to read the daily sports press, watch the evening news, or peruse the numbers that attend sporting functions.

Consciousness and Soul

Almost certainly, the more religious among our readers will dismiss our analogy of sport being a new religion with the comment that while sport has passion, it lacks a soul, and while possessing awareness, it lacks true consciousness. Determining exactly what constitutes true consciousness is, in itself, a major difficulty. Igor Aleksander, emeritus professor and senior investigator in neural systems at Imperial College, London, suggests that there are five axioms of consciousness. Axiom 1 is a Sense of Place, the ability of the mind to place an image in three-dimensional space relative to the body. Axiom 2 is Imagination, while Axiom 3 is what Aleksander calls Directed Attention: that is, the ability of the mind to focus attention so as to more ably depict events and people. Axiom 4 is Planning, the ability to repeat sequences of sensory inputs such as the notes of a song, and Axiom 5 is effectively the ability to feel Emotion.[1]

If these are the hallmarks of true religion, then we will admit that perhaps there is a difference, at least at the moment. That this may always be so, however, is doubted by Francis Crick, the joint discoverer of DNA's double helix and Nobel prize winner, and Christof Koch, professor of neuroscience at California Institute of Technology, who have just published research which explains the human soul and attributes human consciousness to a set of neurons in the brain.[2]

Crick and Koch claim they and their colleagues have found the group of cells responsible for generating consciousness and an individual sense of self. If Crick and his group are correct and the blueprint for life and evolution lie in a simple molecule and a set of biochemical reactions, then there is little doubt that with singularity both a soul and self-consciousness can be genetically formulated.

Sport, like religion, mobilises communities, forges identity, provides meaning, infuses passion and enlivens the soul. It teaches in narrative, in endlessly entertaining weekly stories. It is mythical yet real. It takes the very source of human vulnerability – the body – and transforms it into a vehicle for vicarious experience, for transcendence, for immortality. Enlightenment is always imminent. Who would not seek to be a god or near to a god? And for those who do not make it, there is always next season.

With next season comes the new merchandise. There is a new sponsor, or the pattern of colours has been modernised (again). A new season ticket is available, and for the away games there is the obligatory subscription to a pay television network to cover the majority of matches that do not make it to free-to-air. Of course, if circumstance is unkind, there is also the opportunity to watch that match-changing goal or touchdown via a wireless application protocol (WAP) enabled mobile (cellular) phone, complete with LCD screen. After the event, the entire game can be dissected blow by blow through Internet community chat-rooms with like-minded supporters from anywhere in the world. Some sites even support real-time access to footage, to be manipulated with directorial power (all of these for the appropriate fees, of course).

Thus we arrive at an axiom of Western sport culture: where there is sport, there is also money. Karen Armstrong observed that in order to cultivate an experience of the sacred we do not need to believe in a deity,[3] but we do need to believe in something. The secular Western world has used sport as a substitute for meaning and identity and, in turn, business has used the sport follower for financial gain.

Marcus Bussey argues that in order to be relevant, futures studies must acknowledge spirituality and individual consciousness.[4] He believes that progress is spiritual and the study of the future is concerned with personal change. Moreover, studying change implies accepting future scenarios that will be deficient and complex, as futures will become layered and non-linear. In Bussey's view, what he calls 'meditative empiricism' is a valid research methodology; mystery is a spiritual and empirical reality.

This chapter examines sport as a spiritual experience and highlights the mechanisms through which this 'genuflection' is exploited by sport and entertainment businesses. It also considers how this extraordinarily powerful force might be harnessed within a technological framework and the implications for spiritual and personal development that might result. Ultimately, as we peer into the future of sport business, we will argue that the inexorable technological innovations that will bridge the gap between vicarious experience and actual experience will only strengthen the spiritual nature of sport following. Eventually, sport will provide a vehicle to remind us of the significance of physicality in a world that is mired in the desire for immortality.

The Flow

At its most primal level, the simple joys of participating in sport might be blamed for part of the spiritual experiences with which it has been associated. Like Michael Jordan, who insisted on a clause in his contract that permitted him to play basketball wherever and whenever he chose, even if it was in an unofficial 'pickup' game on a Saturday afternoon, the pursuit of the perfect sport experience seems to be a universal goal, even for some professional athletes. This is part of the confusing aspect of sport business. Athletes, who had once played for the pure joy of the sport, are now preening and whining about contracts and promotional appearances. Have they forever abandoned the spiritual dimension of their activities in exchange for the seriousness of making a living or, better still, making a fortune?

Phil Jackson, one of the most successful US National Basketball Association coaches ever, argues that selfless team play rather than winning through intimidation is the pathway to not just success but also the spiritual plane of sport. Jackson, in the Zen tradition, refers to his philosophy as 'mindful basketball'. It represents a quest to bring enlightenment and self-awareness to the ruthless, competitive world of professional sport. Jackson's book, *Sacred Hoops: Spiritual Lesson of a Hardwood Warrior*, is as much about the human spirit as it is about sport. In many ways, the genius Jackson has demonstrated is that competitive success is less about strategy and more about the ability to convince self-obsessed and pampered young men to work together to achieve a common goal. Even spoilt and ill-tempered super-stars can remember the time when playing was an end in itself.

The sport cathedral houses many denominations. There are those who find the thrill of competition irresistible, and those who fall into that mystical unconscious zone as spectators during their quest for visual pleasure, or in their desperate hope for certain outcomes. One spectator explained the experience that overwhelmed him while watching a game:

> My heart suddenly flooded with joy, and a smile spread itself across my face. Like a Japanese brush painting, the scene embodied complete 'suchness'; it was a small masterpiece of economy and joy, and in its contemplation I nearly wept with happiness ... A moment of pure joy had released energy that washed my tiredness away as if it had never existed ... expanding my heart to a point of self-forgetfulness.[5]

The true power of sport is contained in its capacity to deliver those mystical feelings of being lost in the game zone, being absorbed, being happy and being absolutely clear about the 'rightness' of the activity. There is nowhere else to be and nothing else that it is more important to be doing at that precise moment. That zone of effortless flow is always around the corner, sometimes elusive, but always seductive. As the Zen proverb suggests, enlightenment might be an accident, but some activities make you accident-prone.

This optimal experience, or flow state as it has become known, largely thanks to the research and commentary of Csikszentmihalyi,[6] has not been overlooked by sports psychologists. Their insights help to explain why the flow state is an important part of what makes sport so unique. Perhaps more importantly (from the sport business perspective at least) the findings of psychologists are useful in understanding the sport follower and participant and what triggers their consumption behaviour, as well as their extraordinary product loyalty. For example, the flow state has been speculated to occur where there is a relative match between the skill of the participant and the challenge they are undertaking. Peak performance and peak experience are linked.[7] This relationship might be somewhat obvious for the average athlete, but the link is less considered as it applies to the sport spectator.

In a sense, the implications from research are that spectators are more likely to fall into the state of optimal experience when they can match the challenge of fully understanding the game they are watching with the knowledge they possess. This, of course, explains the cultural divide between many sports, and why others seem universally appreciated. It explains why an Australian and an Indian can watch six hours of cricket every day for five days during a Test match that ends in a draw, and still be amazed at how quickly the time passes. It also explains why it is so difficult for American football to become effortless viewing for Europeans trying to come to terms with NFL Europe.

Education is an essential ingredient in encouraging new groups to attend sport or watch it on television. As technology facilitates this educational process through closed captions or customised commentaries, new possibilities emerge for capturing difficult audiences. Horse racing in Australia provides a good example of how this educational marketing process can work effectively. Targeted squarely at young females, horse racing marketing campaigns appealed to their fashion awareness, social interest and sense of adventure. On-track activities explained the nuances of picking winners and the mechanics of race betting through simplified betting agencies.

Research has also established a relationship between flow states and feelings of spirituality.[8] The two sets of experiences seem to inspire similar emotions and mental states, although it is unclear whether the correlation is also causal, and which direction that causality runs. It might not be stretching the empirical evidence too far to suggest that spiritual experiences and flow states not only have similar characteristics, but that they are mutually inclusive; with one comes the other.

One interesting outcome of the research in this area has to do with the circumstances when flow states come about during everyday activities compared to sport activities. In the USA, for example, it was found that sports provide this experience 44 per cent of the time for teenagers, whereas the occurrence during television was only 13 per cent.[9] This finding implies the relative difficulty in obtaining flow states while not personally participating in an activity. The more that an individual can be drawn into a sport, the more likely that her engagement will lead to the spiritual feelings associated with flow states. Thus any viewing arrangements that enhance the personalised nature of a spectatorship experience are relevant. Technology will play a strong role in this customisation, particularly via netcasting where viewers can manipulate camera angles, follow specific players or watch unusual replays.

The flow state is one of the aspects of sport that distinguish it from recreation and entertainment. As sport entertainment businesses rush to make a killing by acquiring sport content for their pay television and free-to-air enterprises, the question remains as to whether they will ultimately kill professional sport itself by surgically removing its elements of value, either to be sold off separately or because they are not conducive to 'good' business practice. The answer to that lies in the symbolic potential of sport.

The Symbolic Potential of Sport

At the heart of all sport is a symbolic meaning. For the participant, it often has to do with what psychologists call mastery, the never-ending quest for improvement and perfection. Sometimes this opportunity for personal development is supplanted or sublimated by the social meaning associated with the athletic pursuit. This tribal aspect, where meaning can come from ownership to a collective, can have an immensely powerful impact on the 'spiritual' perspectives of group members. It is a default human need to feel part of something bigger. The collective identity that comes from being part of a close-knit sports club can substitute for an absence of belonging to a group that offers meaning more overtly, such as through a church. Psychologists have observed that the tribal compulsions of humans lead to a natural inclination to join groups with more than five and fewer than 50 members. Although many sports clubs have more than 50 members, the larger ones tend to fragment into like-minded factions.

Michael Novak in his book, *The Joy of Sports*, explains that sport satisfies our deep hunger to connect with a realm of mythic meaning, to see the transpersonal forces that work within and upon human nature enacted in dramatic form, and to experience the social cohesion that these forms make possible. Sport is, according to Novak, a faith without explanation. Sport intensifies experience and awakens within us a larger sense of being. Sport is an agent of self-reflection. It is a tool for understanding where we fit into a world that is devoid of evident meaning.

It is this understanding which is at the heart of sport business. The best in the business recognise the power of the transpersonal experience. Sociologist John Carroll has noted that the behaviour of the crowd at a sporting event demonstrates quite unambiguously that something of deep seriousness is being conducted; it is not a consumerist activity. For the last decade and a half, many sport sociologists have argued that the hyper-commercialism and commodification of sport will be its undoing. How, then, can sport businesses survive and flourish into the future if they continue to treat sport as a consumer product?

This question is stuck in a misunderstanding of what it means to treat sport as a consumer product. It is true that some professional sports have alienated important parts of their support bases, but it is not accurate to assume that this has been a consequence of consumer marketing. Rather, it is more accurate to suggest that it is the consequence of poor consumer marketing coupled with questionable business practice. Good business practice leads to satisfied customers, after all.

European football (soccer) provides a good example. The influx of money from Murdoch's Sky television company pushed far more capital into English football clubs than they had earned. Murdoch's lead has been followed, and considerable sums have been invested in the game. While good business practice might suggest that clubs invest some of that money into their future, improve services to members, consolidate their balance sheets, spread risk or improve infrastructure, the majority of clubs spent wildly on players' wages and transfer fees. The result has been unambiguous. Of the 92 English league teams, which had collectively received a 13 per cent growth in revenues, fewer than 20 clubs are actually profitable. Losses are more than 10 per cent of total revenues. Moreover, English soccer is far from being the financially worst in Europe.

The spiralling increase in professional athletes' wages is not confined to either Europe or football. Exorbitant salaries ensure that only a handful of the professional clubs participating in Australia's professional leagues can earn a surplus. Until very recently less than a quarter of Australian Football League clubs and National Rugby League clubs were in the black. The National Basketball League regularly gains and loses franchises, while last season no club in the National Soccer League made a profit. Even the great Australian summer pastime of cricket can only yield a buck at the international level of competition. UK Rugby Union Super League clubs are also struggling.[10] Clubs participating in the 'big' four professional sports in the USA are more healthy, although not as profitable as many would assume. The Salt Lake City Winter Games profit approached US$100 million, which was substantially better than the expected break-even. Despite the impact of its unsuccessful XFL jaunt, WWE continues to be one of the most profitable businesses in 'sport entertainment'.

However, has commercialisation directly led to fewer fans, decreased game quality, and impersonalised sport? Are commercialised sports capable of captivating audiences, enticing them into that precious flow state and providing meaning and identity in a topsy-turvy world? Is sport just another consumer product to be lifted from the shelf and tossed apathetically into the shopping trolley? Will the 'specialness' – the spiritual nature of sport – be destroyed by business in the future? The current evidence suggests that this will not necessarily be the case.

The fact is some sports are improving their audiences while others are going backwards. There is no obvious relationship between the levels of professionalisation and commercialisation and current audience trends of a sport. In the USA, the big recent successes have been the Salt Lake City Olympics, the National Football League (a ratings stalwart: the average audience is around 100 million[11]) and National Association for Stock Car Auto Racing (NASCAR), which is doubling NBA and MLB ratings. In contrast, Major League Baseball[12] in 2002 secured average ratings of 11.9 (Fox), less than half of its 1991 performance (24.0 per cent, CBS), including the lowest rating All-Star game ever (it hit a ratings peak of 28.5 in 1970).[13] The National Hockey League television viewing audiences have also dropped off in recent years.[14] In 2002, the FIFA World Cup final between Germany and Brazil (ABC) accrued a viewing audience of 2,670,000 (live) and 1,555,000 (on tape) in the USA. This represents a renaissance of sorts for the sport in which the USA fields the best women's team. Tennis is more popular, though: the US Open women's semi-finals rated 11 per cent higher than 2001, for example.[15]

In 2002 in Australia, 97 per cent of people surveyed indicated that they watch sport on television, four percentage points higher than in 2000.[16] In the UK, 881,000 viewers tuned in to the 2002 Extreme Games, compared with 1.42 million in 2001.[17] European ratings for Formula One have also been a bit soft recently, but the FIFA World Cup attracted enormous interest in Europe, particularly in Italy, Spain, Germany and the UK. China eclipsed any European country with 330 million viewers watching the China versus Brazil telecast.[18] Broadly speaking, the FIFA World Cup broke a number of national audience records in the USA and Europe, despite non-prime-time viewing. This included an increased tendency to watch 'out of home', at locations featuring big screen public viewing facilities. For example, it has been estimated that 4.2 million people watched the Korea versus Italy game at an official public viewing. Part of this trend can be accounted for in telecast times, which did not always coincide with out of office hours. In fact, up to 10 per cent of audience totals were made up of office workers who had set up makeshift viewing areas during work time. In addition, Internet viewing with FIFAworldcup.com proved to be the most successful sports event site ever, accruing up to 127.9 million page views a day.[19] To all these figures we could add similarly erratic ones for attendances, some going up while others are going down. Despite the inconclusive trends in attendance, prices for attendance are increasing, which suggests that demand might have been reasonably robust.

Although these figures are just a snapshot of a couple of large television markets, it is difficult to reach any inescapable conclusions. Clearly, part of the problem for both sports and broadcasters is increasing competition, both in terms of content and distribution. The escalating cost of television rights has not made profitability easy for broadcasters, although a number of prominent sports have been the beneficiaries of large television rights deals that will not be exceeded for some time. Perhaps the most illuminating trend is that the total number of sport viewers in the world is increasing, largely because new markets are opening thanks to the superior distribution of well established technologies such as television, as well as an improving infrastructure for newer platforms such as cable and optic fibre for the Internet and pay television. Western Europe, Asia and the sub-continent, in particular India, offer exciting new markets for sport. Africa and South America remain largely sleeping giants.

It is difficult to conclude that commercialisation has destroyed sport. In fact, our suggestion is that sport is getting more popular and the moves professional sports have made towards commercialisation have often been for the good of the sport and the fan. It is true that some of the moves – which have clearly been exploitative of the fan – have been damaging or have replaced dedicated and loyal supporters with more fickle but higher-spending corporate sponsors. But these approaches are not sustainable and are not illustrative of sound marketing and management of the sport in the first place.

The marketing of sport in particular, and the business of sport in general, gets a bad reputation as a result of the activities of a handful of sports entrepreneurs, sports apparel companies, leagues, clubs, athletes and player managers. In some cases, sports have been unduly influenced by short-sighted media companies and event organisers who are in it for a quick profit, and who do not care about the long-term implications of their philosophy. For example, it may be strategically sound to include corporate hospitality within a venue's mix of service offerings, but if that decision also means that fans are locked out while unoccupied seats are visible during the television coverage, the ramifications go beyond just marginalised supporters. Leagues will also have to work hard to rein in overspending on players when clubs clearly cannot sustain the increases in salary costs with commensurate increases in revenue.

Good sport business practice, however, does not alienate sport supporters, and it does not detract from that very special spiritual something that sport can offer. In reality, canny business or marketing decisions have augmented the experience of sport and reinforced its spiritual nature.

Similarly, technological advances have allowed sport to be viewed all around the world. In the future, as the opportunities to sell sport remotely increase with globalisation, so too will possibilities for customisation improve. In fact, the trend evidence that we discussed in earlier chapters concerning the impact of a technological singularity will have a radical impact on the personal and spiritual experience of sport and its entertainment value.

The weekly pilgrimage is less often to the church; it is to the sacred turf instead. At its best, it is also leveraged by archetypal characters fulfilling the roles of heroes and sinners. In the words of Carroll, sport is the most prominent form of Western meditation. How might sport businesses of the future enhance this mystical experience?

Virtual Sport Worship

The impact of the symbolic potential of sport is apparent when we consider the future. From an evolutionary perspective, we tend to measure progress in terms of technological development. We can, therefore, rarely comprehend a future that is not defined in terms of a radical new technological framework where science fiction is some sort of inevitable reality. The cultural aspects of society tend to be overlooked or unchanged in these versions of the future. (We return to the most important issue of cultural change in Chapter 9.) Hence little speculation has occurred concerning the future of sport beyond the radical technological interventions that might revolutionise its pursuit.

From a sport business perspective, there is a reason for this. The cultural aspects – the traditions – of sport have never really been associated with the business side. Some sport entertainment and media companies have viewed these cultural elements as obstacles that discourage consumers from experiencing sport in 'new' (their) ways. Thus the exciting areas for the future of sport revolve around the technological developments, where sport broadcasts can reach wider audiences, and existing audiences can be sold more than last time.

The difficulty is that it is the cultural aspects of sport, those parts which are fundamentally grounded in symbology and meaning, that preserve the unique interest that sport receives from its most dedicated followers. But it is a mistake to assume that technology cannot or will not augment the sacred aspects of sport; it simply has not yet come to grips with what is needed.

In an era of computer super-intelligence, with a global wireless Supernet and the capacity to create an interface directly between the organic and the machine, the possibilities seem almost limitless for recreational and sporting activities. For over a decade now, futurists and armchair commentators alike have speculated about the possibilities associated with virtual reality.

In the previous chapter, we presented the argument that, although virtual, this computer-interfaced experience could ultimately be as real as it gets. We projected this technology into the realm of sport and entertainment, and concluded that enhanced sport spectating would probably be just the tip of the technological iceberg. While we might sit in the virtual stands in any seat of our choosing, and in any event being played anywhere in the world, the question is whether the vicarious experience of sport will remain sufficient to satisfy our self-edification when technology will allow more interactive possibilities. Instead, for example, of sitting on the holographic bench, why would we not want to participate?

Since we are considering a time in the medium-term future where human beings can interact with computers, or at least computers with artificial intelligence programs that are so sophisticated that they can provide any environment and any experience, surely many sports fans would no longer be interested in watching the real thing, instead being more interested in participating in the virtual thing? After all, we are effectively talking about a *Star Trek* style 'holodeck'. Any fantasy can be as real as reality. Any programming parameters can be determined. There would be no limitations. Who would want to live in the real world when a fantasy world is so ubiquitous and welcoming?

Not only could you play against the greatest, but you could, literally within your own fantasy world, be the greatest. As a virtual player in this world, nothing would be beyond your fantasy skills. Perfection could be achievable. More adventurous participants could define their own skills set only marginally beyond any other player or athlete, and allow the contests to proceed with uncertain outcomes, subject to the whims of the simulated world. Olympic gold medals, World Cups, Super Bowls, Mount Everest, running with the bulls in Pamplona: the possibilities are endless. And if you want to add a touch of the real to a contest, you could invite some friends into your personal software. Their virtual characters could be adversaries, or together you could take on the world – literally – if you choose.

Moreover, the fantasy need not discontinue off the field. Who wants to live the life of a sporting hero? Money, sex, power. This brings us back to an earlier question: who would not want to be a god? In effect, real professional sport will be over. The sport business world will be ruled by software giants capable of delivering the programming power behind the fantasies. Media and entertainment enterprises will fall away from supporting real sport. Product sponsors will do deals with the software companies instead. The world's leading Olympics software will contain plenty of virtual signage. Instead of observing it as a spectator on television, consumers will see it in their reality, as participants of the Games. No one will ever be bored again, or will they?

On the surface, the question might seem to be technological in nature rather than philosophical. But the purpose of this chapter is to establish the nature of why sport is so attractive. If, in the end, what can be offered to interactive participants is more potent than playing or watching real sport, who would not become addicted to the fantasy world?

The answer has to do with the spiritual dimension of real sport. Ultimately, it is reality itself that plays a strong part in what makes it so special. We have argued that sport can provide a sense of belonging and that it is in the moments of 'flow' that the mystical aspects of the experience can most powerfully manifest.

For the sport theatregoer, seeking exhilaration and spectacle, the fantasy world will be sufficiently intoxicating, but for the genuine aficionado, whether participant or spectator in nature, the virtual world will be vastly enjoyable, but a pale substitute. For those addicted, the spiritual experience of sport is grounded in a sense of the real and the absolute. There is an unambiguous importance; a sense of seriousness, of achievement, of personal victory and satisfaction, irrespective of the playing outcomes. There is the pride of having played or supported well.

The virtual sport world may be compelling. It may even prove addictive for the sport lover, but it will not provide that spiritual dimension unless it duplicates the belief of the real. It has to convince us that it is not a game, but is in fact our true reality. In the new, post-singularity world, sport may provide one of the most important reminders of the very thing that we can never isolate ourselves from as humans, our physicality, and what it means to be *our* best rather than *the* best.

To this point, we have allowed our unambiguous trait of optimism to shine through. To be honest, however, we must acknowledge that the future may not be as bright as we have painted and a number of quite conspicuous clouds may prevent our view of future sport from being seen as clearly as we may have implied.

The world has faced the introduction of revolutionary technology in the past. The results have not always been encouraging. Perhaps the most well-known example was the band of labourers, known as Luddites, who in the period 1811–16 rioted in the industrial areas of England and destroyed newly developed textile machines, to which they attributed high unemployment and low wages. Although harshly suppressed, the Luddites left a legacy of opposition that reappears whenever new technology is introduced.

The Luddite mentality, though frequently apparent, is usually overcome without too much difficulty. Less innocuous, however, is the possibility of such revolutionary technology as the advent of singularity being hijacked for one country, one industry or one group of individuals.

Technologically advanced countries may see an advantage in seeking to restrict AI to the few. This may occur because governments or individuals may see the promise of huge profits or military advantage in the technology. Governments may perceive that singularity may bring with it the possibility of civil unrest, loss of public control, loss of individual freedom or even health issues. Cost alone may cause the use of widespread AI to be basically confined to the richer Western nations. Deeply religious countries may see AI as a 'false idol' and may declare formal opposition to its use. Perhaps the most pessimistic outlook is that the introduction of AI, with all its potential benefits, may create a split in society far greater than any clash of nations Samuel Huntington may have foreseen, and far more costly than any previous division in the world order caused by ideology, the lack of economic equality or warfare. Regretfully, there are sufficient examples in history of new technology benefiting the few at the expense of the many.

Zen and the Art of Sport Business

There are two intrinsic constituents of sport that link it to spirituality. These two are associated with the flow state and the mythic potential. Flow is about matching skills to challenges. If the challenge is removed by computers or simply because the participant is aware that it is not a true challenge in the real world, then sport simply becomes recreation or leisure. For the spectator, the danger lies in allowing sport to become just another form of entertainment, where the emotion and passion of uncertainty is replaced by another permutation of the same filmic clichés, unravelled with the same plot but using slightly different characters.

Sport has its strongest appeal when it mirrors life: uncertain, fragile, painful, breathtaking. The dangers of computer interactivity in virtual sport are sufficient to remove the most appealing aspects of its involvement. This is simply because we will always know that it is not real. While this knowledge does not diminish entertainment, it does compromise meaning. Sport business must never encroach upon the sacred aspects of the sport experience and, if it does, it will remove sport aficionados and replace them with fewer, more fickle theatregoers. We suspect, therefore, that physical prowess pre- and post-singularity will always be coveted and admired, even when the performances are derived in large part from genomic manipulation.

Extrinsic rewards have always been important to athletes, whether they come in the form of money, fame or status. This will continue to be the case. The need to make money will not diminish for sporting organisations, and the need to be relevant will remain essential. Some sport enterprises will occasionally attempt to exploit sport followers, but will be vulnerable to corrections which are subject to the approval of the supporter base. Even participation and extreme sports have been commercialised. The proliferation of fun runs and triathlons testifies to the fact that sport can be run for the average athlete at a profit without their discontent.

The Extreme Games are owned by the national cable sports channel ESPN. It has provided essential and, more importantly, inexpensive content at a time when sport programming is exorbitantly costly, but this does not mean that it cannot deliver the specific expectations of the game's target audience. Its popularity in a target demographic, to use the marketing nomenclature, is utterly amazing. The games are the perfect association for sponsors such as Pepsi.

Despite the increases in ticket prices, and the expense of merchandise and pay television subscriptions, professional sport will never be exclusively for the wealthy. Predictions that professional sport will alienate its grassroots fan groups in exchange for the patronage of the corporate sector are unlikely to come true. Such a strategy is a recipe for self-destruction and, although it may not seem like it sometimes, few sport organisations are so incompetent. Even if they were, they would soon be corrected by the backlash caused by the corporate sector itself. Corporate hospitality and sponsorship can never in itself provide the backbone of revenue for a sport organisation. The majority of revenue comes from television rights. Clearly, media companies are not going to buy rights for events that have marginalised the very viewers they are targeting.

The secondary revenue sources, sponsorship, gate receipts and merchandise, will be similarly declining without the support of the broad base of sport supporters. Without being apologists for the sometimes stupid and political decisions made by some sport organisations, in general, they aim to improve their service offerings to members and supporters. Their fundamental problem has probably never changed, and probably never will. The speed at which they can increase their resources is not as fast as the speed at which those resources are required by the talent they need to achieve their only real objective: victory. Therein lies one of the differences between the sport industry as a business and other constituents of the commercial sector. Large parts of the sport industry are unprepared to risk the consequences of cutting costs due to the fear that it will mean losing the best players to another team more comfortable with debt.

As more sport organisations falter in their debt burdens or succumb to controlling interests that are unambiguously profit seeking, this will change. It will also help to consolidate the sport industry into the hands of businesses that are less concerned with winning at all costs than making money at all costs.

Ironically, despite the frequent lament that media and entertainment companies are taking over sport, and subsequently ruining it, their involvement may help to save some sports. The financial clout of these companies, and their insistence on proper (and usually sustainable) business practices, may help bring some sports back to sensible operations. Whether they completely understand the seriousness of their power is uncertain. In the case of the Extreme Games, the news is good. That which makes the Games special is protected because the event managers appreciate on which side their bread is buttered. The biggest danger facing extreme sports as a result is the likelihood of becoming too mainstream, a risk that is difficult to assess, especially when ratings have fallen in the UK recently. A more obvious example was the lengthy pre-programme show at the 2002 All-Star baseball game in the USA, orchestrated largely to tie up a sponsor. It has been observed that it contributed to the lowest rating All-Star game in prime time.

In the future, those sport businesses which continue to deliver the nebulous but critical spiritual aspects of sport will continue to prosper. Technology will ensure that the integration with sport governance and media-entertainment enterprises is complete, with the radically increased involvement of software businesses. Thus we might expect that sport will remain a pivotal vehicle for meaning-making for both the secular and religious, but this does not necessarily mean that sport will replace religion any more than it already has.

Sociologist John Carroll counselled that sport has risen in its significance for people in inverse proportion to the decline in church attendances, but religion has never been isolated from sport, and neither has sport ever been a direct replacement for religion. In fact, the money in some churches is used vigorously in some sports. For example, the Church of Jesus Christ of Latter-day Saints donated more than US$5 million to the Salt Lake Olympic Committee and the Christian ministry, Motor Racing Outreach, is deeply involved in NASCAR, a sport which has long been heavily influenced by the US Bible Belt. Sport can provide all the essential ingredients in personal development and reflection but, to some extent, the veracity of this possibility in the future will be determined by the broader society or culture in which sport is placed. We consider this important enough to revisit in the penultimate chapter of this book.

John Galtung and Sohail Inayatullah claim in their work, *Macrohistory and Macrohistorians*, that the rise of one, global religious system is unlikely to occur. The new book by the American religious historian, Philip Jenkins, *The Next Christendom: The Coming of Global Christianity*, argues that the twenty-first century will see Christianity replace ideology as the prime sociocultural force. The number of Christians in the world is expected to reach 2.6 billion within 25 years (including 228 million in Africa), mainly as a result of increases in the developing world.[20] In a similar way, increases in population in the Middle East will give rise to substantially more adherents of Islam. The perception that religion is dead is incorrect. However, individuals can convert to sport without relinquishing other religious ties. Only comparatively few fundamentalist groups insist on the avoidance of technology, mass culture and sport, preventing its simultaneous observance with religion.

Full Circle: A New Physicality

The danger of the technological developments that we are predicting in this book is that they might dilute professional sport to such an extent that it will no longer have any meaning beyond that of entertainment and spectacle. The experience of sport will be little more than noisy theatre. It has been observed in research contrasting technologically advanced societies and those with more traditional, 'primitive' structures that little difference is noticeable in self-awareness, thought and happiness[21]. In fact, some might argue that technological advancement sometimes leads to intellectual and emotional devolution. Packaged stimulation is the Western model, and professional sport has been one of the chief packagers. In the USA, for example, the NFL generates US$3 billion, college sports US$2.7 billion, MLB US$2.4 billion, NBA US$1.4 billion, NASCAR US$1.2 billion and the NHL US$1 billion in officially listed merchandise sales.[22] Furthermore, college sport in the USA offers the chance to learn how to worship sport, as well as how to worship capitalism.

Despite the attraction of the fourth place, we believe there will remain sport consumers who will reject the world of the virtual over the real. Some will cling to the participation experience, not perhaps untouched by technology or the commercial realities of the world, but certainly motivated by a different source of interest. This source might be described as a more primal element, mitigated by cultural forces. Chapter 9, on cultural sport business, ventures into this area. In Chapter 8, however, we consider how the sport cathedral is changing physically to become more environmentally aware.

Sport, now and in the future, will always offer more than just recreation or entertainment. It offers, and will continue to offer, a communal experience, either live or remotely. It is, and will remain, an opportunity to care ardently about the same things; to receive personal affirmation. Sport fans are forgiving. During an event, they can forget the drugs and scandals, salaries and attitudes, owners and marketers. They can embrace the spiritual side of the experience. It is this worship in the sport cathedral that provides such a powerful opportunity for the corporate world to demonstrate its commitment to community contribution. We take up this possibility in the next chapter, 'Corporate Sport Citizenship'.

Sport requires from the participant the deft application of skill and creativity within the limited boundaries of the game and, from the follower, it demands a knowledgeable and loving eye, attuned to the aesthetics of effortless perfection that is always sensed but rarely attained. Humanity can use sport as a mechanism for renewing its spiritual edge, because no matter how good we can be in virtual reality, deep down we know it is empty and hollow. There are no shortcuts to true spiritual experiences. It may take some time, but ultimately many people will recognise that cyber-sport is a false god.

Notes and References

1   Aleksander, I. (2003). 'I, computer'. *New Scientist*, 179 (2,404), pp. 40–3.
2   Crick, F. and Koch, C. (2003). 'A framework for consciousness'. *Nature Neuroscience*, 6 (2), pp. 119–26.

3   Armstrong, K. (1999). 'The search for the transcendental endures: Europeans now try to find God in drugs, football and videogames; Where has God gone?' *Newsweek*, 12 July.

4   Bussey, M. (2002). 'From change to progress: critical spirituality and the futures of futures studies'. *Futures*, 34, pp. 303–15.

5   Anonymous. *The Simple Joys of Sport: Where do they come from? Can we cultivate them deliberately?* Available at http://www.oceansofenergy.com/simple%20joys.htm, accessed on 17 October 2003.

6   Csikszentmihalyi, M. (1990). *Flow: The Psychology of Optimal Experience*. New York: Harper & Row.

7   McInnman, A. and Grove, J. (1991). 'Peak moments in sport: A literature review'. *Quest*, 43, pp. 333–51.

8   Dillon, K. and Tait, J. (2000). 'Spirituality and being in the zone in team sports: a relationship?' *Journal of Sport Behavior*, 23 (2), pp. 91–100.

9   Csikszentmihalyi, M. (1997). *Finding Flow: The Psychology of Engagement with Everyday Life*. New York: Basic Books.

10 Gillis, R. (2003). 'UK Leagues bear comparison'. *Sport Business International*, 76, p. 7.

11 Britcher, C. (2002). 'AFL takes a popularity dip'. *Sport Business International*, 75, p. 17.

12 Barrand, D. (2003). 'US viewers play a familiar tune'. *Sport Business International*, 76, p. 7.

13 The Associated Press (2002). 'All-Star TV ratings hit all-time low'. *The Cincinati Enquirer*, 11 July. Available at www.reds/enquirer.com/2002/07/11/red_all-star_tv_ratings.html, accessed on 23 August 2003.

14 Chengelis, A. (2002). 'Hot Wings, Cold TV Ratings'. *The Detroit News*, 3 June. Available at www.detnews.com/2002/wings/0206/03/a01–505146.htm, accessed on 17 October 2003.

15 Available at www.newslink.nandomedia.com/SportServer/tennis/slams/archive/story/527721p 4178040c.html, accessed on 15 September 2003.

16 Hirons, M. (2002). *Media-led Recovery in Sporting Interests*. Sydney: Sweeney Sports.

17 Gibson, O. (2002). 'Grandstand's extreme sports scare off viewers'. *Guardian Unlimited: Guardian Newspapers Limited*.

18 FIFA Marketing AG Media Services. *FIFA World Cup Ratings success – results confirm event as a '24/7' viewing experience*. Switzerland: FIFA Marketing AG Media Services. Available at www.fifaworldcup.yahoo.com/en/020624/2/17xw.html, accessed on 18 June 2003.

19 FIFA Marketing AG Media Services, *FIFA World Cup Ratings success*.

20 Shanahan, A. (2002). 'Opinion: The young are leading the march back to religion'. *The Australian*, 24 December.

21 See M. Csikszentmihalyi (2000). 'The mythic potential of evolution'. *Zygon*, 35 (1), pp. 25–38.

22 Chengelis, 'Hot Wings, Cold TV Ratings.'

CHAPTER 7

Corporate Sport Citizenship: Tigers and Sharks

Citizenship implies community, and 'community' simply is about cooperation between people who vary in their ability, needs and views of the world. We could call it cultural diversity. Before any *business* activity, in the modern interpretation of the word, took place, there was only community. Social capital (the productive value of all citizens) was used to sustain the community.

Today businesses are trying hard to reconnect with the communities they have emerged from; sometimes because they feel they have to, but mostly to avoid alienating their customer base. The reality of life in a globalised world, however, is that big business needs to assume much of the responsibility for the wellbeing of people which in past times was considered to be the role of national governments. Businesses in the 2000s have social, political and economic responsibilities. They need to be corporate citizens. Increasingly, sport organisations, corporations and athletes are not escaping the watchful eye of public opinion. Why should Tiger Woods earn $100 million to get free Nike gear when so many other people cannot afford to buy the sneakers at $100 a pair? How responsible is Tiger for the wellbeing of others as a result of his extraordinary earning capacity?

In this chapter we take a closer look at how the corporate citizenship game is becoming mainstream business for many of the corporate giants around the world, and argue that it will play an important part in the future of sport business. UN Secretary General Kofi Annan's *Global Compact* initiative asks big business to incorporate practices and policies that are based on universal principles. We consider how this trend will impact the profit and non-profit dimensions of sport participation and spectatorship organisations and the athletes they deliver or exploit. We will introduce the concept of social relevance and discuss how this applies to any organisation. We even take the liberty of bringing Darwin into the discussion, to argue the validity of a 'survival of the fittest' metaphor, and that the 'fittest' of the future are those who are the most relevant to the community.

There is increasing evidence that socially responsible and engaged organisations are also those that have the highest potential for business success. This is great news because it means we can do good business and be good citizens at the same time.

In the final part of the chapter we take a closer look at how Nike has dealt with increasing community pressure to clean up its act, and how these developments have stimulated developments which will significantly affect the industry in the future. We conclude the chapter with an example of how former Olympic gold medallist Johann Olav Koss uses sport to enable and stimulate non-sport business to contribute to a better world. In the future, sport will offer the perfect tool to contribute something back to the community.

Social Capital

There are a multitude of associations that the word 'community' takes in the twenty-first century.[1] From a geographical perspective the word implies people living in close proximity, in groups or tribes smaller than a town, state or nation. In technological terms it represents enthusiasts interacting in cyber-space, linked by common interests. One interpretation is that community represents the site where economic globalisation is confronted by social change.

Stevenson suggests that defining community from a geographical or virtual perspective emphasises cohesion and cooperation.[2] He suggests that definitions of community too often ignore the existence of difference because in practice communities accept diverse interests, values, agendas and debates. Community might therefore be best seen as, 'the artful act of cooperation among people with a variety of different abilities, needs and views of the world – cultural diversity'.[3] In many ways, communities are consortia of tribes. We have already argued that tribes are likely to be more important social and cultural conduits of sport in the future.

It has been observed that the social infrastructure of local communities has been eroded by industrialisation and the global economy, leading to the loss of what might be called social capital, or the productive value of citizens embedded within a dense social network.[4] This viewpoint implicitly assumes that communities contain valuable social resources which might be lost if not managed and cultivated. Moreover, the very institutions that rely on communities and their constituents to achieve economic prosperity are the very same ones that are driving their marginalisation. The corporate machine has been slow to find ways of reconnecting with 'grassroots' communities. Increasingly, in the future, sport will offer an opportunity to remedy this oversight.

Sport has a way of becoming part of a society's fabric. Even in the age of 'radical' technology, sport offers the chance to bridge the social and economic gaps, to improve the quality of life and, as this chapter explores, provide an opportunity for large and profitable businesses to share a little of their prosperity. In fact, technology is likely to facilitate the process of sport corporate citizenship, as it will provide new vehicles for transmitting differentiated products, services and sponsorships. In a cynical world, the quiet support of community sport may be one of the few ways to penetrate the sponsorship clutter.

The idea that the wealthy in a society should help those less fortunate is, of course, not new. Corporate philanthropy or charity is valued in the billions. This generosity has tended to be confused with sponsorships, where sporting enterprises are faced with the responsibility of returning the investment made in them through exposure, positive associations, hospitality and product sales. With few exceptions, corporate sponsorship of sport is premised upon decisions as ruthless as any found in business. Corporate citizenship is newer, however, and in its true form is not based on the promise of positive exposure or the drive for an investment's return. Citizenship is about meeting an obligation to put something back into the society in which a business or an athlete operates or performs. In this chapter, we shall consider how this form of activity has taken shape, why it is relevant to the future and why sport might be central to its success.

Fad or Future?

In the current environment of one-hit management wonders, you could be forgiven for thinking that 'corporate citizenship' is just another buzzword, another fad to come and go. Cynical readers may consider it the latest version of empty, philanthropic gestures made by billion-dollar businesses. But there is some evidence to suggest that increasing pressure is being placed upon corporate enterprises to do more than write an annual cheque for charity, or sponsor a football stadium and pretend that their contribution was based on generosity rather than a financial return on investment. Consumers and communities are beginning to demand that business responds to their social, political and economic responsibilities in a strategic rather than superficial way.

Big corporations in the business of sport have not escaped the watchful eye of community opinion. Nike, one of the most vilified companies in the world, has suffered at the hands of an 'anti-sweat-shop' campaign that has forced it to change its outsourcing practices and, by default, citizenship policies. The company has since adopted a strategic approach to social responsibility with dedicated personnel, supply-chain codes of conduct and a policy of public transparency. This example illustrates just how pivotal reputation is in a cluttered consumer marketplace. Other retail giants (including Reebok and Adidas) have experienced similar pressure, and have signed up to social responsibility programmes such as *The Fair Labour Association Charter Agreement* along with Nike. In the future, sport governance organisations, such as the IOC and FIFA, will also face a unique set of challenges, as the public, championed by a ruthless media, demands more accountability. Mounting pressure on the IOC, for instance, has pressured it towards more competitive neutrality and public transparency.

Unlike many other industries, the sporting scene is fertile ground for select individuals to amass extraordinary personal fortunes. Tiger Woods, for instance, may soon become another sporting billionaire, alongside his mega-star predecessor, Michael Jordan. Although sporting heroes do not usually attract the same public cynicism as 'faceless' corporations, it is reasonable to anticipate additional public pressure for athletes to make substantial commitments to social and environmental causes. We, as sport fans, are trapped in a love–hate loop with the business side of sport. We lament the loss of tradition, the selfishness of athletes, the soulless commercialism and the artificial media hype. But we also demand high quality customer service from clubs and from venues, and we expect comfortable seats, good sight lines and reasonable food. We insist on being entertained, we crave statistics, facts and gossip, we lust for our heroes and we savour the vicarious theatre of the modern gladiatorial contest. These do not come cheaply. In short, we are prepared to pay, at least up to a point; but for how long? Professional sport cannot continue to absorb player salary increases and, in our more sober moments, far from the adrenaline and tribalism of the stadium, we might ask ourselves what players are really doing for us.

How many of us think about the fact that we are paying for Tiger Woods' $100 million Nike sponsorship when we part with $200 for a pair of shoes? When it does happen en masse, accountability for the hands that have stitched the shoes will not stop at the manufacturers' door-step. In response, multinational companies and even internationally prominent athletes are likely to take a 'glocal'[5] approach to managing their reputations, such that they invest not only in the geographical communities where they reside, but also in global causes.

In contrast, domestic sporting organisations will maintain a local citizenship focus into the future. Regional, state and national sports bodies are likely to be concerned with local community issues, their own service quality and reputation. As predominantly non-profit service providers, they are unlikely to be questioned about their 'social licence to operate'. Instead, they will be increasingly challenged to meet community expectations, including meeting professional business standards and enhancing local cultural enrichment.

The positive attributes of sport will be increasingly used by sports organisations to address local social issues, not only because they are expected to, but because their membership depends upon it. Several football clubs in Britain, for example, have recently implemented anti-racism campaigns within their regions. Corporations undertaking citizenship programmes are likely to seek similar alliances with sport organisations in order to leverage positive community perceptions about the benefits of sport. In this way, sport will be the recipient of corporate citizenship programmes, bolstering the ongoing viability of grassroots participation and regional events.

In short, the name of the corporate citizenship game has moved beyond the rules of ethical behaviour and charitable donations. The *Global Compact* initiative driven by Kofi Annan is premised upon the Universal Declaration of Human Rights, the International Labour Organisation's Fundamental Principles on Rights at Work and the Rio Principles on Environment and Development. Put simply, big business is asked to incorporate practices and policies that are based on universal principles. This shift has been spurred by the rise of globalisation, and is here to stay.

As globalisation has changed the balance of power away from government and towards multinational corporations, the public has progressively demanded a corresponding weight of responsibility. While anti-globalisation campaigners cling to the idea of turning back the clock on the inequities of globalisation, a growing majority has turned its gaze of accountability away from government and towards private enterprise, believing, perhaps astutely, that people are *more powerful as consumers than as voters*. After all, the market is sovereign.

Based on recent history, sport 'corporations' (including mega-stars) have largely escaped this public scrutiny because they were 'different'. The people-owned sport and its star athletes offered vicarious excellence. But in today's sport business environment, sport organisations are no different from IBM, Coca-Cola or Shell. With FIFA's ability to mobilise billions of people around the world comes the responsibility to reinvest some of the 'for the good of the game' resources 'for the benefit of all'. Similarly, with Tiger's swinging skills and public appeal comes a responsibility to use his influence and resources for the good of his benefactors. Stock markets around the world will ultimately demonstrate that no company can be worth one billion dollars based exclusively on its ability to deliver financial returns. Rather, companies need to show their relevance and community fit to all stakeholders; this task is best delivered through sport. With no disrespect to the impressive sport business success and generous personal disposition of Greg Norman, perhaps the future will yield more Tigers than sharks in the business of sport.

Corporate Citizenship: Getting to Here

In the recent past, well-developed and powerful national and regionalised government systems have regulated the dealings of non-government organisations (both profit and non-profit) to the extent that they could be forced, to a large extent, to abide by community standards. In other words, governments made corporations fit in. When the Berlin Wall came down, with it came the countervailing power of socialist states (and the huge markets they controlled) in which governments were the main drivers of industrialisation, resource accumulation and allocation, as well as product commodification. The post-1989 free market ideology, combined with rampant globalisation, has encouraged big corporations to become even bigger and also spurred on the decentralisation and privatisation of state companies. With governments stuck within the boundaries of geographically determined borders, transnational organisations were free to trade, lobby and invest anywhere in the world where profit seemed plausible. Without comprehensive international control mechanisms, some companies have taken advantage of weaker, poorly developed national government systems in Third World economies, where short-term economic development was (and still is) much more important and attractive for local powerbrokers than long-term sustainable growth that benefits all members of the country. In other words, businesses make money for company shareholders and exploit the host community providers. However, according to Kofi Annan:

> Globalization is a fact of life. But I believe we have underestimated its fragility. The problem is this. The spread of markets outpaces the ability of societies and their political systems to adjust to them, let alone to guide the course they take. History teaches us that such an imbalance between the economic, social, and political realms can never be sustained for very long.[6]

John Ruggie,[7] Kofi Annan's former senior adviser for strategic planning and the UN's Assistant Secretary General from 1997 to 2001, noted that the first golden age of globalisation was from 1850 to 1910. Transatlantic cables between London and New York dramatically improved the speed of communication. In addition, the opening of the first Alpine tunnels and the Suez and Panama canals, combined with the British Industrial Revolution, led to dramatic improvements in transport (especially rail) infrastructure in Europe and North America. According to Ruggie, this unrestrained opening of markets was based on neither social nor cultural needs, and became a situation out of control leading to economic protectionism, depression, anarchy and war. Social market economy systems and social democracy, after much trial and error, emerged as the systems that could effectively be used by governments to moderate, mediate and facilitate international trade and interaction.

The second wave of globalisation that currently embraces us has moved beyond the boundaries of national economies and presents the same problems of a century ago, only on a much larger scale. Corporations are now occupying the driver's seat for the moderation, mediation and facilitation of international trade. Hence the call for a global 'compact' by Kofi Annan, on the back of the anti-globalisation protest movements of the 1990s, and more recent corporate scandals and mismanagement leading to bankruptcies (e.g., Enron, Worldcom, Kirch Media, One-Tel).

Citizenship in the future has to be global to be relevant. Global corporate citizenship has been defined as a company's response to its 'social, political, and economic responsibilities as defined through law and public policy, stakeholder expectations, and voluntary acts flowing from corporate values and business strategies'.[8] Corporate citizenship can include perspectives such as the economic (deliver returns), legal (live by the rules), ethical (advance beyond the rules to higher standards) and philanthropic (give back to the community) responsibilities of companies.[9] In summary, with the partial transfer of power from (national) governmental organisations to multinational corporations has come the need to devise new systems of economic and social control. These systems are predominantly required to ensure a fair (re)distribution of resources, a universal approach to the usage of (natural) resources, and the development of business policies and practices that benefit all stakeholders and can be implemented and applied in the majority of (cultural) contexts. It will not come as a surprise that this is an undertaking of great complexity. The great challenges of modern globalisation are threefold:[10] first, the equal distribution of wealth; second, the balancing of social and economic global rule-making; and third, the identification of a global identity (who are we?). Does citizenship facilitate this process and, if it does, where does sport fit in? In order to answer these questions, we must start by deconstructing citizenship.

Dimensions of Corporate Citizenship

The enforced ambition of multinational corporations to become global corporate citizens is a commendable but troublesome task. If it were possible to apply a corporate citizenship model to all organisations that operate on an international scale, many adversaries of globalisation would ease their protests. However, as argued by James Post, the individual company 'citizenship model' should be aligned with the company's business model, the latter being a direct derivative of the company's geographic business scope and the orientation of the industry that the company is operating in.[11] In regard to the geographic scope, companies can be domestic, multidomestic or global operators. Domestic companies will have acquired knowledge about how they are expected to 'act' in their local market. When these companies expand their operations internationally, they are faced with the task of devising 'local' citizenship practices that are in line with the expectations of stakeholders in the new marketplace. This process often involves the appointment of local personnel and management, or entering into ventures with local partners. Truly global companies have to balance their need to be seen as 'global' brands, produced and distributed in highly complex and integrated globally managed systems, with local commitment to dealing through and communicating with the domestic or regional stakeholding groups.

When considering the industry orientation, Post identifies five industry models: natural resources, industrial/manufacturing, services, retail, and e-commerce. Both natural resource extracting and manufacturing companies face community issues that require a 'social licence' to operate. Pollution, traffic, indigenous land rights and, in the case of company townships (e.g., mining towns), the provision of a range of vital life services are citizenship prerequisites that need strong consideration. For service businesses, the image and reputation of the company is a key success factor. Negative perceptions about service providers will rapidly lead to the demise of the business; hence, positive involvement in stakeholding communities is of critical importance. This is one of the reasons why so many services businesses are involved in the sponsorship of arts, entertainment and sporting events at both the global and local level. The latter holds true for retailing organisations as well. Linking the consumption of consumer goods to public events often will lead to the 'mental integration' of the brand and/or the company in consumers' good books. Finally, the emerging e-commerce model centres on 'interest' communities rather than geographic communities. Without the geographic market boundaries that are used to categorise traditional markets, a whole range of new (and largely unidentified) cyber-citizenship issues need to be dealt with in the e-commerce industry, and these issues will be more likely to be related to the type of products that people purchase online, rather than their respective countries and localities of origin.

Prosperity Factors

Before we take a closer look at the real meaning and purpose of the global push towards corporate citizenship, it is useful to further outline the main reasons why organisations evolve in the first place. According to textbook definitions, an organisation comes into being when two or more people work together towards the achievement of common goals. Stated differently, when it is deemed by an individual that a particular task can better be achieved with the help of another individual, a form of systematised cooperation can be created that we call an organisation. The premise upon which organisations can be (and often are) successful is that the pooling of resources, when used smartly, will deliver greater results than using these resources independently. The first resources are human, but subsequently include financial, natural and information resources as well.

If we, for reasons of simplicity, assume that Darwin was right, and those organisations which 'best fit' their environmental niches will survive, then organisations that are the best at transforming their resources into useful outcomes (most often determined by the marketplaces that the organisations deliver to) will flourish. It therefore comes as little surprise that many organisations (especially in the sport industry) have clearly defined 'survival' and 'growth towards domination' as their most important objectives. After all, is not that the attitude that will lead to ultimate success of the organisational species? What is 'right' and 'wrong' in that process is at the heart of the corporate citizenship debate. Human beings, for that matter, have themselves been engaged in an evolution-long search for the definition of what it means to be human. More specifically, what are the rights of a human being? Are these rights universal? That is, do they apply to all humans in all societies equally? If so, how do we define those rights if the cultural systems and contexts upon which they are based and formulated differ significantly? Which cultural system drives the formulation of human rights in the first place?

The Fittest Organisations are those that are Socially Relevant

In his book, *Our Posthuman Future*, Francis Fukuyama argues that human rights are principally based on the concept of human nature (versus nurture). He defines human nature as, 'the sum of the behaviour and characteristics that are typical of the human species, arising from genetic rather than environmental factors'.[12] Fukuyama argues that if humans, as a 'higher' species, are all connected by something we call human nature, then human dignity – the universal desire by humans to be recognised as members of the group(s) they want to belong to – naturally flows from this. In turn, the rights that we have as human beings are predicated on the principle of equality. In other words, what sets humans apart from other animals is their desire to be respected as human beings, to be treated equally with other human beings, and to be recognised as human beings first and foremost; everything else is secondary (i.e., religion, gender, physical and mental capacity, etc.). Applied to humans, Darwin's 'survival of the best fit' is an optimisation theory. Competition is good because it will bring out the 'best' in the species. What has set apart the human species from other organisms is its genetically-based ability (nature) to compete fiercely for survival, yet base that competition on sets of elaborate, predetermined rules called ethics that lead to an assumption that there must be universal human rights. These assumptions in turn require cooperation and citizenship.

Evolution is based on random mutation, variation, niche survival and procreation. Apply this to organisations: if one organisation follows a new path (say, corporate citizenship) either deliberately or accidentally, and prospers greatly, it will go on to be dominant. In biology, it takes only 4,000 generations for an organism to go from 0.1 per cent to 99.9 of the species population. The difference is that we can see this process is radically accelerated in business today, and we are more likely to see it progress with even greater rapidity in the future thanks to technological developments. Twenty or thirty years ago, the most successful companies in the world had taken 20–30 years to reach one billion dollars of net value. Notwithstanding the impact of inflation, this time has been substantially slashed by relatively new companies, many of which have been associated with technology. The lesson is clear: the pace of business development has accelerated. Companies need to carve out the equivalent of their Darwinian ecological niche if they are to survive and prosper.

If we know that organisations are groups of human beings working together, then surely this would not eliminate the principles upon which human interaction can be defined. Without succumbing to the risks of over-simplicity (we know we are for the sake of the example), when organisations fiercely compete with other organisations in their quest for scarce resources, and methods of efficient and effective resource transformation, how is this different from one human being competing for survival with another? Corporate citizenship is the natural progression of faceless bureaucracies towards realising that they are actually made up of thousands of human beings, interacting with other corporations that also pool thousands of fellow human beings. Principles that drive human interaction, competition and cooperation should also drive the interaction of organisational entities. In other words, survival of the best fitting organisation, and those that will fit best in the community, also return value to those communities.

Corporate Engagement: Bottom Line Community Involved

So far we have argued that corporate citizenship or corporate social responsibility is about the ways in which we expect business to deal with the commercial, ethical, legal and community (public) expectations that societies have about them. These expectations are not based on a fluid set of rules and regulations, but rather are premised upon the universal principle of human dignity; we expect groups of people working together (organisations) to treat all stakeholders of the business as if they were fellow human beings. This brings us back to the UN initiative, Global Compact. The initiative is intended to advance global corporate social responsibility and is founded upon nine universal principles. The principles are as follows:[13]

1 Support and respect for the protection of internationally proclaimed human rights.
2 Non-complicity in human rights abuses.
3 Freedom of association and the effective recognition of the right to collective bargaining.
4 The elimination of all forms of forced and compulsory labour.
5 The effective abolition of child labour.
6 The elimination of discrimination in respect of employment and occupation.
7 A precautionary approach to environmental challenges.
8 Greater environmental responsibility.
9 Encouragement of the development and diffusion of environmentally-friendly technologies.

Advancing the corporate citizenship concept towards implementation, John Weiser and Simon Zadek[14] have introduced the concept of Corporate Engagement (CE). Corporations are truly engaged when they get involved in activities that may have a positive impact on low-income communities, when these activities are part of ongoing community involvement strategies, when the activities offer direct or indirect benefits for the corporation, and when the activities combine philanthropy with the core competencies of the organisation. For example, its ability to use bargaining power, and economies of scope and/or scale, to benefit both the company and those receiving philanthropy. Weiser and Zadek argue that many Chief Executive Officers (CEOs) of corporations have yet to be convinced of the positive impact that CE can have on the company's financial performance.

Irrespective of the disbelievers, however, the evidence is accumulating that CE, or being good corporate citizens, does lead to higher performance in many different areas. Companies that are 'stakeholder balanced', and which excel in managing the relationships with investors, customers, employees, suppliers and communities best, outperform their 'shareholder focused' counterparts four times in terms of company growth, and eight times when it comes to employment growth. Also, publicity about unethical corporate behaviour has a significant downward effect on stock prices for at least six months.[15] The shareholder return of 'stakeholder super-stars' over the past 15 years was 43 per cent, whereas companies with a sole focus on financial shareholders returned only 19 per cent.[16] High returns will also lead to easier access to capital. The perceived price to quality ratio of products and services remains an important indicator of the company's image and reputation in the marketplace, but 89 per cent of all Americans also believe that companies are responsible for things other than achieving business success. For example, 42 per cent believe companies have a growing responsibility towards solving social problems such as crime, lack of education and community health. A further 46 per cent of those surveyed reported that they had purchased products from companies because of their active stance towards social responsibility.[17] Eight in ten Americans feel more positive about companies that support causes which they also support. From the internal stakeholder perspective, 87 per cent of European employees say that they are more loyal to socially-engaged employers.[18] To have loyal employees leads to higher employee retention (or lower staff turnover). Also, improved staff attitudes lead to higher customer satisfaction, in turn leading to higher revenues.[19] Without claiming to be exhaustive, there seems to be sufficient empirical evidence to claim socially responsible and engaged companies will also heighten their potential for business success.

Business Characteristics of Sport Organisations

For decades sport managers have argued that their organisations are different from other profit and not-for-profit organisations. It is, for example, common knowledge that US-based professional baseball franchises have been treated as exceptions to the rule in regard to anti-competitive legislation. Where monopolistic behaviour in the fiercely competitive USA is outlawed as soon as it surfaces in 'normal' business, professional baseball has been granted a licence, by law, to operate as a monopoly. The argument is simply that sport is not a business like any other. There are also numerous examples of football clubs in Europe and Australia which have, on several occasions, survived bankruptcies that would have finished business for any other non-sport organisation. In these instances it was determined that football clubs are vital parts of the cultural and social make-up of local communities and, as a result, community funds (taxes) or pooled competition resources could justifiably be spent on keeping those clubs in 'business'. In more recent times, even when some of those clubs are listed on the Stock Exchange, they remain largely untouchable by the economic forces that determine the fate of other enterprises. In short, sport organisations are often run in a way based on emotional support and attractiveness as much as they are run on the basis of business principles.

We all feel that we know what sport is because it permeates modern life with such penetrating intensity that even for those who loathe sport there is little chance of escape. Beyond describing sport as a simple 'physical contest' or 'game', there are six ingredients that paint a more complete picture of its contemporary flavour.[20] First, it has set and defined rules; in other words, a player must behave within certain boundaries to (questionably) enhance 'fairness'. Second, modern sport is highly organised with fixed structures and often substantial systems of infrastructure. Third, sport remains a physical pursuit that includes an element of 'playlike' activity. Fourth, equipment and facilities are essential features of contemporary sport. Fifth, at the heart of all sport lies an intrinsic uncertainty of outcome. There can be no sport unless there is a chance of either victory or defeat. Finally, modern sport requires (ironically) both cooperation and conflict, within the framework of a competition.

This brings us to discussing the most important performance indicator that is used to measure success or failure of sport organisations. From a financial point of view, sport is no different from any other business, but financial health tends to come second when success is measured in sport. When considering the uncertainty of outcome of the sporting contest, and the consequent competitive and cooperative spirit of sport organisations in the context of a competition, (spectator) sport suddenly becomes a different case. It needs to be noted that probably all organisations that operate in the sport industry, including manufacturers and marketers of sporting goods and apparel, are directly or indirectly dependent on the success or failure of elite athletes. However, those sport organisations that produce competitive sport to be offered to paying spectators (professional clubs, event organisers) are most directly affected. For most of those organisations the most important performance measure is success on the field. The SportBusiness Group Editorial Director, Kevin Roberts, perfectly hit the mark when he described the irrational approach to decision-making in sport: 'the board of directors of major European soccer clubs will smile as they write a cheque for $30 million to buy a new striker but deny the marketing manager $1,000 for some new software'.[21] The logic underpinning 'winning' as the primary performance measure is the (only partly true) assumption that success on the field will lead to more passionate and loyal fans, in turn driving the business off the field.

Within corporate citizenship rules, however, the overriding question remains, who are the stakeholders of the organisation? Too often in sport these have been either the board members of the organisation (enthusiastic, sport-loving volunteers who, next to their – often high-profile business – day jobs, run the professional sport organisation in their spare time) or the high-performing star athletes, who have disproportionate power in regard to the resources the club or event has at its disposal to run the organisation. From the perspective of corporate engagement, sport organisations are at the crossroads, forced to ask themselves who their stakeholders are, and how they can maintain a stakeholder-balanced business perspective. In the next section we outline how the sporting apparel manufacturing industry has come to grips with this dilemma.

Big Brother is Watching: Behave or be Punished

The sport organisation best known for its brash and rebellious advertising campaigns has been subject to vicious global scrutiny throughout the 1990s. Apparel marketer Nike, which outsources all of its manufacturing, was targeted by the Australian-based organisation Oxfam Community Aid Abroad because it was the market leader which pioneered the use of low-wage production countries (with poor human rights records). According to Oxfam, Nike was reaping the benefits of low production cost margins, and it targeted Nike because it felt Nike should use its excess profits to improve the conditions of the workers in the contracted factories.

The Oxfam campaign placed an enormous amount of pressure on Nike, largely because of the power of the Internet. For example, in 2001 an MIT graduate student, Jonah Peretti, responded to a Nike offer to personalise his trainers by asking if they could print the word 'sweatshop' on the side. Nike refused and Peretti e-mailed his response to Nike and Oxfam (and the rest of the world). It read:

> Thank you for the time and energy you have spent on my request. I have decided to order the shoes with a different ID, but I would like to make one small request. Could you please send me a colour snapshot of the 10-year-old Vietnamese girl who makes my shoes?[22]

Oxfam continues to run its NikeWatch campaign, posting updates on the movements of the company on its website on a regular basis.

In all fairness, irrespective of Oxfam's continued criticism of the company, Nike has taken comprehensive action to not only improve its own conduct as an employer and industry leader, but has also set up policies and procedures at the level of the industry, forcing competitors into taking an active stance towards appropriate citizenship as well. Nike was among the first to set up an industry code of conduct in 1992 which included standards relating to the abolition of forced labour and child labour, fair compensation, legally mandated benefits, reasonable work hours and conditions of overtime, a safe and healthy working environment, and the requirement to document and regularly inspect the implementation of the code of conduct. In October 2001 Nike released its first corporate responsibility report. It employs an internal team of more than 30 people who are in charge of coordinating and monitoring the 750 contracted factories (based upon the principles set out by the Fair Labour Association). The company has a vice-president of corporate responsibility, and its factories are independently monitored by a new company called Global Social Compliance. Nike is also a founding member of the Global Alliance for Workers and Communities. The organisation's primary goal is to devise a sustainable monitoring, assessment and development process for the benefit of young adult workers in global manufacturing industries.

After realising that child labour was used to stitch soccer balls in Pakistan, Nike centralised its activities through one contractor, Saga Sports. Saga Sports now operates a number of stitching centres in Pakistan, paying school tuition for former child workers and hiring their family members who are at the legal age to work. In an industry-wide effort to independently monitor the process of eliminating child labour in Pakistan, the Pakistan Soccer Ball Program has brought together more than 50 sporting goods brands (including Reebok, Umbro, Puma, Adidas and Nike) who will only buy from local manufacturers that participate in the program. Reebok also label their balls with 'guarantee: manufactured without child labour', as part of the Reebok Educational Assistance to Pakistan programme (REAP).[23] Indeed, other sporting apparel corporations such as Reebok and Adidas have learned the lesson the easy way. Nike has taken many of the blows, but at least this has led to most global apparel operators now being actively involved in independent monitoring of manufacturing activity, and in the process providing some kind of educational and medical support to local manufacturing communities.

Domestic Corporate Sport Citizenship

Mark Glazebrook is the Corporate Citizenship Manager of BP Australia. He recently joined one of BP's senior managers on his travels to a number of Australia's remote Aboriginal communities in the Northern Territory, to witness with their own eyes the devastating effects of petrol sniffing on the local community. In some of the communities, more than 10 per cent of the population wear permanent sniffing cans attached to their heads. British Petroleum, or Beyond Petroleum in corporate citizenship lingo, through the work of Glazebrook, is looking into ways of helping the Aboriginal communities cope with the problem of petrol sniffing. After all, they do make much of their money from petrol sales. Talking to Glazebrook, he recalled a remarkable story.

A local development officer recently hosted a match in which a team of petrol-sniffing boys played against 'clean' opponents. Their petrol cans were lying conveniently on the sideline in order to take a quick sniff after kicking every goal, but playing football is pretty much the only activity that will get them to remove the cans from their heads for a while. Australian rules football is the only 'new' activity that the Aboriginal people in Australia's north hold close to their heart, and they are pretty good at it as well. During the 2003 pre-season, one of the more prominent teams in the national professional competition, Carlton from Melbourne, came up to play a practice match against a selection of the best Aboriginal players. They were convincingly defeated.

At the start of this chapter we argued that domestic sport organisations will maintain a more local citizenship focus. In the case of the AFL, much time has gone into the debate about the establishment of professional teams in Australia's less populated regions, in particular the football-mad state of Tasmania, off the south coast of Australia, and in the Northern Territory (NT) in Australia's tropical north. The AFL has maintained its view that the 'business' case for teams in either Hobart (Tasmania) or Darwin (NT) simply does not add up. Apart from the fact that crowds will be significantly smaller than in the major cities, travel by air to and from the remote Northern Territory will be draining on the already substantial air travel budgets of the other teams. However, the AFL does spend a lot of money on developing Northern Territory (Aboriginal) talent, organising development camps and bringing high potential youngsters to Melbourne to try out for the big teams. From our perspective, the AFL is in the perfect position not only to make a strong point about the Northern Territory as an Australian community, but also as a sport organisation leading the way in corporate sport citizenship. It may not be financially rewarding to establish teams, but the social gain will far outweigh the investment. The boys in the Northern Territory have already shown there is an abundance of talent available. Not only can talented Aboriginal players stay at home rather than relocating to one of the cities but local communities can congregate at the stadium to support their players, creating enormous *esprit de corps*, with economic benefits for the local economy. But, most importantly, the boredom that leads to petrol sniffing may be replaced with a weekly climax of local 'footy', playing with and against the big boys from Melbourne, Sydney, Brisbane, Adelaide and Perth. This, of course, is a rather simplistic view of the complex situation that is the clash of traditional with new culture in Australia. However, what the Australian government continues to struggle with, giving the Aboriginal people the respect and rightful place in Australian society they deserve, is there for the taking on a platter for one of the biggest sport organisations in the country.

Using Sport to Improve Communities

Let us finish this chapter with the athletes, and one athlete in particular, Johann Olav Koss. A gifted athlete in his time, winning four gold speed skating medals, three of them at his 'home' Olympics in Lillehammer, he has redirected his ambition towards making a better world through sport for disadvantaged children. Koss is the President and CEO of Right to Play (formerly known as Olympic Aid), an IOC-endorsed organisation that funds and delivers sport-based development programmes around the world. Koss argues that sport harnesses a power unknown to other forms of aid. For example, he recalls a group of children who lived in a war zone picking up a soccer ball rather than the weapons offered to them by the local warlords. He feels that team sports can offer children who have nothing else left in the world a sense of belonging and community, offering social development opportunities along the way. Right to Play also operates a development programme for local coaches and volunteers, Coach2Coach, assisting the organisation to develop a sustainable sport infrastructure in local communities. More recently it has moved from being a fundraiser to implementing development projects as well. Koss has successfully been promoting the cause of the organisation world-wide, to both private and public organisations, and he anticipates the budget of the organisation rising from $6 million in 2002 to $20 million in 2004. Admittedly, some businesses will only affiliate with Right to Play because it makes them look good in the process. Call it *enlightened self-interest*, and, indeed, some of the high-profile athletes involved may feel that it does not hurt their ability to increase their sponsorship value. Koss summarises the argument we have put in this chapter perfectly:

If anybody has an interest in promoting the positive role and potential of sport around the world it is the companies which benefit so much from the spending power of the sports obsessed youngsters of the developed world. In some respects payback time is approaching and, on this occasion, everyone will be a winner.[24]

Notes and References

1   Stevenson, T. (2002). 'Communities of Tomorrow', *Futures*, 34, pp. 735–44.
2   Stevenson, 'Communities of Tomorrow', pp. 735–44.
3   Stevenson, 'Communities of Tomorrow', p. 737.
4   Putnam, R. (2001). *Bowling Alone: The Collapse and Revival of American Community*. New York: Simon & Schuster, pp. 40–2.
5   Post, J.E. (2000). 'Moving from geographic to virtual communities: Global corporate citizenship in a dot.com world'. *Business and Society Review*, 105 (1), pp. 26–46.
6   Annan, K. (1999). 'Business and the UN: Address delivered to the World Economic Forum', Davos, Switzerland, 31 January 1999. *Vital Speeches of the Day, 0042–742X*, 65 (9), pp. 260–1.
7   Ruggie, J.G. (2002). 'The theory and practice of learning networks. Corporate responsibility and the global compact'. *Journal of Corporate Citizenship*, 5, pp. 27–36.
8   Post, 'Moving from geographic to virtual communities', p. 28.
9   Carroll, A.B. (1998). 'The four faces of corporate citizenship'. *Business and Society Review*, 100, pp. 1–7.
10 Ruggie, 'The theory and practice of learning networks', p. 30.
11 Post, 'Moving from geographic to virtual communities', p. 28.
12 Fukuyama, F. (2002). *Our Posthuman Future. Consequences of the Biotechnology Revolution*. London: Profile Books, p. 130.
13 Ruggie, 'The theory and practice of learning networks', p. 31.
14 Weiser, J. and Zadek, S. (2000). *Conversations with Disbelievers. Persuading Companies to Address Social Challenges*. Ford Foundation. Available at *http://www.zadek.net/pub_frame.html*, accessed on 17 October 2003.
15 Business for Social Reponsibility website (2002). *Introduction to Corporate Social Responsibility*. Available at *www.bsr.org*, accessed on 23 May 2003.
16 Weiser and Zadek, *Conversations with Disbelievers*.
17 The Conference Board (1999). *Consumer Expectations on the Social Accountability of Business*. New York: The Conference Board Inc.
18 Fleishman Hillard (1999). *Consumers Demand Companies with a Conscience*. London: Fleishman Hillard.
19 Rucci, A., Kim, S.P. and Quinn, R.T. (1998). 'The employee-customer-profit chain at Sears'. *Harvard Business Review*, January–February, pp. 83–97.
20 Shilbury, D. and Deane, J. (2002). *Sport Management in Australia*, Melbourne: Strategic Sport Management; Loy, J.W. (1968). 'The nature of sport: A definitional effort'. *Quest*, 10, pp. 1–15; VanderZwaag, H.J. and Sheehan, T.J. (1978). *Introduction to Sport Studies: From the Classroom to the Ballpark*. Dubuque, IA: William C. Brown.
21 Westerbeek, H. and Smith, A. (2003). *Sport Business in the Global Marketplace*. Basingstoke: Palgrave Macmillan, Basingstoke, p. x.
22 Skapinker, M. (2002). 'Why Nike has broken into a sweat'. *Financial Times*, 7 March, pp. 13–14.
23 Business for Social Reponsibility website (2002). *Issue Brief: Child Labour*. Available at: *http://www.bsr.org/BSRResources/IssueBriefDetail.cfm?DocumentID=394*, accessed on 3 November 2003.
24 Roberts, K. (2002). 'Sport's helping hand.' *Sport Business International*, November, pp. 24–5.

CHAPTER 8

Green Sport Business: Greenbacks and Green Thumbs

Conducting 'green' sport business is an outcome of corporate citizenship. It is one of the strongest demands society is placing upon sport organisations from the perspective of adding value to society, rather than using its resources for economic gain only. The environment has been on the global political agenda for more than three decades. However, it is only since the early 1990s, leading up to the enactment of the Kyoto protocol in 1994, that sport has actively been brought into the equation.

The Olympic Movement's Agenda 21, which was adopted by the Earth Summit in Rio de Janeiro in 1992, sought to encourage Olympic members to play an active part in sustainable development. The 1994 Lillehammer Winter Olympics added the 'environment' as a third pillar to the previous two of Olympism, sport and culture. Lillehammer actively sought to implement a sustainable approach to major event management by using natural building materials, energy conservation designs, recycling programmes and the blending of new and existing facilities with the natural environment. Lillehammer put the environment on the map for future sport business, and Sydney's 'Green Games' in 2000 were a further expression of a changing attitude towards organising mega sporting events.

Green sport business is good for the planet, but it also has great marketing potential. The future of sport business will partly be built on the ability of sport to showcase 'best practice green business'. Sustainable sport will, more than any other kind of business, attract the limelight because of its natural ability to generate interesting stories for the news-hungry media. Sustainability relates to our ability to fulfil current needs without compromising the ability of our children to meet their needs. What better educational tool than sport to teach all of us? Sustainable sport can further be described as being driven by business principles from an economic viewpoint, and driven by social and environmental perspectives from the sport development outlook.

In the context of the singularity we face a number of difficult – if not impossible – choices. If indeed future technology is going to allow us to fix everything we have destroyed in the past, then why bother about the environment now? The other perspective may be that if we lose control of our own destiny in the future, we may at least have 'programmed' the singularity with 'green' attitudes that will lead to a sustainable and liveable planet. The long-term reality is that if we do not find ways to achieve sustainability and biodiversity now, no future technology will save us.

In this chapter we argue that next in importance to sport's ability to secure social, political and economic integration is its ability to encourage better environmental understanding, simply because the natural environment constitutes much of sport's own context. Sport business could be a solution.

It's Easy Being Green (Sport)

The original Olympic Games were held in Olympia, Greece, every four years from at least 776 BC until they were banned by Emperor Theodosius in 393 AD. Inspired by these ancient games, Baron Pierre de Coubertin of France conceived the modern Games, which were first held in 1896 in Athens. From that date, the Games have been held every four years except when interrupted in 1916 by the First World War, and for the period surrounding the Second World War.

In 1948, when the Olympic Games made their first appearance after that war, London (the host city) took the opportunity to use the games as a way to rebuild much of the sporting infrastructure which it had lost during the war. Almost three years after the last bomb had fallen and the last bullet had been fired, Britain saw the games as an opportunity to demonstrate to the world that it remained a powerful nation on the world's stage. The games, as they had been in previous Olympics, remained essentially a way of showcasing a nation's politics and position in the world. The 1980 and 1984 Olympic Games, in Moscow and Los Angeles respectively, demonstrated even more sharply the politics of nations.

Since the initiation of the modern Olympics, the more powerful Western nations, together with their carefully chosen allies, have dominated the selection of host cities. Not until the ill-fated Moscow Olympics did a non-Western or allied country secure the games. Ideology has always been the political motivator. The Berlin Games of 1936 demonstrated this clearly.

Is ideology still the driving force behind such a powerful sports symbol as the Olympic Games? The answer is, undoubtedly, yes. But the politics have significantly changed, almost certainly as a result of the ending of the Cold War and the break-up of the old USSR. National power and national pride remain, of course, as the underlying motivation behind the desire to become the host country; but national power is now illustrated differently. Ideology now demands that the games demonstrate the host nation as a leader in world citizenry.

World citizenry can be expressed in a number of different ways. At its base, however, is the belief that a good world citizen understands world problems and actively seeks ways of helping solve those problems. Opinion polls indicate that the global public regard environmental management as a key issue on the world agenda, second only to the long-term protection of human health.[1] Thus it was again affirmed that it is generally the problems that affect the mass population that acquire mass support, and high on that list of problems is that of the environment.

The global concern for environmental management has found expression in a number of ways. Meetings, marches and mayhem have marked the environmental calendar. Conferences have debated ways and means of moving the environmental agenda along, yet little has been achieved. Despite money for research being made available by the richer countries, general global agreement on how to tackle the problems affecting the environment has yet to be reached.

The United Nations Framework Convention on Climate Change, usually known as the Kyoto Protocol or Agreement, despite being signed by 166 countries and brought into force on 21 March 1994, has still not been ratified by countries such as the USA and Australia. The agreement sought only a modest decrease of 5.2 per cent on 1990 levels by 2012 in the level of greenhouse gas emissions, and that only from 38 industrial nations. Yet current estimates are that by 2010, emissions of countries in the Organisation for Economic Co-operation and Development (including the USA) are going to be 29 per cent higher than the target committed to in Kyoto. Indeed, there is a conviction even among conservative scientists that by 2030, carbon dioxide levels will be about 25 per cent higher than 1990 levels, despite the adoption of all policies under consideration.[2]

Reaction from the public to the Kyoto Agreement was somewhat mixed, as perhaps might be expected. Environmentalists complained that the Agreement did not go far enough, while businessmen were concerned that the reductions would harm industry and might even cause a global depression. There is probably an element of truth in the belief that environmental regulations might create additional costs for business, but there is a silver lining in that the demand for cleaner technologies is also likely to create new jobs and business opportunities.

It was in the context that initiated the Kyoto Agreement that the relationship between 'green' and 'sport' was first forged. Its genesis probably goes back to what was called the Olympic Movement's Agenda 21 which was first adopted at the Earth Summit in Rio de Janeiro in 1992. Agenda 21 sought to encourage Olympic members to play an active part in sustainable development.

Although history would have us believe that the Sydney Olympics was the first 'Green Olympics', that honour actually belongs to the Lillehammer Winter Olympics of 1994. It came about because the Norwegian Olympic Committee saw the opportunity to become good world citizens and was determined to add a third pillar, the environment, to the two existing pillars of the Olympic movement: sport and culture.

The Winter Olympics have not always been a part of the Olympic movement. Indeed, the first Winter Games were not held until 1924 in Chamonix, in France. These games chose to build huge winter sports arenas on once virgin ground and in so doing became known for despoiling the environment. In 1974 Denver, Colorado, held a referendum on holding the Winter Games, the result of which was to turn down the IOC's offer on the grounds that they posed too great an environmental risk. The idea that winter sports damaged the environment was strong. Lillehammer changed all that. Not only did the games preach 'greenness', but the organising committee chose to do so quite boldly. They actively sought the involvement of environmental groups in the day-to-day planning process for the games. It was the beginning of the concept of 'sustainable green sport'.

Lillehammer drew up a four-point plan for the environment. Companies were instructed to use natural materials wherever possible. Emphasis was placed on energy conservation in heating and cooling systems, a recycling programme was developed for the entire winter games region, and a stipulation was introduced requiring arenas to harmonise with the surrounding landscape.

The real challenge for Lillehammer was in securing the support of both the people and of the business community. To aid in this, the city drew up a set of principles and guidelines to form the cornerstone of its 'green profile'. At the heart of these principles was the concept that the environment would be one of the major criteria by which the success of the games as a whole would be measured. Other principles ensured that the environment was seen as an integral part of the activities rather than as a separate programme, and that legal requirements were met in a consistent way. Not only were the games to take place within a sustainable framework, but they should also bring a measure of success for business.

The 'greening' of the games triggered a number of innovations and ambitious environmental projects. Examples included introducing new environmental design methods for buildings and construction projects, and the introduction of the concept of 'green tourism'.[3] Business took the opportunity to initiate a number of what were highly successful innovative ideas. For example, one million plates (together with three million utensils) were made from potato-based starch, all of them to be recycled and used as animal feed and compost.[4]

The effect of Lillehammer was to demonstrate that the 'green' factor did not stand in the way of regional development and business opportunities. For probably the first time, business had achieved a payback for its involvement in the greening of sport and, through its concern for the environment, Norway established itself as an excellent world citizen.

The success of Lillehammer, though not as great as many of its supporters would have us believe, convinced the IOC (as coordinator of the Olympic Movement) to commit itself to extending the range of its activities in the field of the environment and to formalise Lillehammer's decision to make the environment the third dimension of Olympism, after sport and culture. As a result, and in conjunction with a number of public and private authorities and the United Nations Environment Program (UNEP), a Sport and Environment Commission was set up in 1996 to advise the IOC on environment-related policy. Lillehammer signposted the future of sports: that the environment was on the agenda, that it was to be passionately discussed, and that it was to be a measure of sporting success.

Within a short time, the IOC had developed a set of requirements for candidate cities bidding to host the Olympic Games which required, among other things, those cities to:

(a) prepare charts and explain briefly the system of natural resource and environment management put in place by the public authorities and their responsibilities towards the Organising Committees for the Olympic Games (OCOG);

(b) provide an overview, including maps and tables, of the local situation with respect to the state of the environment, protected areas, cultural monuments and potential natural risks;

(c) obtain from the competent authorities an official guarantee that all work needed to stage the games complied with local and international agreements on the protection of the environment;

(d) state whether impact studies had been performed by the competent authorities for all venues and facilities;

(e) provide an environmental plan for the Games;

(f) describe the efforts to protect and improve the natural environment during the preparation for the Games;

(g) describe the environmentally friendly technology to be applied in relation to the Games.[5]

It was no coincidence that the IOC officially initiated a strategy of sport campaigning on behalf of the environment. First and foremost, the backlash from environmentally *unfriendly* games, such as the Winter Games in Albertville, France, where significant damage was caused to the environment by building new facilities in virgin forest, had forced the IOC to revisit bid policies. Negative public opinion also impacted upon the ability of the IOC to attract corporate sponsorship, another compelling reason to be fighting the fight on behalf of the environment. Then the qualified success of Lillehammer sealed the decision.

Sydney was the first city to be materially affected by the Olympic Environmental Guidelines. To be fair to the city, Sydney's Green Games concept committed Sydney to specific environmental guidelines before winning the bid to host the Games and before construction began. These guidelines were developed with the help of Greenpeace and other environmental groups, but with minimal help from business. Indeed, of the many guidelines put forward, none recommended involving the expertise and entrepreneurial spirit of business.

The athletes' village at Sydney was a model of environmental awareness, addressing as it did the problems of global warming, ozone depletion, biodiversity, air, soil and water pollution, and resource depletion. Solar power was introduced for street lighting, water heating and air conditioning. Bathing and kitchen water was treated on-site for reuse on gardens and for washing vehicles, while there was a ban on harmful components in insulation, refrigeration and air-conditioning units.[6]

Following the Sydney success, the Salt Lake Organizing Committee (SLOC) for the Olympic Winter Games of 2002 sought to make this activity a zero emissions event. Emission reductions addressed a range of pollutants caused by energy use including greenhouse gases, sulphur dioxide, nitrogen oxides, particulates and mercury. Salt Lake attacked its problem in two ways. First, it sought to reduce emissions through the use of energy-efficient programmes (this was only partly successful); and second, donations of emission reduction credits were solicited from local and national companies to offset the emissions produced by hosting the games. The donated credits were then permanently retired so that they could not be sold or used again. This innovative approach to sustainable sport was highly successful, with companies such as DuPont, Waste Management, Blue Source and Kennecott Copper all donating emission reduction credits.

Although, truth to tell, Athens was selected for the 2004 Olympic Games primarily on sentimental grounds, the organising committee appeared initially to have made an attempt to maintain the environmental concerns for the games. The city's troubled mass transit system was improved, and a fleet of natural gas buses was purchased. Unfortunately, with the exception of these initiatives, lack of finance (together with slowness of action) has ensured that only lip service has been paid to environmental protection. Critics have complained that lost opportunities exist for the use of solar power, non-toxic building materials, recycling and waste management in large complexes such as the Olympic village.

Beijing, host to the 2008 Olympics, is speeding up its environmental protection work and the making of a sustainable development plan. Xiaoxuan, deputy director of the Beijing Municipal Environmental Protection Bureau and head of the environmental department under the Beijing 2008 Olympic Committee, has declared that the universality of sport should be used to promote sustainable environmental development.[7] Beijing's plans for infrastructure construction include some 142 projects at a cost of around US$19 billion. At least half of this will go to businesses willing to invest in environmental improvements and initiatives.[8] Environmental projects include new sewage treatment plants, urban regeneration, transportation infrastructure and the development of rigid standards for car emissions. Indeed, by 2008 about 90 per cent of Beijing's sewage will be treated, more than half of the city will be serviced by treatment plants, hundreds of kilometres of new light railway will be constructed, 80 per cent of the city's energy will come from clean sources, and environmental investment as a percentage of gross domestic product (GDP) will have increased by over 90 per cent when compared to 2000.[9]

In a similar fashion, cities bidding for the 2012 Games have already institutionalised environmental concerns.[10] All bidding cities, including New York, Madrid, Moscow, Paris and London, are linking their bids to wider urban regeneration plans. London, for example, is already a leader in cutting emissions that contribute to climate change and in eliminating polluting chemicals, while new buildings must pass high standards for energy efficiency and sustainability. The effect of this is that British companies are already building a world-wide reputation for specialising in development that works in harmony with people and the natural world.

According to Stephen Essex, the current 'urban regeneration' phase of the Games is the latest (and fourth) stage in the cycle of development of the event. He suggests that interest waned for the games between 1960 and 1984, before Los Angeles produced enormous commercial success in 1984, and Barcelona demonstrated the urban transformations possible in 1992. So, did the games earn their second lease on life because they proved commercially profitable, or because they can promote environmental management? Are these two imperatives perhaps now inextricably bound?

Environmental Impact of Sport

What is clear is that sport can no longer ignore sustainability issues given that it is now such big business. Large-scale sporting events and facilities can cause damage through the consumption of natural resources, generation of waste, production of pollution and habitat degradation. The viability of sporting clubs, associations and events is increasingly dependent on the support of a public that is highly aware of the impact which large sport organisations can have on their habitat. Sport sponsors are also increasingly seeking added sponsorship value through associations with environmentally responsible events and organisations. Coca-Cola, for example, used the 2000 Olympic Games to market the global introduction of 'Green Freeze', a project scheduled (conveniently) for completion by Athens in 2004.

Green sport today does not begin and end with the Olympic Games. Green Event Policies have now been developed by the 2006 soccer World Cup (FIFA), the International Cycling Federation, the International Motorcycling Federation, the Canada Games Council and the British Open Golf Championship. Formula One motor racing has initiated a programme that provides for greenhouse emissions through tree planting in Costa Rica. The European Golf Association has established an independent ecology unit, known as 'Committed to Green', to coordinate an environmental management programme in 17 European countries with 500 participating clubs. Sustainable Slopes is yet another example. This is the environmental charter for ski areas in North America. In 2002, some 173 ski resorts in the USA and Canada endorsed the charter, representing about 72 per cent of all resorts.[11]

So the message is clear; big sport business itself has to become greener. But the potential to use (profit and non-profit) sport as an environmental messenger provides business opportunities as well. The universal appeal of sport, together with its inherent link to health and wellbeing, makes it the ideal carrier of messages about the environment. Sport, and in particular the sporting event industry, now represents the front-line for sustainable development campaigns. This not only boosts the marketability of sporting events, but it attracts the kind of corporate sponsors who are keen to leverage public approval, in turn funding a sustainable green environment. However, the philosophical thread running through this chapter goes beyond merely achieving sporting and business success: we wonder if sport ultimately can provide a vehicle to mentally programme our global green consciousness until we achieve a singularity that will 'naturally' lead to the course of planet sustainability.

Sport has become green for two reasons. First, governments and other corporate industries have recognised the marketing and education potential of 'green sport'. This is a significant issue which will ensure that the partnership between sport and the environment continues well into the future, and is an issue expanded further later in this chapter. Second, sport is 'greening' because it is an industry that has contributed to environmental damage in the past, and is therefore being called to ransom by the community at large.

The seventh European Roundtable on Cleaner Production in 2001 acknowledged the potential for sport to impact the environment negatively. It noted that large-scale sporting events and facilities could cause damage through the consumption of natural resources, the generation of waste and the degradation of the natural environment through pollution and habitat modification.

It is not difficult to identify other environmental concerns caused through sport participation. Issues include the use of fuels in motor sports, the degradation of waterways in water sports, unsustainable manufacturing processes such as the glassing of surf-boards, the lack of 'clean' transport accessibility to sporting events, and the use of water and chemicals for turf-grass management. Ozone depleting refrigerants in ice rinks, as well as species and habitat loss through facility development (including golf courses and ski resorts), offer further examples.

Prepared by the Department of Canadian Heritage of Sport Canada, the list of environmental issues for sport facilities and sport events (see Figure 8.1) provides an excellent overview of how sport infrastructure and sport activities impact the environment.[12]

It is absolutely clear that the sporting sector will experience increasing pressure to 'clean up' such environmental blemishes. The viability of clubs, associations and events will depend on the support of a public which will demand change, or seek sport-experiences elsewhere.

It is no wonder that the sports industry is increasingly recognising the importance of sound environmental management practices for their events and facilities. The pressure to improve comes, as Davis Stubbs and Davis Chernushenko state, from two directions: external pressure to meet legal obligations and address public concerns; and internal pressures to reduce costs, conserve resources, minimise risk, improve health and safety standards, maintain good community relations and create a positive corporate image. According to Stubbs and Chernushenko, with these pressures come opportunities. They cite efficiency and cost effectiveness as well as improved morale and employee satisfaction.[13] What Stubbs and Chernushenko do not consider are the wider implications for business. Certainly the sports industry has now realised that green issues are not a side show, but are integral to sporting practice. Wider industry, however, has yet to fully realise this. Investment in the environment, even though related to sport, has spin-offs in many industries that will significantly affect the global community.

The Greening of Sport

We need at this stage to be absolutely clear about what we mean by the greening of sport. One of the major difficulties constantly encountered when discussing this topic is our understanding of the word 'green'. Certainly we realise that green when applied to sport relates to the environmental impact of sport, but does this suggest that sport should be banned when and where it is considered damaging to the environment? It depends

Environmental issue
Air quality (outdoor)
Air quality (indoor)
•   Air pollutants
•   Pesticides
•   Allergens
Water quality (open bodies)
Water quality (indoor)
Land and Water use
•   Rehabilitation of land
•   Open space creation
•   Revegetation
•   Pesticide and chemical fertiliser use
•   Refuelling of boats and vehicles
Waste management
•   Demolition wastes
•   Construction wastes and related packaging
•   Solid waste generation (major events)
•   Solid waste generation (facilities)
•   Solid waste generation (administration)
•   Special waste (medical, film)
•   Animal waste
•   Food waste/composting
Energy management
•   Energy consumption (facilities operations)
•   Energy consumption (events)
Facility use
•   Energy consumption
•   Water consumption
Transportation services
•   Use of public transit and shuttle service
•   Active transportation
Accommodation services
•   Energy consumption
•   Water consumption
•   Waste management
•   Green hotels
Facility and accommodation design
•   Renovation
•   Energy conservation
•   Material choices/use
•   Water conservation
•   Adaptability/reusability
•   Durability
•   Maintenance
Transportation design
•   Alternative modes
•   Choice of vehicles
Construction materials/equipment
•   Durability
•   Recyclability
•   Recycled content
•   Hazardous content
•   Reparability
•   Life cycle impact

Figure 8.1   Environmental issues for sport facilities and events

upon how 'green' the environmental critics are. One environmental engineer, Sharon Beder, argues that there are fundamental differences between the two positions she describes as 'light green' and 'dark green'. Light green environmentalists, she opines, work within the alliance of 'moneyed interests, industry and government', while dark green environmentalists consider that it is the existing system, whose priority is economic growth, which is the problem.[14] In sport, it is the light green environmental lobby that holds sway. Because the burden of technological change is felt most strongly by business and industry, it is this alliance of light green environmentalism and industry that must work together to secure a sustainable sport future.

Environment and industry are not natural bedfellows. Dark green environmentalists are often passionate in their belief that industry pollutes, visually or materially, and that the only safe way of maintaining the environment is to stop industry and force it to close down. As movement along the continuum from dark green to light green increases, however, pragmatism comes more to the fore as environmental groups begin to favour cooperation over confrontation, and we have seen the involvement of groups such as Greenpeace in the Olympic bids. Greenpeace and other similar groups sell their viewpoint to industry by reminding them that being part of green sport offers them the opportunity to demonstrate their company's commitment to the environment and to future generations. It is a strong selling point.

Many industries have responded to the environmental message by seeking the endorsement of environmental groups, hiring staff from them and by inviting leading environmentalists to join their board. On the face of it we might reasonably assume it to be a win–win situation. Strangely, it has not always worked out that way.

Several sporting companies with either deserved or undeserved reputations in the area of human rights and poor environmental concerns have been particularly keen to get the endorsement of leading environmental groups. Of these companies Nike, the world's leading sports and fitness company, with sales of around US$10 billion, is perhaps the most famous. Nike does not manufacture its own products; it sub-contracts the manufacture out to several hundred factories in a number of countries, each of which possess one common factor, that of having access to extremely cheap labour. Thus Nike products are comparatively inexpensive to manufacture. The company, however, spends hundreds of millions of dollars on design and marketing. For Nike, therefore, its brand reputation is most important.

In recent years, as a result of receiving extremely bad publicity for allegedly employing both adults and children in sweatshop factories, for paying minimal wages, and for despoiling the atmosphere in less developed countries, it became the target of many protests. The company responded by reaching agreement with several environmental groups to phase out the use of polyvinyl chloride (PVC) from its shoes. Given that this compound can comprise up to 30 per cent of a shoe, this decision was an important step in Nike's path to sustainability. Nike further significantly reduced its use of petrochemical-based solvents, eliminating 1.3 million gallons of solvent a year.[15] This resulted in Greenpeace Australia calling Nike a model of corporate environmental progress and responsibility.[16] Despite this vote of confidence, Nike continues to be haunted by claims that workers making its products are treated as virtual slaves.[17]

Sport business is fortunate that it is the light green variety of environmentalism that holds the current high ground. Were it not so, then sport and the environmental lobby would have difficulty coexisting. As it is, however, the sports industry business now has an opportunity to consolidate its green credentials and, by adopting what is termed 'sustainable sport', can even move to be a global leader in the race to save the environment.

Sustainability

Sustainability relates to doing those things that enable people to meet present needs without compromising the ability of our children to meet their needs. In the words of Tonn, 'sustainability obligates us to act and think in sustainable ways'.[18]

Other than the incidence of natural disasters or natural endings, sustainability ensures the maintenance of conditions that allow the planet to sustain quality and diversity of life. The UK Foresight programme suggests that future sustainability will depend upon our ability to better understand and enable practices that meet the needs of society, whilst simultaneously maintaining the capacity of the natural environment to renew itself.[19] Sustainable sport is where business principles ensure the economic viability of sport, but the drivers of sport development are derived from a social and environmental perspective. Eco efficiency[20] planning in sport, for instance, will incorporate the principles of energy management, materials and waste management, transportation planning, water conservation and integrated pest management. Although preparing for eco efficiency may require upfront investments, the returns in the long run will outweigh these investments many times over. Benefits for sporting organisations will include more than financial returns: they will also facilitate positive image transfer, public perceptions of 'good corporate citizenship', reduced liability risks and the retention of staff and customers.

Environmental Threats

Let us take a moment to view environmental management from a global perspective. Only when we identify the major environmental challenges facing the earth can we consider the impact on the business of sport and how sport business can (and is) impacting the environment. It has become commonplace to hear of environmental threats associated with climate change, fresh water shortage, overpopulation, urbanisation, deforestation, desertification and salinity. Potential climate change, for instance (although still a hotly debated phenomenon in some scientific circles), is largely reported as a threat that could lead to increases in temperature, rising sea levels and more radical weather patterns, which in turn might lead to higher levels of water pollution, deforestation and desertification due to top-soil erosion. Whilst the likelihood of climate change may be debated, there is little divergence of opinion on the issue of fresh water shortage.[21] It refers to the great imbalance between fresh water resources and the needs of major population explosions. Asia, for example, has the greatest need and the fewest resources. Agriculture presents one of the greatest 'threats' to shortages given the enormous water requirements. Management of turf and golf courses relates closely to this concern, explaining the backlash towards the golf explosion in the developing world and the subsequent water requirement of 'sport for the rich'.

The Likelihood of Sustainability

There is probably little doubt that sustainable practice would contribute to an improved future environmental scenario. More uncertain, however, is whether sustainability is a likely outcome. The Foresight programme suggests that this will depend on the relationship between two continuums, the consumerism–sustainability continuum and the globalisation–localisation continuum. The Foresight Environmental Futures scenario set, in fact, examines four possible futures that describe the changes our society might experience along these continuums in the next four decades:[22]

1 *World Markets Scenario*, defined by integrated global trade systems that emphasise private consumption.
2 *Provincial Enterprise Scenario*, where consumerism continues in the context of national and regional concerns.
3 *Global Sustainability Scenario*, characterised by the integration of social and ecological values in economic decisions and corporate

environmental responsibility. Widespread access to education, reduction in working hours, high mobility labour, increased leisure, political and cultural systems converge through global tourism and global training markets. Commercial opportunities occur, particularly through rapidly developing countries. Low interest rates produce high levels of investment, particularly in projects perceived to benefit the economy and society in the long term. A major phenomenon is the greening of business.

4 *Local Stewardship Scenario*, where regional and national governance emphasises social and ecological values in market development. There is an increased consumer awareness of the environmental impact of their purchasing decisions, shifting market emphasis towards sustainability and service-based provision. This service industry would in turn support socially inclusive, local employment.

This can be visualised as a matrix in Figure 8.2.

One of the major drivers that will determine where within this matrix our future lies is technology. Will technology enable sustainable practice (for it has been shown that, given accurate information and means, humans will make sustainable choices), or will it feed the hunger of consumerism (a trend also adequately demonstrated throughout Western history)? Further,

	Globalisation	Localisation
Consumerism	*World Markets Scenario* Integrated global trade systems that emphasise private consumption.	*Provincial Enterprise Scenario* Consumerism continues in the context of national and regional concerns.
Sustainability	*Global Sustainability Scenario* Integration of social and ecological values in economic decisions and corporate environmental responsibility.	*Local Stewardship Scenario* Regional and national governance emphasises social and ecological values in market development.

Figure 8.2 Environmental futures matrix

Source: Adapted from Department of Trade and Industry (2000), *IT, Electronics and Communications (ITEC) Visions* (United Kingdom).

will humans respond to a world saturated with technology by bridging social and national gaps, or by fracturing into tribal units that will provide meaning by reinforcing difference? In other words, the prospect of the singularity brings with it enormous paradox.

A further paradox of the singularity is that it could enable us to exploit the environment now, believing that technology will allow us to fix it later, or is this technology going to 'rule' us, and is programming the singularity in a way that it will naturally lead to a green and sustainable planet the only way to be 'ruled' in a nice and liveable manner?

Eric Drexler (a nanotechnology pioneer), Chris Peterson and Gayle Pergamit, in their book *Unbounding the Future: The Nanotechnology Revolution*,[23] consider the technological developments that could encourage environmental restoration. They believe that manufacturing will be revolutionised in the future, ultimately based upon molecular manufacturing or nanotechnology. This process will rearrange atoms in specific ways and could be made to deconstruct used products and pollutants into their harmless constituent atoms. Take toxic waste, for example. Like sewage it is not the basic atomic elements that are noxious, but their specific arrangement together. Nanotechnology promises to be able to break down these molecules into their original and benign form. From there, they can be built up again into the next product. Accordingly, a population of 10 billion might be sustained in a high standard of living using nothing but waste from twentieth-century industry.

Of all the refuse humans have created, nuclear waste is the worst. It has converted the relatively soft radioactivity of uranium into a type of intense radioactivity that no form of molecular change can reverse. However, theoretically molecular technology provides the equipment which can safely eliminate the problem. Atom-smashing machines can take radioactive waste and produce safe elements. Although terribly impractical and expensive for present consideration, it is possible that future generations will use this sort of approach to eliminate the nuclear waste accumulated in this era. Recycling will take on a completely new meaning, and it will not necessarily be confined to the Earth.

If technology is used as an excuse to maintain degradation and abuse, the outcome could be catastrophic. It is also, one hopes, unlikely that technology will be relied upon in this way; if this were true, sport would not be greening as we write. Instead, the collective human drive towards control and survival is propelling us towards (gradual), sustainable change. Future technology, then, will be used not to redress the problems of our age, but to deal with those currently beyond our grasp: the virulent diseases, radical atmospheric changes and cosmic disasters of Tonn's future epochs.[24]

Perhaps, then, a more pertinent question than 'Is sustainability likely?' is 'What will occur after it?' Sustainability is only relevant to the low-level threats of our present reality. It is today's buzzword, the cutting edge of environmental management, but either it will become the norm in the not-too-distant future, or the planet will cease to be able to support biodiversity. Sustainability merely provides us with a foundation for the extraordinary environmental management programmes of the future.

Sport Carries the Green Virus

We readily accept that at this time sport represents a threat to the environment, though at a comparatively low level, through problems such as habitat destruction, land clearing and emissions. We accept also that the current socio-political environment has demanded a response from sport, insisting that green, sustainable practice becomes the norm. However, we have made clear that these issues characterise our present struggle for environmental management. The threats of the future will demand technological responses that are far beyond our present reach. These future threats will be largely external ones such as virulent diseases and cosmic events that are not created by industry or progress (or sport).

So if sport is only greening today because it contributes, marginally at least, to the environmental problems we face, will it still be green in the future when it is not the cause of more radical threats? We believe that the answer is that it would stay a similar shade of green to its current tone. Sport is not only environmentally conscious today because it represents a potential threat, it is also green because it is one of the greatest marketing vehicles ever known. Perhaps the most influential of all sport stakeholders, financial sponsors, are eager for the approval of an environmentally conscious public. If a commercial company can transmit socially valued environmental messages, through socially valued institutions (such as sport), the legitimacy of their product/service enjoys an instant double-boost. The example of Coca-Cola's 'Green Freeze' project, launched as a result of Greenpeace pressure relating to its sponsorship of the 2000 and 2004 Olympic Games, is a case in point. After an open letter from Greenpeace Coca-Cola announced that it would phase out potent greenhouse gas hydrofluorocarbons (HFCs) in refrigeration by the Athens Olympic Games in 2004. The company also promised to expand its research into refrigeration alternatives and to insist that suppliers announce specific time schedules to use only HFC-free refrigeration in all new cold drink equipment by 2004.

The potential to use sport as an environmental messenger has been acknowledged in the Australian Conservation Foundation's (ACF's) first (draft) Policy on Sport and Environment, released in March 2002. The document predictably aims to encourage participation in ecologically sustainable sport, and to improve the ecological sustainability of all aspects of sports. However, the policy also identifies sport as a vehicle for the promotion of environmental messages. This indeed is where the future of sport and the environment lies. Sport is the ideal carrier for transmitting the environmental virus.

The universal appeal of sports, together with its inherent link to health and wellbeing, makes it the ideal transmitter of messages about the environment. We are already accustomed to 'hearing' messages about national pride and fair play through sport. Sport, and in particular the sporting event industry, now represents the front-line for sustainable development campaigns. Environmental sustainability is not only making sporting events more marketable, but it is attracting the kind of corporate sponsors who are keen to leverage public approval to enhance corporate reputation. The environmental 'virus' is made more virulent when sporting heroes are used to transmit the 'disease'; a notable example being Planet Ark, an Australian not-for-profit environmental group, set up by retired Wimbledon tennis champion Pat Cash.

Can Sport Save the World?

To suggest that sport will save the world is hyperbole at its extreme. To imply, as we have done on several occasions already, that sport (or rather the sport business) can be a major contributor to, if not a leader in, environmental concern, is, however, perfectly rational and responsible. As a universally accessible carrier of environmental messages and campaigns, it is the vehicle that social/environmental activists will use to spread and legitimise environmental messages through both the strong media presence at major sporting events and the willing sporting 'hero' spokespersons. Whilst virtual technology in sport may increasingly sever the link between the sport experience and the natural environment, sport will be used more and more to communicate environmental messages to communities, governments and businesses. The subsequent increase in the perceived social legitimacy of sport will serve to strengthen the sector's stronghold on sponsorship funds, audience numbers (broadcasting) and participation levels. In short, the marriage of sport and the environment will be a long and productive one. Environmental campaigns and activist groups will access the public on a scale unimaginable through other mechanisms, whilst the same public's enthusiasm and interest in sport will be validated.[25]

Whilst some may protest at the increasing commercialisation of sport, it is clear that by attracting impressive sponsorship and broadcasting funds, the industry is also acting as the juncture for social and environmental responsibility initiatives. Sport will help save the environment, and it can do this only because it is a big business that is universally understood.

Involvement of the Sport Industry Business

The business of sports is a vital component of a thriving economy. In the USA, Street & Smith's *Sports Business Journal* estimates the industry to be worth US$213 billion, more than twice the size of the US auto industry. It is little wonder, therefore, that the sport industry is eager to come to grips with environmental technologies. The challenge faced by the sport business is to develop, use and trade its technology in a way which is beneficial to the sports industry, which is sustainable, and which contributes to the economic benefit of the company and the environmental benefit of all humankind. To get the full potential out of its relationship with environmental concerns it is not sufficient that it relies on marketing and sponsorship alone. Fortunately, most businesspeople involved in the industry already understand that this is the case. As mentioned during the early part of this chapter, business has already involved itself in the practical aspects of environmental awareness. Participation in the environmental development of the Lillehammer Winter Games and in the building of the athletes' village for the Sydney Olympics were excellent examples. Now, business must move to the next stage, using innovative and emerging technologies to push the envelope for sustainable sport.

Innovation can come in many guises and may be evolutionary or revolutionary in concept. In Sydney, for example, street lighting, water heating and air conditioning in the athletes' village were solar powered, the result of the development of more efficient and cheaper solar cells. With further development that capability might be extended both to the lighting and to the control of the atmosphere inside closed stadia. From there it is a simple jump to use such technology in homes and factories. Similar technology could be used to power vehicles, and even ships. The reduction in noxious emissions would be enormous and the payback to industry high. The potential of solar power is immense, offering as it does the possibility of virtually unlimited power generation. Where Sydney led, the world will eventually follow.

Sydney also showed early initiatives in treating bathing and kitchen waste water for reuse on gardens and for washing vehicles. Such technology is in its infancy. With innovation it could be extended to the cleaning of playing surfaces and ultimately might be used to clean up oil spills and polluted ocean and river waste. Biotechnology companies are already experimenting with pollution-eating enzymes that will turn waste products into usable energy. In addition, the Sydney technology is being developed to allow for the reuse of water from sewerage waste for commercial use. Such 'renewed' water is already being used on sports fields and is soon likely to be used for domestic consumption.

Progressively more countries and individual businesses are utilising market-based approaches to spur technological innovation and encourage environmentally-sustainable business and consumer activities. Emerging technology-based industries are increasingly receiving the backing of government, either through improved tax incentives or through the removal of tax barriers for activities considered beneficial to the environment. Tax policy is being revamped in an attempt to reshape energy and environmental goals, and governments at last appear to be prepared to acknowledge the seriousness of the environmental crisis. Individual companies are being driven by a clear and coordinated vision of genuinely new markets. The opportunity for the sport business has never been greater and businesses, many with few previous links to the sports industry, are grasping the opportunity.

Take, for example, IriScan, a Princeton-based firm that holds several patents on 'iris scanning' technology. While seeking traditional uses in mass transport identification and in the security industry, the company has realised the potential of the technology for the identification of ticket holders at sports events. Equally it can be used to refuse entry to troublemakers and known criminals banned from the sport. Or consider Hewlett Packard's recent demonstration that notepads, textbooks and catalogues can be printed with a digital screen that can be read by an electronic pen called the 'Magic Wand'. This pen has the ability to capture what is written on a sheet of digital paper directly into a computer. This application has exciting possibilities for sport. A fan could point to a reference in a programme and immediately download statistics and data on her team or favourite player. The technology additionally gives publishers a way to capture revenues from digital technologies used with their printed materials.[26] Or consider that one day, urged on by the new generation of genomic companies, it is likely that everyone will have a personal listing of all proteins and enzymes in their body. While of primary use for doctors, it allows the possibility of identifying potential athletes at a remarkably young age.

Among other environmentally progressive technologies with potential benefits to the sport industry are a number relating to applications connected to the high-temperature superconductivity (HTS) industry. HTS power transformers capable of providing all electricity requirements for large-scale sporting complexes are already in operation. HTS power transformers are more efficient, smaller, lighter, and do not require cooling oil, which eliminates fire and environmental hazards and allows them to operate almost anywhere. According to Rockwell Automation, HTS motors could reduce environmental emissions significantly (including up to 25,000 tons of nitrous oxide and 8,000,000 tons of carbon dioxide).

Sport businesses are also looking to take advantage of environmental breakthroughs. For example, one of the first products to reflect Nike's 'design for the environment' efforts was a tank-top for long distance runners first showcased at the Sydney Olympics. Seventy-five per cent of the fabric in the top was made from recycled plastic drink bottles. It was designed to perform better than a conventional top in keeping runners cool, yet it used 43 per cent less energy in manufacturing. The shirt was left in the natural colour of the fibre (white), which further eliminated the need for dyeing and finishing.[27] In a similar fashion, the Australian Wallabies' shirt for the 2003 Rugby World Cup was designed to weigh less and to naturally draw sweat from the body to the outside of the shirt, thus allowing the Australian players to be cooler in the hot Australian spring. Again, it is a small step for such ideas to be incorporated in a wide range of outdoor or adventure clothing as well as day-to-day conventional wear. Another company of note is Nanogate Technologies, which is involved in chemical nanotechnology and which has already made successful inroads into the production of an innovative ski wax. It considers that a market aimed at advanced and professional skiers will be able to use the synergies developed in the broader leisure products market.

In the longer term the sport business industry will be materially affected by the emergence of nanotechnology. When that occurs, sport may lose its pre-eminent place as a leader in environmental innovation. Until that time arrives, however, business leaders should take every opportunity to test innovative or emerging technological environmental ideas in the fields of sport. Sport is the ideal arena for this. It is already well recognised as a means of securing social, political and economic integration, and the addition of support for the environment adds yet a further dimension.

Sponsors would welcome the publicity, spectators would be prepared to pay for an improved environment in which to watch their preferred sport, and aficionados would readily greet any way in which they could enhance their statistical collection or information on their favourite star. Being attuned to environmental issues and concerns would attract new facilities and a new public, especially among young people. In turn, this would see the company promoting the sport and the owners of the sports arena achieving improvements in their triple bottom line – economic, social and environment – while additional cost savings might be achieved through compliance with legislation and hence reduced liability premia.

Business must be proactive rather than reactive. It must coordinate its efforts and jointly develop a respected voice in environmental policy debates. It must search for public credibility and be prepared to seek advice and guidance on environmental best practice when bidding to host major sporting events and for new facility development. To be a leader in environmental issues will attract new funding sources, while the ability to trial new technologies in a contained location will lower costs yet yield huge credibility to successful products.

All in all, sport must coexist unequivocally and in harmony with the environment. It is a combination that is essential if sport is to grow. Fortunately, the signs are already there that both the sporting and the environmental lobbies understand the need for such a relationship. It is also a relationship that holds great promise for sport businesses keen both to capitalise upon green sport technological developments and to attract consumers who have embedded environmental health within the new culture of sport. The importance of cultural perspectives is the focus of the next chapter.

Notes and References

1 Gallup International and Environics International (2002). *Voice of The People*. Gallup International and Environics International, 29 August 2002; Roy Morgan Research Centre (2000). *Australians Find it Easy Being Green*. Roy Morgan Research Centre, 9 June 2002.

2 Choy, M. (2002). *World Lags behind Kyoto CO2 Emissions Targets*. Planet Ark. Available at *http://www.planetark.org/dailynewsstory.cfm/newsid/18252/story.htm*, accessed on 3 November 2003.

3 Minister of the Environment Thorbjørn Berntsen, *The Lillehammer Conference*, 13 February 1996. Available at *http://odin.dep.no/odinarkiv/norsk/dep/md/1996/taler/ 022005-090070/ index-dok000-b-n-a.html*, accessed on 3 November 2003.

4 American University, The School of International Service (1996). *TED Case Studies: Lillehammer Olympic Games*, Case Number 222, USA, 1996. Washington, USA.

5 American University, The School of International Service (1995). *Sydney Olympics and the Environment (Sydney) Case*. Washington, USA. Available at *http://www.american.edu/ TED/SYDNEY.HTM*.

6 American University, The School of International Service, *Sydney Olympics*.

7 China Advisor, *Environment Goals for the Beijing Olympics* Available at *www.chinaadvisor. com/environment.html*, accessed on 18 July 2003.

8   Heng, L. (17 July 2001). 'Beijing Olympics creates huge business opportunities: Analysis'. *People's Daily*. Available at http://fpeng.peopledaily.com.cn/200107/17/eng20010717_75179.html, accessed on 18 July 2003.

9   Xin, L. (2000). 'One slogan, many objectives'. *China Daily*, 23 November; Brody, M. (2001). 'Green games, green China.' *China Daily*, 18 July; Guo, J. (2001). 'Bejing to spend big before 2008'. *Asisinfo Daily*, 18 July; Ness, A. (2002). 'Blue skies for Beijing Olympics'. *The China Business Review*, March/April; Yilei, Y. (2002). 'Beijing to cut use of coal for green games.' *China Daily*, 6 September.

10 Menary, D. (2003). 'The Regeneration Games: Why the cities bidding for the 2012 Olympic Games share a common theme'. *Sport Business*, 82, pp. 38–40.

11 NSAA (2002). 'Sustainable slopes. The environmental charter for ski areas'. *Annual Report 2002*. The National Ski Areas Association.

12 Green and Gold Inc. (1999). *Environmental Management and Monitoring for Sport Events and Facilities*. Lakewood, CO: Prepared for Department of Canadian Heritage, Sport Canada.

13 Stubbs, D. and Chernushenko, D. (2003). *Guidelines for Greening Sports Events*. Surrey, UK: Committed to Green Foundation. Available at *www.committedtogreen.com/guidelines/greening.htm*, accessed on 3 November 2003.

14 Beder, S. (1994). 'Revoltin' Developments: The Politics of Sustainable Development'. *Arena Magazine*, June–July, pp. 37–9.

15 Beder, 'Revoltin' Developments'.

16 Beder, S. (2002). 'Environmentalists help manage corporate reputation: changing perceptions not behaviour'. *Ecopolitics*, 1 (4), pp. 60–72.

17 Oxfam Community Aid Abroad (2000). *Frequently asked questions*. Melbourne. Available at www.caa.org.au/campaigns/nike/faq.html, accessed on 3 November 2003.

18 Tonn, B.E. (2002). 'Distant futures and the environment'. *Futures*, 34, p. 119.

19 Department of Trade and Industry (2000). *IT, Electronics and Communications (ITEC) Visions*. London: Department of Trade and Industry.

20 Chernushenko, D., van der Kamp, A. and Stubbs, D. (2001). *Sustainable Sport Management: Running an Environmentally, Socially and Economically Responsible Organization*. Nairobi, Kenya: United Nations Environment Programme.

21 UN/WWAP (United Nations/World Water Assessment Programme) (2003). *UN World Water Development Report: Water for People, Water for Life*. Paris, New York and Oxford: UNESCO (United Nations Educational, Scientific and Cultural Organization) and Berghahn Books.

22 Department of Trade and Industry, *IT, Electronics and Communications Visions*.

23 Drexler, E., Peterson, C. and Pergamit, G. (1991). *Unbounding the Future: The Nanotechnology Revolution*. New York: William Morrow.

24 Tonn, 'Distant futures and the environment', p. 119.

25 Ottesen, S. and Stubbs, D. (2001). 'Sustainability and large scale sporting events'. *Workshop Held at the 7th European Roundtable on Cleaner Production*, Lund, Sweden, 2 May.

26 Tomczyk, M. (2002). '4th Annual Emerging Technologies Update Day at Wharton Features Innovations for 2002 and Beyond'. *4th Annual Emerging Technologies Update Day*, 8 February. Pennsylvania: The Wharton School. Available at http://emertech.wharton.upenn.edu/ETUpdateDay-EyeCatchingInnovations.html, accessed on 3 March 2003.

27 Lanahan, B. and Willard, M. (2001). *Nike Inc.: An Oregon Natural Step Network Case Study, Updated January 2001*. Oregon: Oregon Natural Step Network. Available at www.ortns.org/docs/Nike.PDF, accessed on 15 October 2003.

CHAPTER 9

Cultural Sport Business:
The Games Must Go On

This chapter is about the macro perspective of culture. In this chapter we look at sport business from the perspective of globalisation and internationalisation, the 'big picture', the mega-tribes, or (in the words of Samuel Huntington) at the level of civilisations. Culture, as accepted shared behaviour, mostly intended to solve common human problems, involves answering questions such as 'Who are we?', 'What should we be doing?', and 'Are we doing it?' It is widely accepted that universal human problems exist but that solutions to these problems can be local; hence cultural diversity in sport.

So far in this book we have placed great importance on the influence of new technology, but in this chapter we consider the parallel power of genetic and cultural development on the future of sport business. If genes transport genetic material leading to natural human predispositions, then memes (cultural genes) are the cultural values that are transported from mind to mind, which influence the way these predispositions are manifested in sport.

If success in a particular sport leads to social acceptance and even star status, this sport will become more popular and a dominant means to express culturally important values. People with physical features more likely to be successful in that sport will develop dominant roles in society and will be more likely to procreate, thereby affecting the evolutionary pattern of human physical development. But what will happen to this process if we are in a position to actively manipulate the genetic structure towards preferred athletic features? The development time of the perfect athlete for a particular sport would be brought back to one generation at most. Evolution will become revolution, and a violent one for that matter.

However, sport as we know it today differs greatly from the scenario presented in the previous paragraph. Our sport offers opportunities for different cultures to meet on neutral ground, to appreciate and enjoy the difference whilst fighting it out under 'common rules of engagement'. Sport remains one of the few truly global platforms where people of vastly different cultural origins can meet on a level playing field. In that regard the Olympics represents the greatest paradox of them all, bringing people of the world together to celebrate sport and culture whilst simultaneously reinforcing the immense inequities that exist between peoples of the world.

The focus of this chapter is to explore the place of sport business in communicating and expressing political views, ideologies and attitudes in the future. It also considers how sport business can unify nations and fracture them at the same time, and how values can be disseminated and challenged. In the final part of the chapter we take a closer look at how different perspectives and influences on culture such as the economy, government, the media, demographics, legislation and, of course, technology and science will affect the future of sport business.

Sport as a Cultural Vehicle

As we argued in an earlier chapter, sport consumers will increasingly belong to tribal groupings held together by sets of principles and values. These principles and values can be real or imagined. They can change shape or identity based on the most fleeting of reasons and yet, underlying these chameleon-like sets of principles and values, we find that sport (or elements of sport) can hold individuals in thrall, can bind them so tight that its shackles will hold them and their children for a lifetime. What is it about sport which can so grip individuals that, at times, they would place their sport alongside their flag and defend both equally? The reality is that at the fundamental level sport and flag have a common heritage which, although blunted by modern technology, still has strong symbolism.

In Chapter 5 we introduced tribalism as a micro-social experience; here, we consider the impact of the cultural experience as a macro-social phenomenon. Understanding how culture will impact upon sport in the future is founded upon the recognition that culture is not the sole arbiter of sport's expression. We also must consider the relationship with the biological forces that mitigate our encounters with sport.

To understand – really understand – the culture of another (or even your own) civilisation is exceedingly difficult. Indeed, simply understanding the meaning of 'culture' is surprisingly difficult. The word itself comes from the Latin *colere*, meaning to build upon, to cultivate or to foster. Over the last 200 years the word has undergone a subtle metamorphosis as the philosophical debate on the topic has progressed from Leibnitz to Stuart Hall. It has now come to mean a set of specific values and attributes possessed by a common-minded group of people; if you like, an accepted shared behaviour. Determining what that shared behaviour might be is the key to understanding the culture of a group or a society. To anthropologist Clifford Geertz, it involves discovering who that group or society think they are, what they think they are doing, and to what end they think they are doing it. These represent the 'frames of meaning' within which they enact their lives. Perhaps the test is Geertz's final observation: 'It involves learning how, as a being from elsewhere with a world of one's own, to live with them.'[1]

Continuity throughout history has been provided by culture. It started with symbols which, in turn, created the need for language as a communicative instrument that allowed history, knowledge and experience to be observed and recorded. With that history, knowledge and experience as a basis, succeeding generations were able to build upon the work of their forefathers. As society grew, it developed both a material culture, which sought to satisfy the economic and material needs of the individual, and a spiritual culture, which comprised both religious and philosophical perceptions, as well as values and standards. Sport, however expressed, is a product of culture, both material and spiritual.

However, culture does not adequately explain the track of human involvement in sport. After all, inappropriate behaviour from a socio-cultural viewpoint is not uncommon. In other words, although sport is typically considered a cultural manifestation, it must also be mired in the genetic programming of the mind. Sport is hardwired: an outcome of natural selection. For example, a century of serious research in anthropology has identified the presence of what have been labelled cultural universals.

Cultural universals are modes of behaviour that exist in all cultures because people may do the same things for different reasons, or do different things to achieve the same result. By focusing on behaviour, it is hard to detect universal patterns. But culture can be the collective behaviour of groups of people to solve common (universal) problems. Although all people in general are confronted with similar problems, culture determines how these problems are solved. For example, all human civilisations have intrinsically created some differentiation between what is 'right' and what is 'wrong'. These manifest in practices associated with prestige, status, inequality of power and wealth, property, reciprocity, punishment, sexual regulations, divisions of labour, love, aggression, conflict and murder. In some civilisations, issues are affected by religious teaching, while in others it is managed through consultation and collective law-making. These values have manifested as body adornments, cooperative activity such as sport and recreation, funeral rites, marriage rituals, food taboos, healing methods, humour and sexual appropriateness, for example. Cultural universals imply a common evolutionary inheritance; they are cultural expressions of a biological drive. If sport is the product of both genetics and culture, in order to understand its impact in the future we need to start by understanding how the two interact to produce the imperative for sport.

One theory proposed by Charles Lumsden and Edward O. Wilson, named gene-culture coevolution,[2] observes that in addition to the genetic evolutionary pathway there is a parallel cultural track. These two evolutionary mechanisms are inextricably linked. It works as follows.

Culture is formed when groups of people, often (but not exclusively) living in close proximity, come to see the world through the same, or at least similar, eyes. Culture represents the worldview of the collective mind. But this collective worldview is already programmed to an extent, encouraging predispositions towards particular values and behavioural modalities. Culture as a set of common values – or, as Geert Hofstede declared it, the software of the mind – simply would not exist without the hardware to execute it.

Cultural genes, or (as Richard Dawkins has named them) memes, are passed along through the familiar process of selection, bestowing adaptations on cultures. Memes spread from mind to mind in the form of stories and ideas, sometimes mutating in the process of establishing a 'better fit' with their recipient cultures, in turn reinforcing their commonality in the 'meme' pool until they overwhelm and infiltrate the population. Thus ideas evolve, and the ones which fit best, reproduce more easily. This does not mean, however, that humans are becoming more knowledgeable in a biological sense. We are not born with an improving archetypal set of cultural knowledge. Certainly, technological progress has improved the storage of knowledge and has facilitated the distribution of memes, but cultural evolution does not lead to the transmission of knowledge through genetics. However, the concept of memes is a neat way of looking at how cultural ideas are transmitted both within and between cultures. It is particularly useful when imagining the impact of an alien set of memes, the equivalent of trying to develop soccer in the USA. On the one hand, those memes might, like their genetic equivalents, be completely incompatible. The memes would be unable to replicate themselves because they are so different from what Americans understand that they are effectively not even made of the same cultural DNA. On the other hand, the soccer memes might find a particular cultural niche in which they prosper and multiply. This cultural procreation could have a radical impact upon the development of sport in the country. It might usher in a new sport order, cultivate new ways of thinking or encourage even more cultural fragmentation. Because of culture, sport fans and participants do some strange and fantastic things, but the equipment being employed – brains, bodies and hormones – plays a foundational role in how we learn sport through culture and why we prefer some to others.

Separating genes and culture is troublesome, as the gene–culture hypothesis explains. For example, genetics dictate certain survival characteristics, but those who possess the traits rewarded by an existing culture are also rewarded with an overrepresentative contribution to the genetic pool of a population. As a consequence, genetic features can be proliferated by cultural directives. In this way, if success in sport offers social acceptance and admiration, then those who are genetically disposed to athleticism will emerge as the victors in procreation, and the cycle continues with an increased propensity for athleticism in the genetic pool. Of course, the cultural impact of sport on the process of evolution is impossible to measure, being only a single variable, and would only be manifest over many generations unless genetics were manipulated directly in order to meet cultural imperatives. Genetic engineering for sporting performance would represent a major departure from evolution in the development of human biological characteristics.

All of this may sound somewhat theoretical, but its realisation has several practical dimensions. First, when introducing a sport to a new market, or developing it within an existing market, it is important that consideration be given to its appeal at a genetic and cultural level. Professional wrestling is a good example. Once viewed as another cultural by-product of the USA, and firmly placed in the 'only in America' category, the form of entertainment has now become a genuinely global product. The reason is because it meets certain hardwired human, and particularly male, needs. That is why some sports have the ability to transcend cultural boundaries, others need modification before they can elicit a level of appreciation, and some will never be accepted.

Second, sport as a cultural influence may play a part in redirecting the evolutionary development of humans. Once genetics have been altered to make someone a superior athlete, that person will pass on those modified genes to his or her progeny, who in turn might see the need to make improvements. If this were to be the case, the volume of individuals with high athletic potential would increase radically. This would force an expansion of professional sport and would bolster participation, dampened only by groups opposed by genetic tampering and those whose preference it is to experience sport in cyber-space. We have attempted to summarise this visually in Figure 9.1.

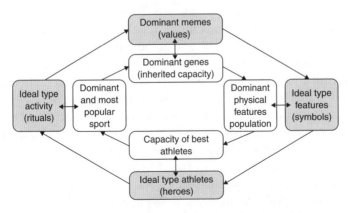

Figure 9.1 Sport gene–culture coevolution model

Sport and Cultural Convergence

Sport is arguably the most pervasive global cultural form we know today.[3] It is also the most flexible, performing community, commercial, political, economic and entertainment functions. It is the success of sport in these domains that will ensure its continued (although modified) existence in the future as the meeting place of cultures. Since technology enabled instant transnational travel, via means such as radio, television and the Internet, sport has become an international phenomenon, used as a tool to assert ideological and commercial imperatives. It is the meeting place of cultures, a common ground where representatives from divergent places engage in a symbolic clash, whilst obeying universal regulations.

However, bringing cultures together, whether they are defined by ethnicity, nationality or another sub-cultural parameter, is not necessarily a 'warm and fuzzy' affair, as it is often portrayed. Cross-cultural interaction remains a problematic space, where intolerance and conflict are as likely as understanding and acceptance. Sport itself is not responsible for creating union or division between cultures; it is merely a space inhabited by humans who bring the potential for both. The generosity of sport is that it provides this highly visible space, although often flawed and politicised, where common 'rules of engagement' allow a physical discourse to occur.

At its most palpable level, sport allows for the meeting of cultures based on regional or national identity. Huazhi Wang of Cornell University[4] points out that international sport is a symbolic frontier for international struggle, and a principal means of national identification in the modern world. Nationalism implies a process of differentiating a sense of nationhood from that of other nations; this process is elegantly executed through popular competitive arenas such as sport. Absolute separation between nation-states is at the core of nationalist ideology.[5] As Tudor notes, 'there must be an Other – better still, Others – in contradistinction to whom the community can sustain its identity'.[6] Sport, as one of the most pervasive cross-cultural phenomena, provides an ideal platform to express nationalist sentiment. The competitive framework and elaborate symbolic system that is international sport leaves it wide open to the idea of nationalism.[7]

According to Rowe and Lawrence sport acts as 'a particularly compelling ideological cement ... it encourages the suspension of ... antagonism in favour of a fabled national interest'.[8] The example of the Gaelic Athletic Association (GAA) underlines this fact. Mike Cronin, author of *Sport and Nationalism in Ireland*, suggests that the GAA has played a key role in expressing Irish cultural distinctiveness and nationalism.[9] Founded in 1884 as a backlash against the British presence within Ireland, the GAA aimed to preserve Irish customs and traditions, and to maintain the physical readiness of its male participants for any future struggle against Britain. Like all successful sports, it has succeeded because it satisfies both the hard-wired and cultural urges of its participants. The Association structured its games around the local parishes, instantly establishing a network of teams with immediate rivalries.

This highlights the fact that national identification is a political issue as well as a cultural one. The GAA's role (or lack of it) in the Northern Ireland Peace process further testifies to this fact. Despite the vitality of the GAA, with its significant local community roots, the Association has been widely criticised for its lack of a role within the Northern Ireland peace process. Cronin explains that as the first cease-fires were slipping into place in the early 1990s, sporting bodies such as the two football associations in Ireland and the Rugby Football Union, among many others, participated in the Peace and Reconciliation Council. Despite offering reasons for their refusal to attend, such as not having responses ready, the GAA was roundly criticised for simply avoiding a role.

If national identification is a political issue, international sport is intensely political. The twentieth century saw sport emerge as a political tool for the promotion of nationalism. Through 'the identification of the sports champion with the nation we are asked to celebrate a country's power and strength'.[10] The promotion of the culture and influence of a nation is emphasised at the expense of others.[11] By definition, international sporting competitions have always been bound up with political nationalism. McGarr highlights the fact that the phenomenon of international games arose a century ago when intense rivalry existed between the world's super-powers.[12] The first modern Olympics took place in 1896, and in 1908 (in the run-up to the First World War) national teams were imposed on the games. Other international events emerged around the same time, including the Tour de France in 1903 and its Italian counterpart, the Giro D'Italia, in 1909.[13]

The Olympics, as the ultimate international event, have been criticised by some as fostering the kind of nationalist sentiment that perpetuates conflicts and intolerance between countries. The structure of the Games requires national identification as a passport to entry.[14] The Olympic party line suggests that the ultimate goal of the games is to bring out the best in humankind, to surmount physical and ideological barriers and contribute to world peace. The cultural role of the games is also emphasised by officials, such as Seh-jin, President of the Seoul Olympic Organising Committee, who reminisces about the function of the ancient Olympics as a cultural festival. It is sometimes difficult, however, to see the culture because it is so obscured by marketing propaganda. The coalescence of culture and mass media promotion was always likely to be an uneasy marriage. Hosting the Olympic Games has increasingly become a tool to generate world-wide prominence and profit for the host nation. This in turn reinforces national boundaries and inequities, leading to cross-cultural clashes and even violence. Does the Olympic institution now act in opposition to the respected de Coubertin ideals of Olympism? Can the Olympics ever aspire to world-wide peace whilst reinforcing differences and inequities between groups of people?

The idea that the Olympics can cure the conflict of the world is based on two myths, the myth of the Olympic truce,[15] and the myth of 'goodness without evil' in humanity. It is the first of these, the myth of the Olympic truce, which interests us here. Abrams,[16] for instance, suggests that the Olympic truce did not even truly exist in the ancient Olympic Games. He points out that no written records of the rules of the ancient truce (*ekecheiria*) exist, although references of its violations are recorded! Modern historians interpret the ancient truce as meaning that in the host state (the city, or *elis*), athletes and travellers were protected. However, warfare continued in surrounding regions. In addition, the truce was not instigated in the name of sport, or the love of homage competition, but in homage to the almighty Zeus. After all, the Olympics began not as a sporting competition but as a religious festival to honour Zeus, and as a ground for military training.[17] In one short century since the emergence of the modern Olympics we have cancelled three games in order to go to war: 1916, 1940 and 1944. It has also been suggested that the modern Olympics were revived with the emergence of international trade, the first four games being held in conjunction with trade fairs.[18]

Nationalism and Factionalism

The establishment of a cultural or sub-cultural identity carries with it the potential for factionalism as much as it carries the promise of celebrating difference. Bell argues that nationalism in itself is not responsible for the conflicts that occur at international games.[19] After all, in-fighting is often reported during national tournaments, such as the China National Games of 2001 and the Nigerian National Games of 2002. Nationalism, then, is one expression of factionalism; factions can occur at all levels, similar to the ways in which ethnic nationalism can transcend or subvert national borders. In other words, human social behaviour, which innately leads us to cluster in groups, has a natural propensity to create factionalism.

The historian James McPherson divides nationalism into two sub-sets, ethnic and civic.[20] Ethnic nationalism refers to a shared identity based on culture, including language and religion, as well as a sense of common decency. Increasingly within the multicultural make-up of global society, ethnic nationalism is not contained within nation-state boundaries. This kind of shared identity can stimulate other, smaller kinds of factions between cities, suburbs, global regions and even schools. On the other hand, civil nationalism reflects a belief in a shared citizenship of a territory, nurturing loyalty to its governing institutions.

The composition of cultural grouping in the future is, of course, unknown, as are the relative importance of ethic and civic nationalism. We have argued in the past that cultural forces will play a significant role in the structure of sport's future.[21] For example, whether countries morph into geographically larger economic and cultural units, such as the European Union, or fragment into smaller independent states, such as the former Soviet Union, will affect the structure and delivery of sporting competitions in the future.

Sport and Conflict

The analogy infamously drawn by George Orwell, that sport is war minus the shooting, represents sport as a political, competitive tool used between nation states. Ironically, it underscores the potential for sport to act as a catalyst for conflict at the same time as it may replace (and thus diminish) armed clashes. The analogy is not an unfamiliar one to the sport-consuming public. The cricket test series between India and Pakistan in 1999 was described, as 'nuclear cricket', occurring in the year both became nuclear powers. Euro '96 featured images of English and German players in Second World War helmets. Wars between football following 'hooligan' groups receive regular media coverage.

For every example of sport performing a global public service, another can be found where sport can be questioned for its role in perpetuating social inequities. In analysing mass media accounts of Venus and Serena Williams, for instance, Delia Douglas suggests that the sisters are portrayed as racialised figures defined outside the dominant definition of womanhood.[22] They are popularly described as too proud and brazen, a challenge to prevailing tennis culture. Their style of play has been described as an intrusion which, according to Hall,[23] reveals the power of the white gaze to determine who belongs and who intrudes. Accounts suggest their success can be defined by physical characteristics attributable to their race, rather than superior knowledge of the game, court strategy or mental fortitude.[24] The media framing of the sisters as unfeminine reinforces the desirability of players such as Anna Kournikova, Elena Dementieva and Daniela Hantuchova.[25] In other words, sport is a contradictory space where black achievement is visible, but where the rationale for their success reinforces black athletes as inherently superior.[26] The resilient idea that sport happens on a level playing field is superficial. Sport in general, like tennis,[27] can be seen as a racialising and engendering institution.

Michael A. Messner suggests in his book, *Taking the Field*, that regardless of significant changes in gender relations in the world of sport, it largely perpetuates its traditional, conservative role in gender relations.[28] He suggests that the rules and hierarchies of sport institutions, the behaviours of sport participants (including the expression of violence) and the major symbols and belief systems that are transmitted by the media maintain the gender status quo. There is disturbingly little evidence that this will radically change in the future at the same pace as technological innovation.

Sport and Reconciliation

However, whilst sport is war minus the shooting, it is also diplomacy minus the neck-tie, and reconciliation minus the 'sorry'. The cohosting of the 2002 Soccer World Cup by Japan and Korea, for instance, was heralded as a great achievement given past friction. 'Show Racism the Red Card' is an anti-racist charity (established in 1996) which is making in-roads into positive cultural change by using professional footballers as role models in educational programmes.[29] There is a prevailing attitude, however, that applying sport to a social or cultural wound will lead to spontaneous, magical healing. Participation in sport itself cannot secure improved social services, civil rights or economic benefits for the general public. Sport is merely a tool, a medium that lies dormant until some human beings take it up and do something with it, while others, with all their prejudices, experiences and motives, go along for the ride. In the 'right' milieu, sport can foster a sense of community, dignity and achievement. In the 'wrong' one, it can reinforce disadvantage and conflict.

It is sometimes observed that providing disadvantaged individuals and groups with access to sporting experiences can have an empowering impact. John Bloom's book *To Show What an Indian Can Do*, for instance, explores the history of sports programs at US boarding schools for Native Americans during the mid-nineteenth to mid-twentieth century. The Federal programme was designed to remove children from their familiar culture and impose mainstream American culture upon them. Bloom describes the sporting success of some participants, including those from Pennsylvania's Carlisle

Indian School between 1899 and 1917: Gus Welch, William Henry 'Lone Star' Dietz and, most notably, Jim Thorpe (arguably the century's greatest athlete) became household names.[30] He also outlines the reflections of former students who describe the sports programme as providing experiences otherwise denied them: dignity, accomplishment and a sense of community. This highlights the fact that sport can offer a temporary reprieve from misfortune, although the context of this programme raises significant sociocultural issues in itself.

This observation is reinforced by the work of Colin Tatz. His research into the experience of Australian Aboriginals explodes the myth that sport can secure improved cultural, social and economic rights and benefits for marginalised groups. Although he acknowledges that sport has enabled some individuals to have access into the social mainstream, he claims there is no evidence to suggest that marginalised groups as a whole have benefited. He suggests that sport is a short-lived activity with fleeting soothing capacities. When the sport system is removed the status quo returns.

Greater interconnectedness needs to exist between sporting organisations and events, and wider social programmes. It is no longer acceptable for sport to claim its presence alone can carve a path out of disadvantage. The community will increasingly call on sporting organisations to link up with other government and community agencies to provide more comprehensive assistance. Does this reinforce the idea of reduced individual responsibility? Reduced individual responsibility is a trend in countries that are able to offer complex social security, compensation and litigation systems (most obviously America), so probably we are going to expect more from sport, and will think that sport 'owes' us more.

The modern phenomenon of media campaigns through sport is worthy of note, however. Marginalised groups are increasingly showing a readiness to use sporting events and competitive success to gain media attention. In the 1994 Commonwealth Games in Victoria, Canada, for instance, the Australian and (later) Olympic champion Cathy Freeman carried both the Aboriginal and official Australian flag on her victory laps following the 400 m and 200 m events, drawing significant attention to the reconciliation cause in her country.

Sport: The History and Future of Capitalism

As observed by Cardwell, the history of modern sport is the history of industrialisation and capitalism. Its future will be the same. Although folk games existed prior to this, they are unrecognisable today. Folk football, for example, had no time limits, no winners and no discernable boundaries beyond those of the village itself. The game could continue for days with men and women playing side by side. When industrialisation revolutionised the Western world, sport was used by 'the establishment' to control the masses. Sporting teams were attached to workforces, churches and public schools to provide the industrial working classes with meaningful occupation. Manchester United emerged from the Yorkshire and Lancashire railways, Arsenal from the Woolwich Arsenal and Sheffield United from the local cutlers. Amongst the motives for establishing these clubs were: 'To keep the young men out of the dram shop'; 'Wherever cricket is played there is lighter crime'; and 'With more curling clubs there would be fewer radical opinions and strikes among the working classes.'[31]

International sport competitions have only existed as we know them today since the beginning of the twentieth century when nation-states became the dominant mode of organisation. FIFA, for instance, was established in 1904 to organise competition between national teams (although the World Cup itself was not established until 1930). The Olympics were revived with the emergence of international trade. The first four modern Olympics were held in conjunction with trade fairs.[32] In other words, sport is a microcosm of global socio-cultural dynamics. Today we also know how capitalist ideology has further enabled the exploitation of sport for commercial gain.

The emphasis on commercial gain has hardly wavered and shows no signs of diminishing in the future. Cultural imperatives have enhanced the marketability of sport, promoting the combative nature of opposing values, ethnicities, nationalities or geographies. Technology in sport offers the potential to take this cultural marketing power to a new level where tribal bands can unite across disparate locations on the basis of self-proclaimed membership of a higher-order family. Commercial sport will continue to possess the power to unite and fragment, to disseminate or challenge values brought about through ingrained historical relationships.

Arjun Appadurai[33] refers to the decolonisation of sport in India as a process of indigenisation, changing the way the sport is managed, patronised and publicised away from its colonial past as a tool of socialisation that communicated Victorian, upper-class values from England. He claims the media have played a crucial role in the indigenisation of cricket in India, with radio commentary broadcasting in the major vernacular languages, and the arrival of television deepening national passion for the game along with the star status of players. The commercialisation of cricket and the commodification of players have also played a role in decolonisation. Cricket is now mass entertainment, demonstrated clearly in Packer's commercially entrenched World Series Cricket (WSC) business model. According to Appadurai, WSC was the first major threat to colonised cricket, and the post-war cricket nationalism.

Appadurai suggests that cultural forms can be either hard or soft. Hard forms are those that are difficult to transform because the behaviours and values that make them up are difficult to tease out. Hard cultural forms change the participant more readily than they can change themselves. On the other hand, soft cultural forms allow values to be separated from behaviours, and more easily facilitate transformations in both values and behaviours. Cricket, he suggests, is a hard cultural form, because it represents puritan values. Of course, definitions of hard and soft emerge from a context; hard may become soft over time as the context changes. It is not as accurate to say that sport has changed from one mode (colonisation) to another (decolonisation); it is more that new phenomena are being layered over the old. First there was the colonial code, and then came nationalist concerns (indigenisation), commercialisation and technologisation. Future changes to nation-state boundaries, global governance, capitalist business models and new technologies will be layered on top of the existing sport–culture relationships. So while some elements of sport will change, such as its accessibility and commercial features, not all things will, including the importance of particular sports to a cultural niche.

Sport and Politics

Sport is sometimes viewed inaccurately as a neutral medium that transcends politics. The ideas of 'fair play' and 'struggling against the odds' are important aspects of sport rhetoric for marketers and educators alike. Sport is held to operate according to a unique set of unassailable rules despite a world corrupted by politics and inequality.[34]

The lead-up to the IOC's selection of the 2008 Olympic Games host city exemplified the role that sport can play in international politics. The Chinese Government, clearly seeing the Olympics as an opportunity to showcase their country, poured considerable resources into Beijing's bid. The political ramifications of Beijing's success were underscored by the US-led debate over whether to influence the IOC decision, in addition to arguments by human rights groups that selection would condone the government's questionable track record. In the end the Bush administration did not oppose the bid, suggesting that hosting the global event was likely to provide the Chinese Government with an incentive to improve human rights policies and deter aggression against Taiwan.[35]

Keys observed that sport and international relations have enjoyed a long courtship, colliding during the Cold War.[36] Olympic medal tallies became a metaphor for the legitimacy of the respective political and economic systems of the Soviet Bloc and the USA/Western world. International sporting success was also used by the German Democratic Republic to gain recognition as an independent country. Boycotts have been used as sanctions, such as the ban against South Africa in 1960 because of apartheid, and events have been employed as a tool of diplomacy, such as Nixon's 1971 'ping-pong diplomacy' with China.[37]

Sport also plays a critical role in global economic exchange, acting as a pivotal component of the US-dominated commercial and media empire.[38] The lure of hosting an international sporting event stretches far beyond any purist desire to see good sport. Political, ideological and economic motives are always thrown into the mix for good measure. The Berlin Olympics in 1936 demonstrated this clearly, with the swastika 'logo' marketing Hitler's fascist Germany.[39] More progressive political causes have also been showcased in the sporting arena, such as post-apartheid reconciliation in South Africa as Nelson Mandela presented the 1995 Johannesburg Rugby World Cup to the home side.[40] Some historical examples of politics and sport follow to lead us into a discussion on its future role as a cultural variable in sport.

Politics and Sport[41]

France, 1789

The first international cricket match on non-English soil, scheduled to be played in Paris, was cancelled when the French Revolution broke out on the morning England was scheduled to leave.

Berlin Olympics, 1916
The Games were cancelled because of the First World War.

Antwerp Olympics, 1920
Austria, Bulgaria, Germany, Hungary and Turkey were banned from participation due to their role in the First World War.

Berlin Olympics, 1936
Jewish communities in various countries called for a boycott of 'Hitler's Games', but the proposal was narrowly defeated in the USA. Hitler attempted to use the Games as a vehicle for propaganda about racial superiority, but was undermined by the success of Jesse Owens.

1940 Olympics
The Second World War extended to the sporting stage. The summer games were withdrawn from Tokyo after the Japanese invasion of China, rescheduled in Helsinki, but finally cancelled after the Soviet invasion of Finland. The Winter Games were cancelled when Germany invaded Poland.

London Olympics, 1944
These were cancelled because of the Second World War. After the war the Olympics took on greater political significance, with participation becoming a symbol of political recognition and legitimacy.

London Olympics, 1948
Germany and Japan were banned because of their role in the Second World War. For the first time ever countries with Communist regimes participated in the Games.

Helsinki Olympics, 1952
The USSR and West Germany participated in the Games for the first time. The People's Republic of China was not yet recognised as a member of the Olympic community.

Melbourne Olympics, 1956
Boycotts over the Israeli-led take-over of the Suez Canal (by Egypt, Iraq and Lebanon), and the Soviet invasion of Hungary (by Spain and Switzerland) made these the first Olympics to be hit by sanctions.

1958
The People's Republic of China withdrew from all international federations and the Olympic movement.

Rome Olympics, 1960
The Games became a showcase for the host country, with the Rome Organising Committee spending a reported $30 million to impress the rest of the world with their facilities.

Mexico City Olympics, 1968
Best known for the Black Power salutes of USA runners Tommy Smith and John Carlos, stimulated by the civil rights movement and resistance to the Vietnam War.

Munich Olympics, 1972
Eight Palestinian terrorists broke into the Olympic Village, killing two Israelis and taking nine others hostage. They demanded the release of 200 prisoners from Israeli jails. In a clash with authorities all nine Israelis were killed, in addition to five terrorists and one policeman. The Games were suspended for 34 hours.

South Africa, 1961–1991
South Africa endured sporting exile from most international organisations due to apartheid.

Montreal Olympics, 1976
Twenty-two African nations boycotted the Games over the refusal to ban New Zealand after its rugby team toured South Africa.

Moscow Olympics, 1980
Boycotts led by the USA, Japan and West Germany occurred in the name of the Soviet invasion of Afghanistan.

Los Angeles Olympics, 1984
The Soviet Union and 13 other socialist countries boycotted the games. Western interpretation of the boycott suggests it was motivated by reprisals for the US boycott of the Moscow Games, as well as a protest against the commercial management of the Los Angeles Olympic Committee for violating the Olympic spirit.

Edinburgh Commonwealth Games, 1986
Following Britain's refusal to impose sanctions on South Africa, 32 nations pulled out of the Games.

Seoul Olympics, 1988
North Korea, Cuba, Ethiopia and Nicaragua boycotted the Games.

European football championships, 1992
Just prior to the finals in Sweden, Yugoslavia was expelled over the war.

Sydney Olympics, 2000
Indigenous leaders suggest Olympic officials should be toured around Aboriginal camps to show the appalling disadvantage of many indigenous Australians.

Salt Lake City Winter Olympics, 2002
Great controversy sparked over whether a torn American flag from the World Trade Centre could be used in the opening parade. Although the IOC initially denied the request, unhappy with the potential for precedence, US athletes, as well as New York police and fire-fighters, ceremonially carried the flag into the stadium.

Japan and South Korea Soccer World Cup, 2002
Japan and Korea (historic adversaries) cohosted the 2002 World Cup.

South Africa Cricket World Cup, 2003
Two Zimbabwean cricketers wore black armbands as an act of defiance against President Mugabe's regime and the death of democracy in their country.

Sport and Culture

Governments are increasingly acknowledging the role that sport can play in the community. The Scottish Government, for instance, argues that:

> Sport and culture are important to our quality of life and the development of Scotland as a modern dynamic society ... Sporting and artistic excellence can inspire; participation can support the development of essential skills in Scotland's people while bringing them and their communities together. Participation in sport links with our priority objective of improving our health and sport is also important to our local and national sense of identity.[42]

But according to John Hoberman,[43] politicians and the media are obsessed with competitive sport rather than the social role and obligations of sport. He argues that sport is primarily a tool of entertainment, and cannot replace other national and commercial institutions to achieve social, economic and political objectives. Andrew Jennings and Clare Sambrook add that sport reporting has been held hostage to powerful media interests and sponsor-driven agendas. They describe the sports sections of newspapers, for instance, as the 'soft-end', with little regard for accuracy (except for the scores, of course). They claim, as a result, that corruption in sport, such as doping, continues largely unchecked. They even go so far as to suggest that the media are pressured to suppress and censor reports in the interests of their national team, and their country's international image. Jennings has made a career out of documenting Olympic and sporting corruption, and his future earnings seem in little jeopardy.[44]

Competition creates, or at least reinforces, nationalism. The more likely aetiology, however, is that the innate human drive towards survival (hence competition) finds expression through mechanisms such as sport. Historically, sport has expressed the internal conflict of good versus evil with heroes representing the external conflict of empires and the competitive 'spirit' of a nation. Future social configurations will also be expressed through the symbolic conflict of sport, whether in the form of nations, empires or, as we suggest, tribal sporting clans. It is also prudent to remain aware that nationalism is a cultural and political phenomenon, and therefore comes burdened with an agenda. According to Juan Antonio Samaranch, former President of the International Olympic Committee, the meaning of the games needs to be constantly re-defined to reflect global socio-cultural changes, presumably including the domestication of technology. Certainly, under Samaranch's governance, the contemporary Olympic era has embraced the political messages of consumption and Western capitalist ideology. Politics and commerce can contaminate sport, but it is a serious misinterpretation of sport to assume that it can respond by providing the same favour.[45] In the words of Weiner: 'In case you haven't noticed, sport is controlled by money, men, and global capitalism – sort of like everything else.'[46]

Culture and the Future of Sport

It seems appropriate at this juncture to redirect our discussion away from the present and to focus it upon the future. Pure prediction needs an underpinning, however, and in this case it will be provided by looking at those factors we consider to be the most important influences upon culture in sport and the impact those factors might have on how culture might develop over the next few decades. Of those factors, we consider six to be of overwhelming importance: government, the economy, the media, demographics, legislation, and technology and science. At all times, however, those factors will rarely act in isolation, as they will relate and interrelate with each other.

Government

To understand the present and contemplate the future we must first look at the past. Fifty years ago, Cold War politics and Cold War ideology provided the environment in which sport was to grow. In Europe, US/Soviet relations were close to an all-time low. The West accepted the Truman Doctrine, that the USA would defend democracy, while the Soviet camp perceived capitalism as the root of evil. The Iron Curtain descended across Eastern Europe, and Germany, the major country in mainland Europe, was divided into two states, one Western, one Soviet. American liberalism saw itself as the protector of the free world, while Soviet communism saw itself as the single entity standing between the free world and American domination.

In Asia, civil war had encompassed China, and a repressive Marxist/Leninist regime had taken control. North Korea had invaded the South, and Europe and the USA was again involved in war in Asia. In the 'Third World', decolonisation issues were generating warfare and unrest in Africa, the Middle East, India, and throughout South East Asia. Capitalism, communism, Marxism and nationalism were all overshadowed, however, by the spectre of living with, or dying by, nuclear weapons.

Over the past 50 years, government ideologies have changed, economies have matured, and countries have gained independence and freedom.

Sport played a role in these changes, most noticeably as an instrument of government purpose. In Communist China, for example, sport, politics and ideology have been closely intertwined. So-called ping-pong diplomacy first allowed China to interact with its perceived Western enemies in a non-hostile manner and allowed it to strengthen relationships between it and its socialist allies. Sport provided China with the opportunity to begin a transition to a more liberal society. The 2008 Beijing Olympic Games will add distance to the journey.

Sport brought change to post-colonial countries such as India, Pakistan, Sri Lanka and Singapore. Cricket in the first three of these countries proved to be the foundation of a national identity and a source of international acceptance. Governments used sport instead of diplomacy as a way of inculcating values and to reinforce and challenge existing cultures. Laws which promoted democracy encouraged the free and democratic establishment of sport alliances.

Today, the violent disagreements of yesteryear are disappearing. Nations still argue but, except for a few still committed to extreme causes, are far less likely to engage in hostile thought or action. Governments have moved closer to the centre of politics. Economies, while still suffering significant differences, are far more robust than 50 years ago. In all, liberal democracies are gaining ascendancy.

Over the next 50 years, this trend is likely to continue. Values and standards, and thus culture, will increasingly be driven by government ideology which, in turn, will be influenced by the media which have always served as an important cultural tool that not only reflects but also initiates the way in which we live. Public perceptions will be guided by an increasingly small number of individuals. Social conservatism will reduce personal freedoms, using the legitimate reasons of terrorism and world unrest. Governments will seek to control sport through financial grants, legislative conditions and other support while the media will seek control through the written word, advertising, sponsorship, and ultimately ownership. Opposed to both of these functionaries of society will be the rise of interactive technology which will allow ideas and thought to become widespread rapidly. Governments will legislate, media will translate and technology will ignore. In this conflict between government, media and technology, sport is likely to become a potent weapon. It is probable that it will be used by all three elements of society to reinforce specific ideologies and by so doing, as we pointed out in an earlier chapter, will strengthen the idea that sport is a significant element of the spiritual culture of a nation.

As the spiritual culture of sport becomes embedded in society there will be those who will seek its emancipation, who will seek to deconstruct the values and attributes of society. This group may be particularly strong in those societies who once lived under socialist regimes or who dwell in less developed nations. If sport produces a group of athletes whose lifestyle and earnings grant them fame and undue power there is likely to be a backlash from others in the community. Countercultures and sub-cultures may emerge which may threaten aspects of sport or promote suitable conditions for that threat to emerge. The values that we accept today as inherent in sport, free speech, democratic decision-making and the right of all to compete, may be endangered.

The Economy

At the macro level, trade, the degree of market accessibility and the growth in global business can affect the culture of a nation. At the micro level, full employment or easy access to welfare, to good and inexpensive health facilities and educational opportunities will all strongly contribute to the way in which the individual relates to culture. But, for both nation and individual, the biggest test will come with the growth of globalisation.

The globalisation of sport,[47] while not something evil in its own right, has the potential to collapse the system if only Americanised or Westernised values in sport are considered, and this appears to be increasingly the case. With the growth in globalisation comes the culture of Western hegemony, and in turn a culture of intolerance to external points of view. The world economy and international business applaud increased homogeneity in sport and thus conformity of values.

Over the next decades, the rise in global business will encourage other nations to create similar sports cultures in order to compete with the USA and Europe. The media will encourage the growth of specific global sports in order to maximise advertising and sponsorship. Cities will continue to compete against other cities for the right to hold major sporting events, to build similar sports facilities, to promote similar sports and produce similar athletes. Brand image, whether for a city, a nation, a sport or a sport product, will be paramount. Smaller sports will die or become confined to fewer and fewer countries or areas. They will become symbols of past cultures. They will become 'old-fashioned'. Even some major sports, such as American football (confined basically to one nation, the USA), will lose popularity to be replaced by soccer. Already, more juniors in the USA play soccer than American football.

Governments will note the global trend and will manoeuvre funds and subsidies into those sports that give the country the widest exposure on the world scene. In so doing they will align themselves with the media. Individual cultures will become moribund, and with the rise of virtual reality and the loss of human interrelationships the real possibility exists that hate and distrust of foreign cultures may grow, causing hostility and extremism among the disenfranchised.

As the global economy increases, economic pressures on sport will continue to be a challenge. To overcome this, some consolidation within competitions could occur in order to generate an elite of elite factions and leagues. Instead, for example, of there being 92 professional teams in the English Football League, there may only be a dozen, comprising the finest players in the country. Remaining teams may simply be local amateur sides. The selected teams will play in a consolidated European or world league. This will have the effect of giving each of these teams a huge supporter base. Budgets for players, facilities and security will jump enormously, but a larger support base, together with increased ticket prices, will compensate. National pride will be strengthened to the delight of the government, while advertising and guaranteed television rights will satisfy the media. Selected cultures will be reinforced.

The Media

Among other things increased globalisation suggests there will be a stronger link between the manipulation of culture, sport and the media. Indeed it is no coincidence that several countries have a designated governmental Department for Culture, Media and Sport which involves itself in disparate arenas such as youth, the economy, science and technology and the arts. In the UK, for example, the culture, media and sport sectors comprise around 15 per cent of GDP, generating revenue of around £140 billion and providing employment for some 4.5 million people.[48] It is an area large enough to wield much influence.

According to David Rowe, sport, particularly 'visual broadcast sport', transfers 'across society and culture in a continuous feedback loop' creating an 'amoeba-like cultural capacity to divide and reform'.[49] This situation, we suggest, stems from the emergence of the mass circulation daily newspapers over 120 years ago. Prior to this date newspapers occupied a secondary place in the formation of public opinion but, with the introduction of the Linotype typesetting machine in 1886 and the application of the halftone process to the rotary press in 1897 (which made photography an integral part of news reporting), newspapers gained a mass audience of readers. Over the last hundred years new technologies of communication, radio and television, have lessened the role of the newspaper but have served to strengthen the role of the media in general. In the process, areas of popular culture, among which sport has found a paramount place, have become dependent upon the media for economic survival.

Reinforcing the role of the media in the formation of culture has been the phenomenon of convergence which began a decade or so ago and appears set to continue into the foreseeable future. Digital compression creates technological convergence in the transmission of signals and the standardisation of equipment, and mergers and take-overs translate into market convergence, while liberalisation in broadcasting is bringing regulatory convergence. The effect has been not simply to give greater power to fewer and fewer in the media, but to give overwhelming power to the US media who possess a massive structural advantage in terms of production and distribution of US products. In this process, the US cultural identity has become paramount, social cohesion in non-Western countries has been endangered, and culture has become globalised.

Over the next 50 years there is likely to be an increasing link between the formation of culture, sport and the media. The US bias will probably lessen as China and India become far more formidable players on the world scene and a number of smaller media players emerge to grab a hold on niche sports markets. Public expectations, however, are almost certainly likely to be shaped more by the media rather than by government or, indeed, by what is morally or ethically right. Nonetheless, the media giants will need to listen to the public voice if they are to avoid a public backlash from an increasingly leisured and educated society.

Demographics

According to the US Bureau of the Census, International Data Base, there are some 6.3 billion people in the world at the present time. Of these almost 3 billion are under the age of 25 years with a further 3 billion between 26 and 65 years. By 2020, total population is predicted to increase to 7.5 billion, of whom only 3.04 billion will be under the age of 25 years and 3.1 billion between 26 and 65 years. The bulk of the increase in the population will be among the group above 65 years old. By 2050, total population will have risen to 9.1 billion. Again, slightly fewer than 3.1 billion will be under the age of 25 years. Those in the 26–64 year old group will have increased marginally to 3.5 billion with the overwhelming increase in the population numbers made up of people over 65 years old.[50]

Regionally, China's birthrate has already declined past 2.1 children per woman, the 'replacement rate'. At this level population is likely to stabilise and fall to, perhaps, 1.2 billion by 2050. India's fertility rate is nearly 4 children per woman and this suggests an increase in population from its current figure of 930 million to 1.5 billion by 2050. In Latin America, fertility is around 3 children per woman, thus potentially increasing the population by 70 per cent to 810 million by 2050. In the West, the US population is expected to grow around 30 per cent to 384 million by 2050, while the population of Europe and Japan should decline by about 10 per cent over the same timeframe. In Africa and the Middle East, despite the AIDS epidemic, population is likely to come close to tripling over the next half century, giving the region a mammoth 2.5 billion people.[51]

The statistics are interesting for they tell us where the greatest viewing audience will be and where the largest market for sporting goods will be located. The statistics also tell us that the growth in the youth market in developed Western countries is facing strong downward pressure, while the growth in the 26–64 year range is not much better. The growth market for the West is in the over-65 end of the spectrum. Broadly, this has implications for sport, government and the media. Logically there should be an increased demand for spectator sport and less participation in sports. Realistically, however, improved health and nutrition will significantly increase the capabilities of the older folk and they may well choose to partake in the less physical sports such as bowls, walking and hiking. In Africa, the Middle East and in India, the youth population is set to explode.

Throughout the West, increased immigration will change the ethnic and racial diversity of the population. More women will populate the workforce, increasingly seeking and finding gender equality. Immigration and gender may well affect the culture and impact upon the type of sport portrayed by the media.

In the immediate future, before technology makes its dramatic impact, a major crisis is likely to arise. In the Western world, increased longevity (combined with higher retirement expectations) will put downward pressure on the stock market as baby-boomers sell assets to finance retirement. Retirement and welfare will increasingly become a burden upon the decreasing workforce. This will create the need for increased taxation with an implied reduction in savings which will disrupt the growth of the market and thus the economy of the developed countries. The brightest of the Western youth are likely to vote with their feet as did their forefathers, creating an even greater problem.

In the less developed countries, the enormous growth in the youth population is likely to perpetuate the cycle of political instability and anti-regime activities that already affects many of these countries. In addition, rapid population growth will create enormous problems as countries struggle with the simultaneous challenge of educating the young, finding jobs for them and dealing with the huge increase in environmental degradation brought on by the swelling population.

Governments in all countries are likely to recognise the inherent dangers in having too many or too few young people and working population. Non-democratic regimes will probably face the biggest challenges as the young seek greater freedom. Governments are likely to respond in several ways. One of these will be to seek any way possible to enforce or reinforce national identity and culture. In so doing they may choose to substantially increase funding for sport, returning to the days of the Roman circuses and finding an outlet for the steam of the more rebellious youth. For the media there will be real business opportunities in the emerging markets and with them the chance to spread Western values of Coca-Cola, Nike and consumption. Fortunately, in the longer term, technology will come to the aid of the world and society.

Legislation

In the short term there is likely to be less financial assistance from government but increasing pressure for additional accountability. This will result in increased legislation and regulation. Legislation concerning safety will increase, as will legislation regulating the use of drugs in sport, particularly those that stimulate genetic change. Many governments also believe that a distinct regulatory approach to the Internet is needed and although they are still grappling with this issue, additional legislation will at some time be enacted.

In Europe and in Australia, many television sporting events are considered to be of such social and cultural importance that legislation is in place to guarantee that such events remain freely available to the general television audience. These events are not chosen by the people but rather by the government.

Within sporting organisations equal opportunity legislation is gradually occurring. At the moment older organisations governed by traditional practices ensure that management is male-oriented and that feminine styles of management are discouraged and undermined. This will gradually change, allowing gender relations to be more equitable.

Over the next few decades we may expect that market incentives will be accompanied by an increase in the volume of legislation both in terms of regulation and regulatory tools. Owing to the rapid increase in professional sport and in the media outlet for that sport, strong pressure will develop for governmental interference in the decision-making processes connected with sport. As a result we might expect the rise of 'sports charters' which will seek to satisfy the needs of sporting organisations, fans and allied business interests. Such charters should lead to improvements in the information and knowledge base for sport development and should ensure that unhealthy relationships between sport and the media or sport and the gaming industry do not develop.

Technology and Science

Over the next 50 years the world will enter a new era, one in which artificial intelligence and molecular and genetic engineering will dominate. It will herald a revolution in business and society greater than any which may have preceded it. We wrote of this new era in detail in an earlier chapter. Rather than repeat our earlier words, let us simply state that AI and nanotechnology will create opportunities for sport, sports business and the sports fan beyond anything previously imagined. Enormous medical advances will underline performance enhancement.

Along with the revolution in technology is a likely revolution in culture. Materially, nanotechnology will allow for society to be healthier and more affluent, while spiritually philosophical dilemmas will emerge. Humankind will increasingly question the roles of God and technology in society and whether science can now replace the natural laws. Exposure to the thousands of niche television channels will impact upon the way in which society considers sport, technology and art, and governments will find it increasingly difficult to influence the development of culture. Nostalgia may, for a while at least, move society away from a feast of visual sport and back to activities such as walking and hiking.

With the new technologies and the growth of a happier, more satisfied society, a reduction in traditional conflict and rivalry will occur. Prejudices and stereotypes emphasised by history and politics will shrink, and this may translate into the sporting arena. In the event that this occurs, both government and the media are likely to adopt strategies leading to the incorporation of manufactured nationalist attitudes. Old games, such as the 1966 World Cup between England and Germany, may be re-screened along with sports highlights such as the 1980 USA–USSR Olympic hockey final. Government requires nationalist prejudices in order to reinforce cultural values, while the media needs rivalry to continue for sport to maintain its viewer base.

The timing of some of these developments is, of course, unknowable. However, the impact of technology on the sport business is undeniable.

In the final chapter, we consider the role of imminent technologies on the sport business future.

Notes and References

1 Geertz, C. (2000). *Available Light*. Princeton, NJ: Princeton University Press, p. 16.

2 Lumsden, C. and Wilson, E.O. (1981). *Genes, Mind and Culture: The Coevolutionary Process*. Cambridge, MA: Harvard University Press.

3 Keys, B. (2002). *Sport and International Relations: A Research Guide*. Ohio, USA: Ohio University. Available at: http://www.ohiou.edu/shafr/NEWS/2002/MAR/SPORTS.HTM, accessed on 13 March 2003.

4 Wang, H. (1999). 'Fighting for the nation, fighting against the nation: literary and cinematic representation of sport in post-Mao China'. *Proceedings of the 1999 Association for Asian Studies Annual Meeting*, 11–14 March, Boston, MA.

5 Rowe, D. and Lawrence, G. (1998). *Tourism, Leisure, Sport: Critical Perspectives*. Rydalmere, NSW: Hodder Education.

6 Tudor, A. (1998). 'Sports reporting: Race, difference and identity'. In K. Brants, J. Hermes and L. van Zoonen (eds), *The Media in Question: Popular Cultures and Public Interests*. London: Sage, p. 154.

7 Wang, 'Fighting for the nation'.

8 Rowe and Lawrence, *Tourism, Leisure, Sport*.

9 Smith, A. (2003). 'Irish sport and nationalism'. *Interview Transcript: The Sports Factor with Amanda Smith*, 19 January 2001. Australian Broadcasting Corporation. Available at: www.abc.net.au/rn/talks/8.30/sportsf/stories/s226378.htm, accessed on 13 March 2003.

10 Rowe and Lawrence, 1988, p. 198.

11 Bell, D. (2002). '"Factionalism" or nationalism? Are nations to blame for disputes at International Games?' *International Games Archive 1998–2002*. Available at: www. internationalgames.net/topics/nationalism.htm, accessed on 12 March 2003.

12 McGarr, P. (2002). 'World cup: Show red card to nationalism'. *Socialist Worker*, 1805, 22 June, pp. 8–9.

13 McGarr, 'World cup', pp. 8–9.

14 Wang, 'Fighting for the nation'.

15 Abrams, H. (2000). *The Olympic Truce – Myth and Reality*. Centre D'estudis Olympics; Barcelona, Spain. Available at: http://www.blues.uab.es/olympic.studies/dir/op.html, accessed on 13 March 2003.

16 Abrams, *The Olympic Truce*.

17 Cardwell, J. (2002). 'It's not just cricket: Sport and nationalism'. *Socialist Review*, 265, July/August.

18 Cardwell, 'It's not just cricket'.

19 Bell, '"Factionalism" or nationalism?'.

20 Bell, '"Factionalism" or nationalism?'.

21 See Westerbeek, H. and Smith, A. (2003). *Sport Business in the Global Marketplace*. Basingstoke: Palgrave Macmillan.

22 Douglas, D. (2002). 'To be young, gifted, black and female: A meditation on the cultural politics at play in representations of Venus and Serena Williams'. *Sociology of Sport Online*, 5 (2), November/December.

23 Hall, S. (1981). 'The whites of their eyes: Racist ideologies and the media'. In G. Bridges and R. Brunt (eds), *Silver Lining: Some Strategies for the Eighties*. London: Lawrence & Wishart, pp. 28–52.

24 Crenshaw, K. (1992). 'Whose story is it, anyway? Feminist and antiracist appropriations of Anita Hill'. In T. Morrison (ed.), *Race-ing justice, en-gendering power: Essays on Anita Hill, Clarence Thomas and the Construction of Social Reality*. New York: Pantheon Books, pp. 402–36; Crenshaw, K. (1997). 'Color-blind dreams and racial nightmares: Reconfiguring racism in the post-civil rights era'. In T. Morrison and C. Brodsky Lacour (eds), *Birth of a Nation 'hood: Gaze, Script, and Spectacle in the O.J. Simpson Case*. New York: Pantheon Books, pp. 97–168.

25 Douglas, 'To be young, gifted, black and female'; Hammonds, E. (1994). 'Black (w)holes and the geometry of black female sexuality'. *Differences. A journal of feminist cultural studies*, 6 (2 and 3), pp. 126–45; Healy, M. (2002, October). 'Three more reasons to forget about men's tennis'. *Gentleman's Quarterly*, pp. 262–5.

26 Douglas, 'To be young, gifted, black and female'.

27 Douglas, 'To be young, gifted, black and female'.

28 Messner, M.A. (2002). *Taking the Field: Women, Men, and Sports*. Chicago, IL: University of Minnesota Press.

29 Show Racism the Red Card Campaign, Whittle Bay, UK. Organisational website at: http://www.srtrc.org/srtrc.htm, accessed on 12 March 2003.

30 Bloom, J. (1997). *To Show What an Indian Can Do: Sports at Native American Boarding Shcools*. Minneapolis, MN: University of Minnesota Press.

31 Cardwell, 'It's not just cricket'.

32 Cardwell, 'It's not just cricket'.

33 Appadurai, A. (1995). 'Playing with modernity: The decolonization of Indian cricket'. In Carol Breckenridge (ed.), *Consuming Modernity: Public Culture in a South Asian World*. Minneapolis: University of Minnesota Press.

34 Cardwell, 'It's not just cricket'.

35 Keys, *Sport and International Relations*.

36 Keys, *Sport and International Relations*.

37 Keys, *Sport and International Relations*.

38 Keys, *Sport and International Relations*; see also Rowe, D. (1999). *Sport, Culture and the Media: The Unruly Trinity*. Buckingham: Open University Press; LaFeber, W. (1999). *Michael Jordan and the New Global Capitalism*. New York: W. W. Norton.

39 Happold, T. (2003). 'The Politics Game'. *Guardian Unlimited: Guardian Newspapers Limited*, 11 February. Available at http://sport.guardian.co.uk/news/story/0,10488,893309,00.html, accessed on 12 March 2003.

40 Happold, 'The Politics Game'.

41 Wilson, J. and Jeffery, S. (2002). 'Special Reports: Sport versus politics'. *Guardian Unlimited: Guardian Newspapers Limited*, 31 December. Available at http://www.guardian.co.uk/zimbabwe/article/0,2763,866874,00.html, accessed on 12 March 2003; Australian Sports Commission (2003). *Sport Information. Olympic Factsheet: Politics and the Olympics*. Canberra: Australian Sports Commission; http://www.ausport.gov.au/info/Factsheets/pol.html, accessed on 23 March 2003; Cardwell, 'It's not just cricket'. Campbell, D. (2002). 'Old glory fans Olympic flames.' *Guardian Unlimited: Guardian Newspapers Limited*. 10 February. Available at: http://sport.guardian.co.uk/olympics/story/0,10308,648048,00.html, accessed on 12 March 2003; see also Proceedings of the *Global Games: Sports, Politics and Society An International Symposium*. Available at http://www.epiic.com/archives/2000/sympos00/sympos00.html, accessed on 23 March 2003.

42   Scottish Executive (2001). *Working Together for Scotland: A Programme for Government: 2.14 Sport and Culture.* Scottish Executive Publications/Her Majesty's Stationery Office, p. 32.

43   Hoberman, J. (2002). 'Fools for sport: The nationalist games politicians play'. *Proceedings of the International Conference for Media Professionals in a Globalised Sports World: Play The Game.* Available at http://www.play-the-game.org/2002/articles/hoberman.html, accessed on 7 March 2002.

44   Jennings, A. and Sambrook, C. (2000). *The Great Olympic Swindle.* New York: Simon & Schuster.

45   Galllacher, L. (1999). 'Conference claims sport can decontaminate politics'. Interview Transcript from The World Today, 1 September 1999, Australian Broadcasting Corporation. Available at http://www.abc.net.au/worldtoday/s48483.htm, accessed on 23 March 2003.

46   Weiner, J. (2000). 'Building towards a political sports movement'. *Education for Public Inquiry and International Citizenship.* Available at http://www.epiic.com/archives/2000/sympos00/VVarticle00.html, accessed on 12 March 2003.

47   Westerbeek, H. (2002). *Interview with Amanda Smith on The Sports Factor,* 6 December. Radio National, Australian Broadcasting Corporation.

48   Ministerial Statement by Estelle Morris, MP, Department for Culture, Media and Sport, October 2003. Available at www.ost.gov.uk/research/forwardlook, accessed on 12 March 2003.

49   Rowe, *Sport, Culture and the Media,* p. 165.

50   US Bureau of the Census, International Data Base, 2003, www.census.gov.

51   Tunisia Daily (2002). *World Demography.* Tunisia Daily. Available at www.tunisiadaily.com/answers/world-demography.html, accessed on 12 March 2003.

Chapter 10

The New Frontiers of Sport Business: Sport Business as Unusual

In this final chapter we try to bring together the content of the previous chapters by focusing on the short-term future. It will not come as a surprise that our concentration will be on imminent technologies as these will signify the major transitions that will take place in the business of sport over the next few decades.

Our overview will range from wireless roaming connectivity between people to bio-interactive systems within people; from brain-enhancing cognitronics to the atom-by-atom building of new performance tools that will assist athletes in their quest for victory, or the genetic building of the athletes themselves. We will consider the super-computers that will help marketers in mining their consumer data and preview the possibility of satellite interactive computers that will relay all available individual consumer information to salespeople all over the planet. Digital platforms will integrate with gaming platforms allowing people anywhere to participate in sport online games that will develop into the new 'Champions Leagues' of the common world: that is, the champions of those leagues will be 'common' but as much revered as the talented athletes who kicked the real ball in the past.

Consumers will become active players, drawn into the experience rather than the passive spectators they are today. Fans will not be limited to geographic location of the club or the team because there will be no fixed geographic location. Hubs of fans will be created in a cyber-environment and fans will be able to find each other in every corner of the world, willing and able to meet at any time of the day. Even more akin to 'science fiction' of the past, advertising and the playing of sport in space is perhaps only decades away.

We will propose the notion that ultimately the sport fan will gain more control. With the potential to access any information at any time, information combined with choice is power. Only those sport businesses that can meet the tribal needs of fans will survive and prosper. As we all struggle to define our respective roles in this technological future, sport business may well help to help remind us of what it means to be human.

The Wave of Technology

Nascent technologies lure us to believe that the future of sport business and entertainment will be digital and progressive. We have speculated that, in part, this technological imperative will threaten to diminish the essential competitive and physical spirit that is the life force of sport. Within the next half century, the development of technology may reach what has colloquially become known as the singularity, and we have noted the implications for sport and entertainment in a post-singularity culture. But even the extreme view that the singularity paints, where sport is merely another manifestation of a personal digital experience, may be too pessimistic for those of us who covet sport in its present and past forms. Without unduly clinging to this past, we have argued throughout this book that despite the potential for sport to be subject to a radical technological reinvention, sport may prove more robust than other cultural institutions and forms of entertainment.

The essential human condition is caught up in the physical. Despite the extraordinary possibilities that the singularity implies, we have suggested that sport has the potential to remind us of our humanity and the joys of a physical connection to a real rather than digital environment. Chapter 6 was an attempt to distil the spiritual potential of sport and argue that, irrespective of its form and the role of technology and business, sport will maintain a special, almost religious quality that is as vigorous and stout as any human cultural or entertainment invention.

In the future of sport business and entertainment, we have also envisioned other effects of technology and the implications of changing cultural values. In Chapter 3, we discussed the pre-singularity sportsperson, professional and recreational. Genomic profiling and restructuring, surgical intervention, drug therapy and technological training apparatus would all seem likely elements in a sporting future driven by commercial 'progress', economic institutions and the insatiable media appetitive for lucrative content. The post-singularity athlete may be nothing more than a digital construction, the labour of a programmer's expertise rather than the realisation of athletic potential, training and fortitude.

In Chapters 7 and 8, we turned our attention to the obligations and opportunities associated with sport business for society's corporate constituents. We argued that prescient corporations will proactively direct resources into their local and global communities and into environmental issues, not merely out of a sense of obligation or with the expectation of reciprocal sponsorships and beneficial exposure, but because they recognise their responsibilities as key community members.

Chapters 5 and 9 took a more cultural and values-based perspective on the future of sport business and entertainment. In these chapters we argued that the future of sport marketing will be driven by tribal affiliations, some of which are unlikely to yield common demographic or even psychographic characteristics within the tribal segment. We have called for a revised approach to marketing segmentation where the traditional criteria, such as income and geography, are far less important than values and experience outcomes. In a future world where virtual spectators are 'placeless', the distribution of sport entertainment through conventional stadia and venues will be less important as a result of digitally changeable environments. As an imminent technology that is presently being explored in the form of virtual advertising, the notion of virtual, placeless fans, is further discussed below.

In this chapter, we return to the technological variables and seek to tease out the key technologies that will affect sport business and entertainment. Unlike Chapter 2, where our focus was on the radical but uncertain possibilities, this chapter is concerned with the almost inevitable consequences of the present incarnation of technology, some of which is likely to prove quite radical as well. In particular, we are interested in reaching some speculative conclusions about the nature of the sport business in the future and the ways in which the sport and entertainment business will be marketed. To do this we need to come to terms with imminent technologies and the effect they will have on sport consumer attitudes and expectations.

Imminent Key Technologies

There is no shortage of prognosticators when it comes to imminent technologies in sport entertainment. Nevertheless, it is worth briefly sketching a picture of those which will play a role in changing the way sport business will be conducted. The technologies underpinning holography, artificial intelligence, virtual environments and actors are well on the way to commercial development over the next decade. In addition, a range of more impressive technologies is also inevitable within several decades. As we noted in Chapter 2, it will be the convergence of these with the achievement of genuine artificial intelligence that has the potential to change the world.

Sport Anywhere

Wireless Local Area Networks act like Ethernets, the technology that links personal computers together in offices. Wireless allows roaming connectivity between different portable and permanent technologies such as phones, laptops, handheld computers and diaries and the Internet. It will prove a strong force for the convergence of technology. This integration will make portable real-time and recorded sports viewing from virtually any location in the world a possibility in the short term and an inexpensive one in the medium term. Handheld, wireless computers are already available and will shortly be pervasive enough to display sporting events, replays and highlights. It is also likely that they will be employed during events for similar functions. As we have noted, the ubiquity of sport through these media will leave networks vulnerable to overzealous broadcasting and could undermine the value of the sport properties they own. This, however, will be offset to some extent by increasing opportunities facilitated by inexpensive receiving technologies slowly permeating the enormous Asian and sub-continental marketplaces.

Towards Cyborgs

Bio-interactive materials is the technical term for the use of computer chips capable of monitoring human activity, ultimately located within the human body. Bio-interactivity at its most sophisticated is premised on the idea that miniature computers and other electronic sensors can be used in and around the body to relay information about identity and health. This form of technology has already been touted as the new 'Big Brother', assumed sooner or later to replace everything from driver's licences and identity cards to currency, where purchases can be completed with a thumb or eye print rather than a swiped credit card. It represents the next stage of smart sensors and monitoring chips that are presently being employed in long-distance athletic events such as marathons. Prototype smartshirts are already around that measure and relay the wearer's vital signs via a wireless transceiver to a laptop or network. US Army-funded research is seeking to develop changing camouflage battle-suits that interact with the environment in which they are placed.

The most exciting possibilities for bio-interactive technologies are associated with use internal to the body. Materials are being designed that can be inserted into bones to help their repair after breakage and to facilitate rehabilitation after injury. The ultimate goal of bio-interactive science is to develop artificial organs and body parts that bionically replace damaged or malfunctioning systems. For example, in addition to the next generation of implantable hearing aids, sophisticated prosthetic limbs made of electro-conductive plastics capable of interacting with the nervous system are under development. In the future, such replaceable limbs and organs are likely to be appealing possibilities not just for health and longevity but for improved athletic performance. These bio-interactive materials might also be used in concert with gene therapy in order to facilitate the growth or modification of new body parts. As genomic profiling isolates the genes responsible for certain characteristics, they will be used to play a role in manipulating physical traits, longevity and preventing disease.

Brain Enhancement

We discussed advanced possibilities of artificial intelligence and cognitronics in Chapter 2. Cognitronics refers to linkages between the brain and computers. At present the development of this field is primitive compared to expectations honed in popular science fiction. However, even without the singularity, this area is the backbone for virtual sport environments of the future where all sporting performances will be undertaken in the digital world through cognitronic interfaces. Although it may seem a far-off possibility, researchers have already demonstrated that linkages are possible between the brain and computers. Medical scientists have had success with converting computer commands into neuro-electrical stimuli to move paralysed limbs. Aside from the first steps in aiding the disabled to be active and, indeed, eventually engage in sporting endeavours, the technology offers the potential for interaction with the environment. We will be able to drive the car and operate the computer with thought control. This will introduce an intermediate range of sporting pursuits in a world that will have moved beyond physicality but not yet developed exclusively virtual environments. For instance, the batting robot will step up to the plate, ready to swing when the batter initiates the right thought pattern. However, first person experience is the hallmark of sporting participation and will offer unprecedented opportunities in virtual settings.

Technological Lego

Molecular manufacturing or nanotechnology, as we noted in Chapter 2, is the science of building structures atom by atom. It involves developing molecular machines that can use atoms like building blocks, as bricks to be restructured into any physical element. At its most sophisticated, it is theoretically plausible for molecular machines or nanobots to construct replica armies of themselves to assemble anything for which they are programmed, whether it is food or complex equipment such as super-computers.

Although the whole idea sounds like modern alchemy, scientists have successfully positioned individual atoms together (the equivalent of placing a few bricks on top of each other in the quest to construct a skyscraper). Assembling atoms is significantly more troublesome, but it is probably only a matter of time before it can be undertaken commercially. The science is where nuclear physics was at the middle of the last century: dangerous but showing remarkable potential. Enough is known to be aware that some of the by-products of nanotechnological activities are toxic, as well as (for all practical purposes) impossible to detect.

The implications for sport and the entertainment business are profound. The ability to develop any structure or substance from scratch should eventually mean the removal of poverty and famine. At the very least, those nations which covet the technology, presumably from the West, will find their citizens endowed with more discretionary leisure time than ever before. This will naturally increase the importance of the leisure, recreation, entertainment and sport industries.

Super-computer Data Crunching

As a process of seeking knowledge, the scientific method has yielded unparalleled success. Roughly, it works by establishing a broad hypothesis, or a set of ideas about how and why things are the way they are, and then sets about gathering data to disprove the hypothesis. If the hypothesis withstands the tests of empirically collected evidence, then it holds its place as the best explanation until the evidence suggests the need for modification or replacement. Conventionally, the method is deductive. It begins with a theory and uses data to test that theory. Some branches of social inquiry use more inductive approaches, where data is collected first and is synthesised into working theories. This works well in confined sets, but is impractical for voluminous amounts of quantitative data. Advances in computer processing and intelligent software design are beginning to highlight some new possibilities. Known as combinatorial science or data mining, super-computers with intelligent software will be able to crunch through mountains of different forms of information including Internet material, books, published research and raw data, looking for patterns that no human has the capability of noticing.

Advances in combinatorial science have some exciting implications for sport marketing and the sport and entertainment industry in general. Marketers will be able to use their super-computers to understand more about their customers and opportunities in the marketplace than ever before.

Going well beyond the rudimentary information provided by customer relationship marketing software, computer software will be capable of making connections and seeing patterns between millions of superficially unrelated data sources. It will even tap into the AI systems managing the Supernet in order to access further information. For example, the computer system might notice that John Brown did not access the game live at his usual time, and subsequently might track down some transactions he has just made in another country, note that he purchased a train ticket several minutes ago, surmises that he might have some time available to watch a replay and contact him via phone, watch or mobile computer to solicit his interest and to ask if he has remembered that it is his nephew's birthday in three days and that no one has yet bought him the new club scarf. The power of super-processing and intelligent data mining software to analyse individual sport and entertainment consumer activity will revolutionise the market research methods of sport organisations and their subsequent product and service offerings.

Digital Transmissions

Presently fans typically access two information streams that are transmitted from a sporting event: video and audio. The potential of the third stream, digital, is only just beginning to be tapped. There are several ways in which digital technology can be used to enhance the sport watching experience. First, it can be viewed like ordinary video or television transmissions, but it is more flexibly accessible so that events may be watched over the Internet. Although at the moment Internet viewing is second rate in some instances where streaming video connections are slow and of dubious quality, the quality gap is diminishing. In addition, there are a number of niche sporting events that are not broadcast on television or televised live but are available on the Internet. As wireless connectivity to the Internet improves in quality, cost and convenience, the option of watching a sporting event on the run through a personal computer, phone, diary or pad will become more prevalent.

Second, digital technology can be used to cover specific players or aspects of the sporting event. Because of the nature of the data, the choices concerning its use are more easily transferred to the viewer than in conventional broadcasts. In other words, the viewer can be the director if she chooses, selecting camera angles, players, activities or replays at her discretion.

Third, digital can be employed to create new statistics associated with the event. The technology provides more options for measuring and monitoring. For example, the viewer might wish to know the exact distance that a golfer's ball is from the pin, the comparative speed of two opposing running backs or the power with which a striker hits the ball during a penalty. These statistics can also be stored for each player or team and revisited later for analysis or even for use in game play.

Finally, the most recent – and possibly the area of greatest potential – is the use of digital for real-time gaming data. As viewers watch the big game, they can link in to play in direct competition through their home gaming console or computer interface. They can attempt the same putts as Tiger, drive against Michael or box against Lennox. As data is stored historically, game players will be able to create their own teams based on real game performances. As learning software becomes more intelligent, historical athletes will be able to participate in new scenarios governed by complex behavioural algorithms based on the meta-analysis of their career performances. Not only will fans be able to play with or against their sporting heroes, but they will be able to create genuine 'teams of the century'. We can find out whether Ali really was the greatest.

Sport Gaming

International Sportsworld Communicators (ISC), the company that owns the commercial rights to the World Rally Championship, has formed an alliance with a real-time three-dimensional graphics creator, Virtual Spectator, in order to provide cutting-edge content to bolster the rally broadcasts. The technology allows the viewer to see replays of cars' performances in video game style graphics that show the participants side-by-side on screen during each stage. It is a lucid demonstration of the power of technology for enhancing the viewing experience. Even the most unsophisticated of rally fans can instantly see where each stage is won and lost, and where each of the cars is fast or slow. Although it has not yet been offered, it is just a matter of time before viewers can race directly against recorded performance of the drivers, or even in real time.

Motor sport is a good example of a sport vulnerable to radical shifts in technology that render actual, real performance unnecessary. Race simulations are already advanced, but another two decades will probably see them progress to the point where they can be used as proxies for actual racing. Although we would argue that real sport will never be completely overrun by virtual sport, there will be enormous opportunity for sporting organisations and broadcasters to offer simultaneous, real-time but virtual participation in events to online gamers. It will be possible to qualify and race in a Formula One Grand Prix or in a World Rally Championship stage. This will lead to a second level of sporting content where it will be possible not just to watch the actual race occurring in reality, but also to watch the simulation race occurring in cyber-space, where the best cyber-drivers compete for the cyber-championship in the same conditions. In some events, this second level activity will be just as compelling as the real thing and just as many spectators will tune in to see their cyber-sporting heroes perform. We can be certain that the rights owners of these secondary, simulation events will brand them, offer sponsorships and market the successful participants just as forcefully as those in the real championship if they can see the commercial benefits. Just do not be too disappointed when the world heavyweight cyber-boxing champion turns up to a promotional event and is a 98-pound (45 kg) 12-year-old.

Cyber and Digital Sport Gaming

Online sport game playing could become the recreation of the future. As a result of increased average bandwidth and improved visual and audio quality of software and computer hardware, the entertainment options with networked gaming are increasing exponentially, as are the number of participants. Even in 2000, an Interactive Digital Software Association survey revealed that over 60 per cent of Americans play video games and 30 per cent of all Americans consider playing computer and video games to be the most fun entertainment activity of all. Increasingly, these game players are using an online environment in which to solicit human interaction. By forming teams, known as clans, groups can play against each other in different leagues. Competitive online gaming has become known as cyber-sport.

There are a growing number of organisations which host cyber-sport events, some of which offer prize money of up to half a million US dollars, provided by a combination of entry fees and sponsorship from hardware and software companies (particularly CPU, video card and network manufacturers). Television networks and media groups have also shown great interest in accessing this market via cyber-sport. As the production quality of video games has improved to rival Hollywood in some cases, media enterprises are recognising that it could be profitable to produce television content in a digital virtual environment. In other words, it is probably just a matter of time before cyber-sports are televised. Recently, the World Cyber Games was the beneficiary of some insistent lobbying by its organisers, sponsoring companies such as Samsung and Sony, and participants to gain entry into the Olympic Games. Unsurprisingly, the IOC has taken a dim view of such an entry.

Spectatorship of cyber-sports is presently troublesome. To date, none of the commercially successful games and their software environments offers the opportunity for uninvolved spectatorship. However, this extension is merely a matter of time and interest. Although recorded demonstrations of the games are available after the fact, the opportunity to watch, say, a live cyber-football game will soon be possible. Technologically, the infrastructure is available and can theoretically sustain a virtually unlimited number of spectators, although Internet Service Providers do not typically provide the multicast transmissions that are needed to send a reliable data stream to an unlimited number of clients. They could, though. Shortly, commentators will provide audio explaining the game and tactics of players. In addition, spectators will have directorial options for replays, special angles, slow motion and even the opportunity to record the moves of a particular player to study or play against later.

For conventional sporting event broadcasting, networks drive their production trucks containing the live 'feed' and mobile editing studio to the venue. Here the director can simultaneously view all of the camera footage and decide which he wants to go on air at any given time. Commentators in the venue can provide their feedback while watching the event live, or by reviewing the edited footage. The director can also add in special effects, replays and slow motion analysis. It is a well-tested approach, but also an expensive one that requires significant resources and expertise. In the virtual cyber-sport world, however, camera footage is unnecessary. Furthermore, an unlimited number of angles can be accessed by the home director, determined before, during or after the live event. Intelligent programming could also play this role autonomously if home spectators have no interest. This could be augmented further if the feed was buffered (delayed) for anything up to a minute. It would still effectively remain live, but would also allow the intelligent programming system to see what events occur in real time and switch to an appropriate viewing mode. Unlike real television broadcasts, the intuition and experience of a director in anticipating the future would be unnecessary in the virtual world of cyber-sport. Camera planning is a well-understood computer science. Applications such as 'Virtual Cinematographer' can provide encoded expertise, and newer systems are emerging with learning intelligence which are able to study and mimic favourite directorial styles of the user.

Cyber-sport as the New Modality

In the future, people could purchase a console or computer games/Internet access principally to watch games rather than actually play themselves, in much the same way as they might buy a television set. Sport broadcasting techniques are being applied to the games and cyber-sport environment and in so doing are providing rival entertainment modalities to conventional sport broadcasting. Like professional sport, spectators are interested in the entertainment that comes from observing skill mastery. With sufficient audiences, sponsors and merchandise will emerge as important elements.

The key issue with both sport broadcasting of the future and cyber-sport broadcasting is the ability to provide an enhanced entertainment experience, particularly one where live or delayed remote viewing is more rewarding in at least some ways than live attendance. While this has typically been easy with television as it has traditionally provided the only alternative to live attendance, which can be costly, inconvenient or geographically impossible, the online environment must leap ahead of conventional television coverage if it is to gain a foothold. It can achieve this by focusing on a number of key elements of the user experience which are difficult to duplicate via the rigid delivery of television broadcasting. Sport broadcasting can learn from the cutting edge movements in the online world of cyber-sport.

The Future of Sport Broadcasting: Unlocking the User Experience

Part of the premise of successful sport broadcasting is that it offers something more than the sporting participant receives when she plays. In general, as a species, humans are doers rather than watchers. Playing provides a certain set of experiences, but watching provides a different set that has the potential to be just as rich and powerful as actually being involved. Moreover, with the addition of new broadcasting digital technologies, there are opportunities for sport spectators, both cyber and real, to have a level of control and interaction that even players, coaches and managers currently do not have. In this sense, the spectator is no longer merely a passive viewer, but becomes a new kind of *player*.

The New Player's Experience

Cinematographical control is the first key to enhancing the new player's experience. As we have already noted, through digital streams, viewers can manipulate angles, replays, follow particular players and events and even record the performances of individual stars in order to duplicate their actions in one-on-one video game competition later. This is just the beginning, however. For example, once sporting performances can be isolated from their environments, they can be replaced anywhere. In practice this will mean that virtual environments can be created by the spectator. They might choose to relocate the venue, add or remove fans, manipulate team colours, add some extra green to the grass or choose between the virtual advertising sponsorship configurations offered by their team and the opposition. The data might be transformed into three-dimensional virtual reality to give the impression of actually sitting in any given seat in the stadium, might be seen directly through the 'eyes' of a specific player, might be projected on to a table so that viewers can watch the stadium as though they were giants, or might even be relocated altogether to some fanciful location and circumstances peculiar to the viewer.

Eventually, post-singularity, when the games themselves do not exist in the real world and are played inside the Supernet, all possible cinematographic possibilities will be available to the viewer, even to the point of substituting themselves in favour of any given player. Each game will be genuinely unique with different outcomes. Players will participate remotely and cyber-space will digitally fulfil every conceivable playing environment. Commentary will also be subject to the whim of the new player, who might choose a different (or even a non-human) commentator programmed with certain charismatic traits and idiosyncrasies. Some will end up with followings as substantial as the most popular human commentators. The power of the viewing experiences could also be magnified through an awareness of the size of the audience and some interaction with them. A virtual stadium containing millions of fans might be constructed. The new player might choose to virtually sit only with his clan comrades and participate in discussions during the games with these like-minded tribe members.

Virtual Fandom: From the Actual Club to the Virtual Hub

An implication of the virtual environment is an enforced 'placelessness' on sporting fans. The future for sport support is likely to move away from the geographic focus of a city in favour of an artificial, virtual organisational hub. In this sense, sport fans are destined to follow homeless teams in the future, attached more closely to virtual locations (such as media networks) than cities or countries. Fans will form trans-geographic 'clans' in the same way computer gaming affiliations work. Professional sport will exist as media software and will be deliverable through a range of distribution services depending upon user preference and purchasing power. This will also encourage the further fragmentation of fans whose tribal affiliations will differ slightly or greatly depending upon their method of access and interaction. Virtual clans will determine their own preferred virtual environments for sports watching and will create their own virtual geographic replacement: a hub of cyber-space. The virtual nature of spectatorship will offer dramatic opportunities for sport enterprises to improve their revenues, particularly if they are a genuinely international property. For example, virtual reality will allow remote users to 'sit' anywhere in the stadium. Like pay television, the number of virtual reality participants will determine profitability, except virtual reality provides more opportunities for discriminatory pricing. After all, a virtual view on the 50-yard line or ringside is worth more than a virtual view from the back of the grandstand, which in turn is a different experience from watching the event on a conventional broadcast.

Outer Space for Place

The United Nations Committee on the Peaceful Uses of Outer Space[1] recognises the likelihood that marketing and sponsorship will move anywhere and everywhere. Their report on *Obtrusive Space Advertising and Astronomical Research* considers the need for international cooperation to limit space advertising that could interfere with astronomical observations. They cite the proposal by Space Marketing Inc. (based in the USA) as 'potentially devastating'.[2] The proposal featured a 'Space Billboard', measuring approximately one square kilometre, rivalling the full moon in size and brightness when seen from Earth. A similar project was proposed for the Atlanta Olympic Games in 1996, with a reflector measuring 1,000 × 400 m. Fortunately for astronomical observatories (and others?), neither of these projects proceeded due to a lack of funding. Other, smaller-scale projects have been proposed under the guise of cultural celebration. The French 'Ring of Light' for instance, was to include a ring of bright satellites celebrating the centennial of the Eiffel Tower (1989) and the bicentennial of the Revolution. Another French proposal was the 'Star of Tolerance' to celebrate the fiftieth anniversary of the United Nations Educational, Scientific and Cultural Organisation in 1999, comprising a pair of balloons in low orbit. Unlike other forms of promotion (or celebration), no individual or nation can refuse exposure to space advertising. Imagine, for instance, a satellite that filters the sun to create shade spelling 'Coca-Cola', or a neon sign orbiting Earth encouraging us to buy Nike shoes.

  Space tourism and the possibility of sport facilities in space is also being seriously considered for the first time in decades. Thirty-five years ago, Pan American Airlines took nearly 100,000 reservations for paying passengers to the moon. Despite the marketing hype, it was a vision many people in the industry believed would become reality.

Although the National Aeronautics and Space Administration's shuttles may no longer be the most convincing prospect of future space tourism, its problems have not discouraged an emerging number of space tourism enterprises such as Space Adventures, which have received a tremendous boost from the US$20 million fee-paying trips of Dennis Tito and Mark Shuttleworth which they organised to the International Space Station via a Russian Soyuz rocket. A recent study by Futron based on a survey of 450 US millionaires concluded that professional space travel could attract more than 15,000 customers and over a billion dollars within two decades. Development has also been accelerated by the consortium offering a US$10 million 'X-prize' to the first team that can send three people to a sub-orbital altitude of 100 kilometres and return them safely twice within two weeks. It is a successor of sorts to the prize that Charles Lindbergh claimed for his transatlantic flight in 1927.

If space tourism can become a reality, there will shortly thereafter be the need for space sport. After all, wealthy tourists cannot be expected to float around all day. Collins, Fukuoka and Nishimura from Tokyo's National Aerospace Laboratory and Hazama Corporation have speculated on the composition of zero-gravity sports centres. While it presently costs somewhere in the order of US$6,000 per kilogram to launch cargo into space, Collins, Fukuoka and Nishimura believe it would be viable to consider the construction of a space leisure and sport facility in low Earth orbit when the costs drop to around US$200 per kilogram. They go so far as to explain the construction methods for three facilities: first, a gymnasium for individual and group entertainment; second, a large swimming pool; and third, a stadium suitable for team sports. Notwithstanding the design requirements of swimming pools with no gravity, it is interesting to contemplate how conventional sports might be modified for a weightless environment. Most goal-based sports could be redesigned, but it remains difficult to imagine a chamber partly filled with enormous globs of water.

Fiction on the Field

One question repeatedly asked about the future is the degree to which technology will facilitate the 'wrestle-mania' of the remainder of professional sports. To be blunt, to what extent can we expect professional sports to become fixed, scripted theatre for the maximal entertainment pleasure of the spectator? Enough has been observed about professional wrestling to make it clear that it is both enormously successful despite its obvious and now unhidden fiction, and not limited in popularity to the USA. Professional wrestling does not fall into the 'only in America' category any more. Its appeal, the television and pay-per-view evidence would suggest, is surprisingly universal.

It may be reasonable to expect that some sports, in desperation, decide to venture down the professional wrestling path. Perhaps we might rate sports by their degree of fictitious content. Say, for example, that professional wrestling scores 10 out of 10 on the McMahon Scale. Presently, professional boxing might earn a rating of five. Professional football (soccer), although not fixed, might still achieve a McMahon rating based on the pseudo-injury performances of its players. Those few sports that fragment and venture towards the dark side of sport entertainment might choose to give fans exactly what they seek. League champions may well be determined by focus groups and consumer panels.

However, despite the rhetoric, there are few signs that sport consumers are ready to fully relinquish genuine outcome uncertainty. It is disempowering for die-hard supporters to accept that the fate of their team, and indeed their happiness, lies in the hands of a Vince McMahon. It is bad enough that commercial imperatives drive professional sport. Money determines the player lists, the manager, coach and support staff. Despite this, and the weight of evidence which suggests that money does buy success, there is always a chance that money will not always buy the championship trophy. As pervasive as technology might become in the future of sport business, and notwithstanding the fact that money and technology reduce the variables governing uncertainty, sport must always have an element of the unknowable in order to satisfy the fan's soul.

Implications for the Future Delivery of Management and Marketing in Sport

The progression of sport and entertainment business towards a digital reality heralds a number of important changes in the expectations of sport consumers and the nature of the delivery of sporting products and services. Information and choice have not traditionally been the hallmarks of sport, but the imposition of technology brings with it the power of improved customer knowledge. Thus, first, sport consumers will have more leverage than they have ever had.

More Powerful Sport Consumers

This leverage will manifest itself in several ways. Increased access to information means that sport consumers will be more knowledgeable about the activities of their favourite athletes and teams. As a consequence of the information revolution, they will also have ready access to more sports and sport entertainment alternatives than ever before. Hundreds of sporting events will compete at any given time for the interest and discretionary spending of potential fans. Some individuals, driven primarily by a desire for an entertainment experience, will divert their interest to lesser-known sports and events. Others will find the participation opportunities in cyber-sport more compelling than watching 'old-fashioned' events. Others still will look for less expensive entertainment options; but competition between sports will be relative. The larger, more popular sports will get larger and become more pervasive, while hundreds of others will continue to battle away for attention amongst the enormous clutter, surviving only through the targeted sponsorships of a handful of interested companies and government grants.

Non-traditional forms of sponsorship will help to mitigate the clutter and noise of the sporting marketplace. For example, although sport properties enjoy the lion's share of sponsorship now, in the future we can expect that companies look for other options that better cover the consumers interested in the knowledge and technology markets, who may be less interested in traditional sport. This will shift some sponsorship from sport to arts, cultural, intellectual, educational and community interests. In part, this will help to satisfy some company's corporate citizenship imperatives. It will also mean that companies will be more prepared to hold a set of sponsorships across a range of interest areas. Traditional sport sponsors may well be just as prepared to support a university in its SETI program as it is to sponsor a sporting event. Other companies will take a stronger line with sponsorship in an attempt to nail down and manage their return on investment. More will become owners or co-owners of events, prepared to take a share of the risk, but also demanding control of the pie and how the brand is used to maximise their exposure. Notwithstanding smaller corporate hospitality packages, more companies will only be prepared to make significant investments in clubs, events and sport properties if they receive an equity position in return. Corporate sport philanthropy ended a decade ago. Fee for service sponsorships will diminish, to be replaced by business models where ownership is a core prerequisite.

A new class of sport fans will emerge. Driven neither by entertainment nor by the need for identity, they will grow up in a world where the support of a club or sport is not necessarily for life, or even a season. Loyalty will weaken. They will change their affiliation with fashion, as quickly as they buy a new pair of shoes or a new telephone. The implication for sport enterprises is that there will be no single way of structuring value. It will be perceived differently depending upon the clan that an individual belongs to. Consumers are overburdened with choice, and sport marketers are going to have to invent new ways to become intrinsic to the purchasing habits of their supporters in an environment that discourages (and sometimes even punishes) loyalty.

Virtual Fans

Sport consumers will be more distant geographically in the future. Their location dependency upon particular stadia and venues will decrease. Clans will cluster around virtual hubs of sport interactivity where cyber-sport, fora and broadcasting will take place. Presently rights are tied up with networks which are terrified of allowing Internet broadcasting to take place, especially by offshoots of the sport properties themselves such as Manchester United or Real Madrid television, which can only provide information around games rather than any actual content. Nevertheless, this will change, albeit slowly for the larger sports. Smaller sports will find that web broadcasting and all its digital opportunities are their best bet for finding a stable niche. Future spam will include highlights from games or events and invitations to participate in the cyber-version of the sport in real time against the best in the world. They may indeed discover that viewers find it more entertaining to watch a fencing or archery tournament when they can actually compete along with the athletes. Professional wrestling may even take on a new appeal for those of us who prefer our sport entertainment to contain fewer steel chairs. But who knows: if we can actually command our own likeness to wrestle against the champ without any scripting, it may just be more fun than folly.

One of the difficulties that will come with distant, virtual fans lies in the distinction between transactions and people. Sport fandom needs to be more than just a receptacle for sport viewing and the occasional purchase of merchandise. If they are virtual fans, they need virtual locations where community building and social interaction can take place. Sport organisations must be a virtual place of social experience: a hub of activity and tribal identity. Communities are about tribal values, and the virtual communities for sport must provide the opportunity for these values to be exposed and encouraged. This means that sport organisations must have the tools to ensure that the relationships they have with their customers bridges the gap between commerce and community.

In turn this necessitates the careful management of customer input into products and services. Through the virtual environment, fans have the power to create a fully customised experience rather than a pre-packaged one that the organisation thinks is more or less appropriate. This means that the organisation must integrate fans into the decision-making process about the products they offer until technology can allow them to bypass the need to provide generic product choices. There is also the need for caution because the biggest trends are not necessarily the ones fans demanded. Fashion can sweep over sport fans just as quickly as over consumers of everyday products.

Sport enterprises will have to work hard to ensure that experiences are created for sport consumers that are superior to those they might receive through other discretionary leisure pursuits. Technology has the sometimes unwelcome potential of converting services or customer experiences into commodities. In order to fortify the sporting experience, organisations must continue to focus on understanding the emotions and feelings of supporters. This reinforces the importance of marketing segmentation based on tribal affiliation rather than convention demographic or other criteria. Sport consumers do not organise their emotions around the industry or the sport, but around the experiences of belonging to the club. Humans are experience-rather than consumption-driven. This explains why new industries can be created by packaging services around existing consumables. There is value for consumers in reducing search costs – as with merchandise – making sure the products are compatible with their lifestyle – as with corporate hospitality – and removing impediments from the quality of the experience (as with technologies that allow patrons to assess the view of any seat before purchasing tickets). Sport consumers are not units of demand or potential transactions; they are passionate 'experiencers', seeking emotional validation and spiritual revelation from their sport entertainment.

Sport will continue to expand beyond its conventional role and will increasingly fulfil other needs beyond belonging and entertainment. For example, it has the potential to meet wellbeing needs through health, spirituality and psychological interaction, learning needs through sport management and marketing education and the acquisition of street skills, time savings through mobile access to games, events, highlights and scores and even security needs through clan protection and membership.

A Sport Business Future

We hope to have presented enough evidence to convince even the most techno-cynical reader to at least consider the radical involvement of technology in sport to be a part of its future. However, will sport continue to march forward in this way, inexorably towards the singularity? In the end, we think not. Sport exemplifies humanity; physicality, challenge, fragility, triumph, failure, belonging, comradeship and combat. Even if technology overwhelms sport in the medium term, it will bounce back in its pure form. Humans will always want to actually play, irrespective of how real the virtual world is. Although many of us will embrace the opportunity to play alongside the greats in virtual sport, we will always want to watch the real thing and marvel at the skills of the best, if for no other reason than to remind ourselves what it is like to be human.

Notes and References

1   United Nations Committee on the Peaceful Uses of Outer Space (2001). *Obtrusive Space Advertising and Astronomical Research. Background Paper by the International Astronomical Union, 18 December 2001.* A/AC.105/777. United Nations General Assembly.
2   United Nations Committee on the Peaceful Uses of Outer Space, *Obtrusive Space Advertising*, p. 3.

Vincent and Leonardo

'... And it was only in the last ten minutes of the game that England scored two more tries to win. Let me think, it was the Rugby World Cup of 2003 in Australia and the game was in Sydney ... no, it was in Melbourne ... or was it Sydney? No, I'm sure it was Colonial Stadium in Melbourne. Oh, by then it probably was called Telstra Dome. That sounds right. And it must have been before it became the Microsplit Arena.

'Yeah, we took some clients to the game and I still remember talking about how good it would be if Samoa could beat England. Very unlikely of course with England being the tournament favourites. And did the Pom next to me let me know ... Carrying his tray full of beers, having already downed at least half a dozen before the match. "ENGELAND, ENGELAND!!", he was shouting. Drove us mad! It was good to smell the Pommie fear when Samoa was still leading England 15 minutes before the end. Some good kicking by Johnny Wilkinson and two late tries saved the day for England, but the Samoans gave them a hell of a fright!

'It was a sold out stadium, 55,000 people there on the night. Spring time, but it felt like winter. $5.50 for a Heineken and a meat pie for $3.50. Yeah, those were the days. There is something romantic about lining up for a drink and a hot dog. I remember realising at the front of the queue that I didn't bring any cash which, of course, was the only thing they'd accept. They even had two big so-called video screens for people in the stadium to watch the match in close-up when you can't follow the action on the field. And referees! They had referees running along with the players, ruling on pretty much everything that happened on the field; tries, penalty kicks, violations of the rules of the game by players. Yeah, son, those were the days of real sport, when the players were still made of flesh and bones, when you didn't know which sport you would be best at until you actually played it.'

It took Vincent a while to focus after his grandfather's ramblings. 'Why would people go to the trouble of actually playing sport themselves, grand-dad?' he asked. 'Isn't it much easier to load a *fluidchip* to kick a few goals?

Besides, I'm not interested in this thing you call rugby union, otherwise I would've gone to *McSportals* a long time ago, to order a takeaway *sport-fix* and get a feel for what it is. But being there and doing it all yourself, that seems so ... dirty.'

'Vince, I suggest you have a word with Uncle Hans's dad', Aaron replied. 'He comes from a time when they didn't have computers growing up.'

'Why should I talk to him? I can travel back to that time to experience it myself!'

'Pfff.' A deep sigh escaped from Aaron's enormous, genetically enhanced chest. Why couldn't he make Vincent and his other grandson Leonardo understand that everything they programmed their mind to do was not the 'real' thing? That only those who had lived in the previous century could really explain to them how different it was to move and feel outside a programmed environment? Hell, what does it mean anyway to live outside the *Supernet*?

Aaron's parents were still alive because they had been 'lucky' enough to regenerate their bodies back to biological youth. And now the constantly upgrading *'life-after-life'* programs made sure that new ways were always being found to sustain life beyond natural biological use-by dates. His colleague Hans had gone even further. With some genetic material from his late father's shaving razor, they were able to construct an exact copy of him from the time when he passed away in 1997. Now Hans and his father were catching up on lost time, or better, interrupted time, and reliving the old days as much as discussing the new.

Hans's father is not happy, all the same. He feels that life was not meant to be like this. In his original genetic structure he had always been naturally inclined towards respecting nature. He really did not want to be revived, brought back to a life that is not life anyway. Life, according to Hans's dad, is about the unknown journey, about exploration, learning, amazement, finding love, losing it and finding it again, about the excitement of the unknown, about finding solutions and realising they lead to even more of the unknown. And as all journeys come to an end, so does life. And that is how it should be, because if it doesn't, there is nothing to live for. Why live if life is eternal? Why live for today if we know we can leave everything till tomorrow? Or the day after? 'Let me be', he said one night to Hans. 'Unplug my mind and cherish our moments of intense happiness and mateship from the days of limited time left. Because what is limited is precious.'

'Granddad, granddad!!' Vincent aroused Aaron from his self-generated daydreams. It was a habit from his youth that had been all but eliminated except for a handful of his generation. Very few people are still able to think and dream outside the 'productive dreaming mainframe' that has been constructed by the *Clone Consortium*. Only those who are genetically predisposed to meditation, enabling absolute separation of the soul from the body, can still enjoy the sheer pleasure of sometimes thinking for themselves. But even that rare skill is now being targeted by the *Consciousness Deconstruction Company* to make sure future generations are better adapted to populating the outer vicious and violent non-Earth territories.

'Granddad', Vincent whispered. 'Look what I've painted.'

It is quite amazing to enjoy the skills of grandchildren who have been constructed in ways to please their parents and grandparents. Named after the Dutch painter who lived a couple of hundred years ago, Vincent Smith is the materialisation of Clare's dreams, Aaron's wife for some 89 years now. His paintings not only rival van Gogh's art, they build on the brilliance of the master in a way which has led to pictures that are of such intense beauty that they make onlookers burst into tears of sheer joy seconds after looking upon the canvas. Clare, of course, has made sure she is mastering the combined skills of some of her heroes herself.

'Hans, ... Hahaans! ... Hans!' Loes was vehemently shaking Hans's arm, trying to wake him up from what seemed to be a very deep sleep.

'Hans, it's 9.30! Weren't you going to meet the boys for a round of golf at Albert Park at 10.00?'

'Hmmm? What? Where am I?'

'What do you mean, where am I', Loes said. 'You're at home of course, and you're late! You're going to miss your tee-off time.'

Hans suddenly realised that much more than just a late arrival on the golf course was at stake. Today was the long awaited match against the boys from the Yarra Valley golf club; the match would decide who was going to win what was to be the culmination of 12 events played throughout the whole year! He leaped out of bed, straight into his golf gear and, with a few doughnuts in his pocket, jumped on the autotransit and immediately made an illegal visio-link to Aaron.

'Sorry to disturb you on a Sunday morning, mate', Hans said, trying to keep his eyes on the express zone, 'but can you do me a favour?

'Can you load a Nike Tiger program and wire it to me by link? I could use the extra support today.'

'You're still playing physical golf, eh?' Aaron said. 'Besides, I thought you purists weren't supposed to use any link supports.'

'Everyone uses them. Can you send the program?'

'Yeah, but you might do better if you gave up that old Tiger program and tried using something a little more modern.'

'I prefer the classics,' Hans observed.

Everything in this epilogue is based on the truth. All characters are real and all events have occurred, or will.

smith@manage-to-manage.com
westerbeek@manage-to-manage.com